S.W. Seventeen

a prairie girl remembers

by

Carol Schroeder

Order this book online at www.trafford.com
or email orders@trafford.com

Most Trafford titles are also available at major online book retailers.

Printed in the United States of America.

ISBN: 978-1-4120-6297-8 (soft)
ISBN: 978-1-4122-3771-0 (ebook)

Our mission is to efficiently provide the world's finest, most comprehensive book publishing service, enabling every author to experience success. To find out how to publish your book, your way, and have it available worldwide, visit us online at www.trafford.com

Trafford rev. 6/17/2010

www.trafford.com

North America & international
toll-free: 1 888 232 4444 (USA & Canada)
phone: 250 383 6864 • fax: 812 355 4082

Preface

So much has been written of our pioneer heritage, and rightly so, as it should be recorded for all posterity. Without those roots and humble beginnings of those brave souls, our country would not have been settled, and become the proud nation it is today.

It is a later era of which I write—a "linking time" between then and now—an age when my husband and I were youngsters, growing up at our respective farm homes north of Neudorf and Wolseley, and the many remembrances we have of those "olden days", as our children now refer to them!

To both of us it seems important to set down the events of this small space in time (our childhoods—approximately 1943 to the 1960's), for our children, grandchildren and their children, so that perhaps some day this small link with their past heritage will be interesting and meaningful to them in establishing their roots and identity, recalling through these jottings the way things were for us in an era about which very little has been written.

When we think back, it seems like another lifetime ago, and yet recalling events and happenings of those days, some seem like they took place only yesterday…so much has changed since then.

While I will endeavor to include excerpts of Gordon's heritage and memories from time to time, this journal will, for the most part, encompass the recollections of this writer.

Naming this collection of memories South West 17 (A Prairie Girl Remembers), seemed especially appropriate to me as it was this quarter section of land that became the "home quarter" to our family, and is where the majority of the following recorded memories took place.

In 1994, my sister Connie and I became joint owners of the South East and West quarters of Section 17, when our mother Margaret no longer wished to manage the farm business, and in 1997 I became sole owner of these two parcels of land, buying out Connie's share, as she wished. The decision to own this half section of prime farm land, once owned by our parents, has been an especially meaningful one for me, and makes my heart glad. It will always remain dear to me because of our parents struggle first to obtain it and then to maintain it and make their living from it. It wasn't easy, but provided a good life for us all I think, and a wealth of memories, looking back…

Table of Contents

Gordon and I almost qualify as post-war "Baby Boomers", both having the birth year 1943. I am an Easterner by birth (heaven forbid), being born at McKellar Hospital in Fort William (now Thunder Bay), Ontario, where Dad worked at Canada Car prior to being posted overseas with the Regina Rifles during war time. What a joy and thrill for me to finally return to this birth place in September 1996, when Gordon and I visited there on holidays.

Prior to that I had no idea how emotionally rewarding it would be to see places including McKellar Hospital, St. Paul's Anglican Church, where I was baptized, and best of all Christina Street, where we had lived, still lined with well-kept war-time homes. Lake Superior with the Sleeping Giant, and of course Kakabeka Falls—all landmarks in the area I had heard Mom and Dad speak of many times while we grew up, but had never seen until we visited. How thankful I am to have been able to make that sojourn back. I now feel everyone should have the opportunity to visit their birthplace, at some time in their life, especially if it differs from the place where they have grown up and now live.

Gordon's experience was somewhat different to mine in that he was born and has lived in the Neudorf area and later Regina all his life and could easily visit his birth place each time he went home to his family's farm. He had the unique and rare distinction of being born at home and laid to warm on the oven door in the kitchen. Apparently, modern medicine had not yet reached this little pocket of prairie habitation, as it was not that much of an unusual happening in that area. The doctor was called but missed the delivery and still collected his fee, while the mid-wife and Mom Schroeder had done all the work!

Because Gordon's parents were established on the farm land that had belonged to his mother's parents, William and Katherine Issel, Gordon spent all of his childhood years at this farm home, five miles north of Neudorf, with this town providing a centre for Church and supplies, while he attended Pheasant Hills rural public school. It was hard work helping with farm chores, but he and his older brother Helmuth seemed to accept this as a norm of the times, thus providing much needed help to their farm operation, both outside and in the house, as there were no sisters. Many skills were thus learned, still very evident in Gordon today. (The ability to fix almost anything, and make it work, of being a diligent and hard worker, and also being very helpful as a "house-husband", a term we working wives have coined these days!)

I on the other hand, had more variations in my young life, moving as a baby from Fort William with Mom when Dad went overseas, coming West by train to Wolseley, which was home to both parents Gordon Sexsmith and Margaret (Teasdale) Sexsmith.

Several years were spent living at Gran Teasdale's cosy home in Wolseley. I have only snatches of memories from this period in my young life, although by all accounts it was mostly happy for me, except that my Daddy was not present. I do recall relishing eating the frozen crystals of cream that expanded and popped the round cardboard caps off the glass milk bottles left at the back door by the milkman in Winter (milk was pasteurized but not yet homogenized!) Also I remember falling off the narrow ledge around the trap door in the kitchen floor leading to the cellar (its only access), and the huge bump on my head that resulted.

Apparently, being the first and only Grandchild in my maternal family had distinct advantages. (Chris Teasdale born shortly after me to Harry and Dorothy lived "away" in Montreal and was no real threat to my position). Also being the first and only niece to my doting single Aunts Alice and Elsie (Mom's sisters) my little life was happy, carefree and "pampered" to say the least!

By all accounts, I was "the darling" of the town, with many friends that liked me, among them the Gibsons, who ran the Red & White Store, Frank Vincent, the Post Master, Albert Murrell, Mr. Sargeant's care giver (neighbor of Gran Teasdale), who left me my Charlie McCarthy replica when they went to reside in B.C. Little girls like Jane Howell, Janet Danvers, Betty Whitney as well as Maxine Cole and Judy and Bonnie Bacheldor (Knight's grandchildren—who were also Gran's neighbors) were friends. Cousin Audrey used to come and play with me, when they visited from the farm.

Hundreds of snapshots (black and white only) were taken of me for Dad's benefit, and sent to him, while he was away stationed in England, Holland and France. I was always dressed in white ankle boots with white socks folded over the tops, and beautiful silk dresses quite often delicately "smocked" over the bodice, with full gathered or pleated skirts and bows that tied in the back. I can still recall the delicious and naughty pleasure I got from scrunching up the skirt of these silken dresses and biting into it to make a hole—don't ask me why? I don't know to this day! Apparently, I also had a fascination with dirt, liking its smell and tasting it. Again, to this day, I still love the smell of the damp, moist, black earth, but now resist the temptation to eat it! (Perhaps I was already a "Green Thumb" then!) Earth worms were no problem, and apparently I had no qualms picking these wriggly creatures up off the "cigarment" (cement) sidewalks after a rain.

During this time, I came to know and love my Gran Teasdale very much, living in her home

FORM-18 16

WARTIME HOUSING LIMITED
FORT WILLIAM, ONT.

HOUSE RENTAL RECEIPT V-1057

NAME D G Sexsmith DATE OCT 18 1943 194
ADDRESS 274 Christina
AMOUNT Twenty three XX/100 DOLLARS
PERIOD Oct 1-31/43
#2965
WARTIME HOUSING LIMITED (AGENT)
$ 23.00

MEMORIES OF FORT WILLIAM and CANADA CAR (see page 1)

EMPLOYEE'S NAME: Sexsmith, D.G.
EMPLOYEE'S CHECK NUMBER: 2965
PAY PERIOD ENDING: May 13

DEDUCTION DETAILS	DEDUCTIONS	
Tax	11	10
Un. Ins.		54
	11	64

EARNINGS	
BONUS	
GROSS EARNINGS	79 66
TOTAL DEDUCT'NS	11 64
NET EARNINGS	68 02

DOLLARS CENTS

32.07
100.09

CERTIFIED CORRECT
CHIEF TIMEKEEPER

NET EARNINGS

THIS IS TO CERTIFY THAT THE ABOVE EMPLOYEE WAS PAID OFF ON THE ABOVE DATE AND RECEIVED THE ABOVE NET EARNINGS.
ANY ALTERATION RENDERS THIS CERTIFICATE VOID.

EMPLOYEE'S RECORD

NO. 19418
CANADIAN CAR AND FOUNDRY COMPANY LIMITED

As a baby with Mom and Dad in Fort William, Ontario, 1943-44

At Gran Teasdale's in Wolseley--growing up

With my Gran at front of her house (before insulbrick on house)

With my Daddy (see the "ginnell")

With Gran in the back yard by the garden

I loved purses (still do!)

With cousin Audrey, beside Gran's garden

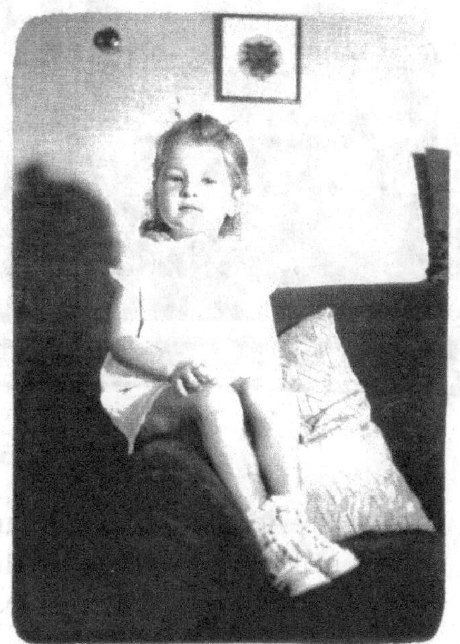
Little Miss Carol taken at Grace Conn's (Aunt Alice arranged)

Our horses Prince and Babe by barn—with Carol at reins!

Aerial Photographs
Box 13 - REGINA
July 21, 1950

Aerial Photo of our farm (buildings all finished and
multiple trees planted to the west—Dad is weeding in them)
Dad always felt sorry the garage door was open slightly

Our farm home under construction

Gordon as a boy

Carol with Buoy, the pet dog, on her birthday (note: wearing 2 birthday gift outfits–and unfinished barn in background)

with Mom. Gran and Grandad Sexsmith came to visit often and I loved them dearly also. I remember liking my two Aunts, a lot, and loved to be in their company. Also their two future husbands, who were later to become my two favorite Uncles, Don and Clifford (the Swailor) as 1 used to call him (he was in the Navy). Uncle Wilfred (Grandad Teasdale's brother) was also a favorite, and I loved to be in his company whenever he came to visit from Vancouver. Other Aunts and Uncles (Herb and Ruby Sexsmith, Gladys and Norman Bowers, Lloyd and Winnie Sexsmith, Dad's brothers and sister}, and Harry and Dorothy Teasdale, (Mom's brother), weren't as well known to me then, but because of close proximity, after we moved to the farm I came to know and love Aunt Ruby and Uncle Herb, and Dad's cousins and their wives Raymond and Isobel, and Harold and Eileen, who were almost like Aunts and Uncles, because we were all close farm neighbors also.

The only traumatic event to mar my young life up to this point, that I remember was having to have my tonsils out, (a common surgical practice at the time, to avert sore throats, tonsillitis and the like) and I was no exception. Apparently, the Wolseley doctor Isman arranged for the procedure to be done at Indian Head Hospital, as there was no hospital in Wolseley at the time. Only snatches of the day come to mind, laying on a white table surrounded by a white-masked doctor and nurses, them holding me down, and struggling to place a black, rubbery, foul smelling piece of equipment over my face (the ether mask, commonly used to anaesthetize patient's for short-term surgery at the time). Apparently the actual tonsillectomy went quite well, but the recovery period was very difficult for my Mom, having no place to lay me down, and having to hold me in her arms for most of the day, and trip home, not an easy task with a crying, troubled three year old, with an extremely sore, bleeding throat, who couldn't really understand the reason behind it all!

The war ended, Dad returned, unharmed, much to everyone's relief, and a sense of normal returned to our lives. Another favorite memory from this period comes to mind. Apparently, we were in Winnipeg for Dad to obtain his official discharge from the Army, staying with Ila and Stan Stanley (family friends). I recall Ila playfully chasing me behind their couch, and picking me up, saying she would eat me all up—to which I apparently squealed "No, please don't do that, or my Mommy won't know where I are!" I also have fragments of remembering their beautiful garden area, with bird baths, flowers and a lovely round gold fish pond with golden fishes darting around in the water, hiding under the round ledges. It must have been this memory that prompted a life-long desire to someday have a similar pond with gold fish in our own yard that has now become a fond reality, thanks to my husband's efforts, the waterfall and edging made with field stones from our Neudorf farm.

Dad decided to farm, and arranged to buy the south half of section 17, north-west of Wolseley, from his father Dave Sexsmith, through the Department of Veteran's Affairs, who were assisting veterans with re-entry into civilian life. A home was built, and in 1947, we moved there to live and farm. (It is ironic that in 1948 when Grandad passed away, this same 1/2 section was then bequeathed to Dad, I am told.)

As I recall, we moved ourselves and belongings to our new home on a stormy, snowy winter day, taking the "Main Road" (the name commonly given to this road leading to the valley west of Wolseley), using Ted Lewthwaite's red box truck. We became stuck and slightly tipped over, and I remember thinking of it as an adventure. I recall riding on Mom's knee (car safety seats weren't invented yet) and asking her if she thought my red toy table and chairs were safe in the back of the truck? How we ultimately arrived and became settled I do not recall. According to what I've been told, Henry Scheibler, Irvin Arndt and crew did construction on our house and other buildings. I remember Henry always joking around with us and Irvin always being nice to me like a big brother. I would have liked an older brother.

Apparently a lot of construction went on after we moved in to our new home, including cupboards, shelves and general finishing. Out buildings included a barn, hen house/pig pen, and garage built as time and funding permitted, none of which I recall. Mom was always amazed Dad hammered and sawed late at night in the house, after I was asleep and the noise didn't awaken me. I am now also surprised by this, as for most of my adult life, I have been and continue to be a very light sleeper!

The only other vivid memory that comes to mind prior to my school years took place soon after our arrival at the farm, perhaps the next winter (before Connie, my sister was born at least). I recall being alone in the house while Mom and Dad tried, in vain, to coax our old Chevy car into motion, for a much-needed trip to town. Were they cranking it or pulling it with our huge old horse Babe, or with the tractor or both I don't recall; all I know is as they left our lane, turning East and got as far along the grid road adjacent to our oat bin (not even 1/4 of a mile), I became petrified they were in fact going to go on to town without coming back for me, perhaps ever, and I must get to them immediately. Not stopping for outer clothes or boots, and leaving the door wide open, I plunged out across the field towards them, into snow drifts as deep as I was high! I was flailing my arms, crying and floundering along, as best as I could. I recall Dad running to "rescue" me, reprimanding me all the while for being so utterly careless and silly as to think they would leave me behind, and for neglecting to dress properly and worst of all, leaving the house open to the winter-breezes! Whether we ever got to town that day or not I can't recal1. (I am told this huge amount of snow resulted from the Blizzard of '47, that paralyzed the area that winter.)

[illegible] Sask
Nov 23rd 1950

Dear Uncle Norman + Aunt Elsie

Well don't drop over dead because you are hearing from me I often think of you all over there many times, but I'm such a poor hand at writing + just keep putting it off so you will excuse me for my negligence

Am sending you a photo taken from the air of our buildings + I will explain them as best I can to you.

bording the picture are the three fields each 110 acres

The wheat field you see if the frost hadn't of hit us would have easy gone 50 bushels to the acre but only did 32 bushels to the acre

You will notice the tracks in the field of wheat They are made by the

This letter has a colorful history—it was originally written by Dad in November 1950 and sent overseas to Mom's family (Grandad Teasdale's sister Elsie and her husband Norman) whom Dad had stayed with while in England during the War. The letter accompanied an aerial picture of Mom and Dad's farm home. Both were later returned to Mom after Dad's passing, as a keepsake to us. It is included here with a copy of the same picture, because of Dad's detailed description of the farm, fields and buildings plus dimensions of each. He was obviously proud of his and Mom's accomplishments, wishing to share this information with the overseas relatives. I have included the letter in its entirety as felt it was a "thumb-nail" sketch of the life and times of our family in 1950!

I hope you can understand that jumble drawing might help to give you a better idea.
Well to start with the house is 20'x 24' fully insulated + full sized cement basement with cistern + furnace, both kitchen, dinning room two bedrooms + a small room that can be made into a bathroom. not very big but we are nice + comfortable, The barn is 24'x 26', ~~ga~~ double garage for the car + tractor which is 20'x20' with double doors. The hen house is 16'x 24' + 8' on the left side facing the picture devided off for a pig pen + for our spring chickens. The dugout, that is our water supply is 175' long 65' wide + 12' deep so it hold a good supply of water. The well is 12' deep + just a ~~sochage~~ soakage from the dugout. You can see the four cows grazing just opposite the dugout. This has all happened since 1947, so you can see Margie + I have spent no idle moments. There wasn't anything here when we started.
Well I guess that's about enough about that eh you will be getting bored or else crazy trying to figure this all out. so if you can't straighten it out the best thing to do is to come on over + see us
How are you making out anyway. Still carrying the mail ~~get~~ across the fella

3

And Aunt Elsie, I suppose you are going as fast as ever what with the store + your work besides. Sorry to hear that Aunt Margaret eyes are giving her so much trouble. Say Hello from us all to her + also Uncle Billy + Aunt Mary I should write them to. I do hope they won't be offended about not getting a picture, but we only had three done. One for ourselves one for Gran Teasdale + one for Gran Sexsmith + when I mentioned I would like to send one over to you folks Mother said I could take the one we gave her, so here it is.

Carol + Connie are sure both growing. Carol goes to school everyday, is in grade 2 since summer holidays. She sure loves going to school. Right now they are getting their Christmas concert ready so she is quite elated. Connie is a cute wee mite. Almost starting to walk. She can stand by herself + push a chair in front of her + does she ever love to try + climb. She has ten teeth + is cutting two double ones right now + they make her a bit crusty at times. Margaret is always busy, Carol to send off to school every morning + the baby to look after, besides her house work. I help her quite a bit with Connie

4

in the winter time but when summer comes I haven't much time to be in the house

Right now we are having a terrible cold spell. It was 20 below last night with a horrible north west wind & its 19 below now so the radio says but there is very little wind. We haven't a lot of snow yet. The cars are still running yet. Hope they run all winter, because the winter is sure going to be a long one if it keeps this up

Do you still keep your hens uncle Norman? If so do you keep them in the same place?

Margie & I were killing some chickens to-day Killed 6 this afternoon & have 8 more to kill to-morrow. We still have plenty more to kill but that's a start. Right now we must have over 100 hens & 25 or so roosters that we are fattening to kill. I don't mean ~~that~~ we are killing all the hens just the roosters, so come on over & we will have a d---- good feed

Well folks my hand is just about giving up as I'm not very used to writing much now. Hoping this finds you all in the pink & we often talk about you all. Say hello to the Thompson folks eh Guess those three kids Margie Jim's will be grown up now eh. Wishing you all the very merriest Christmas & a very Prosperous New Year lots of love

Gordon

Looking back, it seems the whole focus of my life back then was attending Allindale School. Now when I look at the spot on the corner of that grain field where that school yard and trees (planted with the assistance of both Grandads Teasdale and Sexsmith) and sturdy brick landmark once existed, in all my girlhood years, and still in memory does, I become extremely sad and melancholy. The fact that every shred of evidence of its existence has been erased forever, except in the minds of former students, seems awfully sad to me. To this day, many of my dreams still take place within those hallowed walls. I loved school, my teachers and learning, so understandably, the place where all this took place has left an indelible mark on my memory. Students that I recall that were in attendance during the years 1949-1961 were as follows:

Debenhams: Lorne, twins Linda and Jean
Spaniers: Tom, Billy, Thelma, twins Shirley & Sharon
Luthers: Norma, Eddy, Victor, Gordie & Susan
Sexsmiths: Elaine and Wayne, Dwight and Wes, Audrey
Carol and Connie
Balfours: Cecil, twins Clifford & Stanley
Listers: twins Maureen and Meredith Bradley: Clayton
Ganders: Robert, Ronald & Mary (English) Reid: Grant
Browns: Ron & Noreen
Livingston: Darcy
Turpin: Ross

During my era, more students came and went, before and after, but these children were present for some or all of my time there. We had a different teacher almost every year, usually just out of "Normal", or with a basic teaching certificate, obtained by attending a one year course in Moose Jaw. To think those girls were only in their late teens (19) almost seems impossible to believe—that they would have enough authority and/or knowledge to be put in charge of an entire classroom of eight grades, with 2 or 3 pupils in each grade, must have seemed awfully frightening to them, as well as to our parents, come to think of it!!

It seems we were blessed at Allindale though, with reasonably good teachers, compared to some of the horror stories Gordon has related to me re: his elementary school teachers, and their sadly lacking abilities. No wonder he was "turned-off" school by Grade 9 and didn't care to continue then.

For Grade I, I recall having two teachers; Miss Powell, who became ill after several days and didn't return, to be replaced by Miss Lois Weatherald (to remember her name Mom told me to think of the "Weather"). For Grade II Miss Clarke began the year and Miss Dicken) completed it. Grade III we had Audrey Adams, who was very musical, played the piano, sang and helped teach cousin Dwight and I to sing the song "Sometime" in harmony for some contest in town. For Grade IV Miss Mary Thompson came teach, and ended up marrying Ivan Brown, eligible bachelor at the time, giving up teaching at the end of that year for family life. Miss Jeannine Railton came to teach Grade V and VI, teaching me among many other fine things to crochet, and finally Miss Edna Nelson for Grade VII and VIII. Years later this same nice teacher also taught our two girls Heather and Michelle (unfortunately, Michael missed having her) at Rosemont Public School in Regina. We couldn't get over the fact that she had been teaching all those years, with the exception of time out to have her family, still looked great, still a good teacher, etc.

To ease the load on these youthful teachers, the Curriculum was arranged in these one room school houses for two grades to take the same Science, Social Studies and Health, as well as Art, Music (singing and tonette or recorder) were taken by all grades once or twice a week, as I recall. With the "two-grade" arrangement, the teacher could take this group with her "up to the board" (blackboard), for individual instruction, while the other grades remaining in their desks were given their assignment and then expected to work independently, until she was available to help them. It must have been quite a challenge to keep everything going at once! Probably, quite a lot of this instruction rubbed off on the Grades working in their desks, as a review for older children, who had already taken the work, or as preliminary information for those younger.

These youthful teachers seemed almost entirely on their own, as far as our instruction was concerned, and usually this arrangement worked well, except for the occasional "problem child" whose individual instruction was then "worked out" with that child—parents weren't usually involved. There was no Home and School or parent/teacher interviews, etc. "Meet the Teacher" was on the first morning of the new school term, at the end of August and the only other contact with the teacher was at the annual Christmas Concert. There was a School Board, comprised of volunteer parents, that negotiated contracts and saw that school grounds and buildings were maintained over the years, but they generally did not interfere with the teacher's actual instruction. Teachers always boarded at Raymond Sexsmith's in earlier years, and later at Uncle Herb Sexsmith's, probably because they both boasted the two largest homes in the district, and were willing to provide a good home for these young girls.

Several times a year, the School Superintendent came to call, always without warning. I recall only one gentleman, by the name of Mr. Penny ever holding this position, who was based in Indian Head, I believe, and whose jurisdiction was all the surrounding public schools. Our teachers were under Mr. Penny's direction, much as a school principal presides over each school today. Thinking back, what a big job he had, over many miles of countryside, in all weather!

He was a very kindly gentleman, very unobtrusive to our classes, usually taking notes, etc., as to what chapter we were taking, in several subjects, probably to compare with other students in other schools. I expect our teachers looked on these Superintendent visits with a bit of trepidation, but of course we were never aware of it at the time.

We had recess morning and afternoon for 15 minutes, with an hour for lunch, beginning at 9 and finishing at 3:30 just as is usual today. No one went home for lunch, mostly because of distance, and a long grey painted bench housed all manner of lunch kits, bags and syrup pails filled with lunches. I recall receiving a dear little lunch kit of lime green, trimmed with white, with a lid and two little handles for my sixth birthday, just prior to beginning my school experience, that I proudly took my lunch in for several years, (although much to Mom's distress, I hardly ate, try as she might to prepare and send whatever she thought would tempt me). There was always too much urgency to get on with whatever particular game had been chosen to play, collectively, over the lunch hour, I recall just abandoning lunch in favor of being part of the group! (No wonder I was always so skinny). Later, I graduated to Dad's black lunch box (Canada Car), as it had room for a thermos, and I began to eat more sensibly.

The teacher had a large silver bell with a black handle and a make-shift metal nut clacker (wired in place) to call us back to class at the end of recess and noon hour. We were encouraged to spend our free time outdoors when the weather was clement, but during winter we had indoor games, played in the basement. A favorite of everyone was "Snake". Wayne was always "It", starting the game off from the centre post, the snake tagging children, becoming longer and longer until everyone was "caught", which didn't take long as there weren't many hiding places! A ping-pong table upstairs was very popular, with contests—the boys usually being declared winners over the girls. Of course only 2 or 4 could play at a time. Outdoor games of Hide & Seek, Mother May I, Red Light, Pump Pump Pull Away, Tug of War and Anti-I-Over were all played, the latter occasionally resulting in a broken window. Ring Around the Rosie and Fox & Goose were also played. Snow angels were made in winter. Several of us girls loved skipping and became very adept at it, chanting endless rhyming ditties that continued on and on until a missed step ended their turn, and another girl got to try; each girl had her own plastic jump rope, (mine was yellow). A sample of the silliness of these rhymes:

> Stella, Stella, dressed in yellow,
> Went downtown, to see her fella,
> How many kisses did she get? One, two three, etc.

We played several games bouncing little multi-colored rubber balls against a wall in a series of intricate patterns, each girl owning her own ball. A cement pad poured directly around the circular steps leading up to the door on the southeast side of the school, like a patio of today, was a great area for us girls to play on, and was well utilized for both of the above mentioned recess pass-times, for us girls.

Two swings made with huge telephone poles, chain-link ropes and wooden seats, were very popular with both boys and girls. It was a great day when one could finally "pump" oneself up, first sitting and then finally standing, and not having to be "pushed" by someone else. Because of their constant use, there was a depression in the dirt under the swings, that always filled with water when it rained, making them inaccessible until the sun dried it up, or else whoever played on them usually ended up with very muddy, wet shoes and feet! Thelma, Billy and I spent many happy hours on these swings. Not having a swing at home until I was grown, the swings were a particular favorite pass time for me during recess, noon hour and even after school.

At the back of the school yard, a ball diamond existed, with old discs (from disker seeding implements) for bases and home plate. The boys often played ball or scrub, each taking turns at positions, because of lack of willing players (usually the girls). However, everyone was more or less recruited into playing near Field Day competition in June, as each school entered a team. Ball always proved an elusive pursuit for me as my heart was never in it. I never seemed to be able to throw, catch or bat, all requirements of the game of course. Running was my only saving grace, but without the other components didn't mean too much! I always felt owning a ball glove would have worked wonders for my prowess as a player, however that wasn't a priority in my parent's eyes, since I wasn't a very good player any way.

A huge maple tree stood in the northwest corner of this yard which was often climbed by many of us, or just sat under for shade. Large fir trees had been planted on the north, south and east perimeters of the yard, and it was fenced with three strands of smooth wire as opposed to barbed wire used to fence pastures, etc. Wild grass, fragrant yellow Buffalo Beans and Brown Eyed Susans grew in the school yard in summer; it seems to me the ball diamond area must have been mowed when we wanted to play ball on it, or did we just trample it down as we played, I don't recall.

A wooden barn, painted red with a black roof and white trim, stood southwest of the school, and served as a shelter for the horses ridden or driven by several of the children over the years, namely cousin Audrey's old mare Nelly, Spaniers horse that pulled their red cart and the Balfours and Debenhams horses.

The school building itself was a sturdy brick rectangular structure, set on a high foundation. There were large basement windows on the east, north and west sides, the glass covered with mesh wire to guard against accidental breakage, I guess. The main level of the school had huge wall to ceiling double windows all along the west side, and two on the south east corner. No windows existed facing south, to prevent glare on the blackboards. The front door at the north of the school, faced the road and was accessed by wooden steps painted grey. This door was boarded up and not used for a number of years while I attended, being opened up at the time of major inside renovations when I was in Grade V or so. A white flag pole stood tall and proud on the east side of these steps, equipped with a rope and pulley system to raise and lower the flag (then the Union Jack) each day…we were very patriotic and depending on the teacher's wishes and time of year, all students went outdoors to stand at the base of the pole to sing "0 Canada" in the morning when the flag was raised and "God Save the King/later Queen" as it was lowered, by the student monitor assigned the task for that week.

The back or side door in the middle of the east wall was always the main door used by students and was accessed by an aging set of wooden steps, later replaced by a lovely set of curved cement steps and the a-fore mentioned cement pad base, we all loved to play on. Wooden basement stairs led from this side door landing, and a step up to the left led to the one room class room. A partitioned area all across the north wall housed both girls and boys separate cloak room/wash basin area in the centre and separate toilet areas on each end. (Apparently, indoor toilets that could be used all year 'round, were a luxury some students didn't even enjoy at home, at the time, outhouses being the norm at some schools). Two of the same huge windows were located on the exterior north wall, providing light to this area.

The inside of the classroom was boring plaster, painted beige, later covered with plywood and varnished during renovations, the floors were green colored linoleum, over wooden board floors. Heating was originally provided by a pot-bellied stove, that burned wood and coal, vented to the chimney by a long series of stove pipes, suspended from the ceiling with wires. Students lucky enough to be near this stove were toasty warm, even too warm, while others seated farther away were cold. Central heating eventually replaced the stove, with a wood/coal burning furnace in the basement (later converted to oil and electricity), with a centrally located floor register, much more efficient and warmer. The heat that came up from this register also served to dry sodden mittens, boots and to warm water brought in syrup pails by Spaniers for hand washing prior to lunch break. (I recall the horrible smell of manure on some boots, as it warmed and filled the room!) Graduated sizes of desks were bolted to long parallel 2x4's for stability, six to eight to a set. Younger children always sat to the west side of the room, near the windows, while older grades filled the rest of the room towards the door.

Other furniture consisted of the piano and stool, the teachers large wooden desk and beige swivel chair with adjustable back, the large gramophone (donated by Spaniers) a brown wooden cupboard at the southwest corner, and later a beautiful plywood, varnished cupboard that sat all along the south wall, that served as a library/art supply centre. A map storage cupboard was located above the blackboards, (Both of these cupboards, as well as the ping-pong table, mentioned previously, were built by Mr. Luther during Miss Railton's term there.) A large globe was suspended at the right front of the classroom by a thin rope and pulley system, weighted by a 4-6 inch steel ball, used to raise and lower it. (This same steel ball was on occasion used for amusement by the older boys seated beside it, being swung back and forth like a pendulum between them until the teacher put an end to their antics!)

In order to keep school-life running smoothly, the teachers drew up lists of student monitors, to do those little tasks, like keeping blackboards and brushes clean, sweeping floors, flag raising and lowering, health inspection—keeping hands and nails clean, and having a clean handkerchief (because tissues weren't in common use yet) to display hands on each morning, keeping washbasins and area neat and clean, library/art paper helper, etc., rotated each week. Older students were assisted by younger ones, and eventually all students had been "trained" in all these little jobs, with the exception of sweeping, which usually fell to two students in older grades. This task had to be performed each day as school was dismissed, and was even a paid position! All the rest were volunteer. Ten cents a week didn't add up very fast, but it was a little source of income. Families who supplied water for drinking and hand-washing each day were also paid a nominal amount, I recall. (Spaniers later supplied a white thermal-lined cooler that kept this drinking water much cooler). Floor sweeping was carried out with two soft brushed push brooms, with each student required to sweep half the floor surface, demarcated by a join in the linoleum at approximately half the width of the classroom. Dustbane, sort of an oiled pencil shavings-type of material in green or brown, (that smelled clean and fresh—supplied to the school by the school board and always sat in the corner of the girl's cloak room in a large cardboard barrel) made sweeping up the prairie dust and grime a bit easier. Sweepers would begin at the south end of the classroom and proceed to the front or blackboard area where all the dirt and dust pane would be pooled and swept into dust pans, to be discarded. Every once in a while the units of desks (described earlier) had to be moved over a little and the dust pane and dirt accumulated underneath would be swept away also. I recall sharing this job with Thelma and then Dwight for several years during my tenure at Allindale. Whoever was on cleaning brushes had to take them outdoors to the step and pound them together with great fervor to release the chalk dust accumulated over the day's cleaning of blackboards. Usually more chalk dust settled on the students clothing, hands, arms and hair than into the air, unless the wind helped out. The brick school walls were also employed at times to pound the brushes on, resulting in chalked walls, especially around the back doorway left to the elements to wash away. (Needless to say, being a clean and neat little girl, I didn't particularly like this job, but took my turn willingly with the other students).

Keeping basins and the wash-up area clean and tidy wasn't a particularly inviting job either, with 12 to 15 students washing over lunch hour and supposedly after toilet duties, in the same two basins of water over each day, made for some pretty grimy water and basins. We either dumped the water outside over the step or down the toilets and cleaned the basins with Bon Ami, or some such common cleanser. I suspect the teacher often helped out with this unpopular job oftener than we realized! As mentioned earlier, in winter when the furnace was running on a regular basis, we warmed the water over the heat register in the floor, right in the tin syrup pail it was transported in, but in summer cold water had to suffice. The flag monitor was responsible for putting the flag up each morning and taking it down after school hours, all year long, even when not accompanied by the student body, as mentioned previously. The flag was always treated respectfully, had to be folded "just so" and had to be hung right side up, (a very difficult task to figure out, with the Union Jack having so many stripes, that could foul up a young mind!) Caretakers now do this task I am told—made much easier by the red maple leaf/red bordered flag!

I recall Mom and Dad arranging to clean the school over several summer holidays, when I was older, not so much for the money, but so it would be done "properly" according to Mom, as it was difficult to get someone to perform this task. It was a big job for $25, but Dad helped her, as well as us girls. Isobel leant us her electric floor polisher to assist with the floor-waxing, and I recall Mom and I having a hilarious time trying to figure out how to run it, as we couldn't find the release for the handle position, (other than upright, so it just spun around) until Dad returned from an errand at home, and helped us figure it out! We often laughed about it afterwards.

Blackboard duties involved cleaning the boards each night with brushes or rags with the exception of borders of printed and written capital and lower case alphabet letters that most teachers kept written in colored chalk along the upper edge of the blackboards, for young minds to refer to, while doing their assignments each day. Allindale was blessed with a box of brown paper stencils (probably brought and left by a teacher at sometime) that were often used to brighten and enhance the side edges of the blackboards for certain special occasions. This job usually fell to the older grade girls with the help of the teacher, and I loved to help with it, when I was finally old enough. Not all teachers felt this was necessary, but if we girls wanted to put up the stencils, there was usually no objection, provided we left her enough room to carry on with the lessons she wished to instruct using the blackboard. The design was incorporated on the brown paper in a series of pin-pricks; by holding it onto the blackboard, and patting the pattern with a blackboard eraser or brush filled with chalk dust, the design would be transferred to the blackboard underneath. It was an exacting job, the transfer having to be held by several sets of hands to keep it from moving, and disturbing the fragile design before it was completed. Once it was in place, a white chalk outline made it more visible, and finally the design was filled in with colored chalk. I remember especially, an Easter lily design we often used in Spring as well as fall leaves, Christmas and all other special occasions, were remembered in that box of stencils, always well-used during my time at Allindale. In order to "trace" a picture for a school project, etc., we had to employ light at a window, holding the picture to be traced under a plain piece of white paper and tracing around the design with a pencil (a very cold job against cold windows if it was winter). I recall loving to have a piece of tracing paper, an almost impossible commodity to "own" at the time, on the farm, and my only access to it was when Uncle Don Morton would bring me discarded pieces no longer needed at his office in Regina. Then I would use and re-use each piece at school and at home for my tracing. Still to this day, it bothers me to throw carbon paper away, especially the long sheets from forms at work, etc.

Added to the "usual jobs" mentioned previously, and common in many country schools at the time, I suppose, was the job of stoking the furnace, prior to classes each day and after school. This job usually fell to a Grade VII or VIII responsible boy, whose job it was to maintain the school's heat at a satisfactory level during the cold winter months, quite a big job for a boy of this age, but because it involved a bit of pay, was willingly taken on. Gordon tells me he did this job for several years at his country school, and it is from his recollections that I can write with any authority on this. Wood and coal burning pot-bellied stoves in the classroom were later replaced by furnaces in the basement, the heat reaching the classroom by forced air through a large floor register. Each school morning, the ashes formed by the burning wood and coal had to be removed from the furnace and disposed of on an ash heap outdoors, and if embers were still apparent, inside the furnace, kindling, wood and then large blocks of coal could be added, for the new day. At noon, more fuel was added, and after school to last the night. Over the weekends, the fire was allowed to go out completely (there were no running water pipes to guard against freezing then), so on Monday morning an icy cold school greeted that boy, whose task it was to come early to school, and have the fire burning and the school somewhat warm, before other students and the teacher arrived for classes. I think on occasion, this job also fell to the teacher, if male, or fathers of students, willing to assist in this way.

School supplies, like pencils, pens, erasers, crayons, scribblers, pencil crayons, ink, etc., were all the responsibility of each student, however text books, library books, all manner of paper, and chalk, were supplied by the school. Only when the curriculum changed, requiring special texts, or when workbooks were required to go along with school-supplied texts, were parents asked to provide them. I recall at the start of the school term in Fall, some parent usually went to Regina to Canada Drug and Book Store, and bought these extra supplies for several families, or mail orders would also be filled, but not as quickly, of course. Library books could

Allindale school. 1893-1964.

My Beloved Allindale School attended 1949-1957

New brick building 1921-1964--227 pupils over the years.

During the sixty years of operation David Sexsmith and his nephew, Raymond Sexsmith, were the only two chairmen of the Board. Members of the last school board for Allindale were Raymond Sexsmith, chairman, Ivan Brown, Gordon Sexsmith, and Herb Sexsmith, secretary.

Carol, with cousin Audrey

Invited to the Halloween Party at Allindale prior to beginning attendance there in Grade I--I must have been cross at not having a costume like everyone else!

l. to r. Carol, cousins Audrey, Elaine, Jean and Linda Debenham and Thelma Spanier.

Allindale School picturing those in attendance in 1950--back row: l. to r. Tommy Spanier, Jean, Linda and Lorne Debenham; middle row: Audrey and Billy Spanier; front row: Carol, Thelma Spanier and Clayton Bradley.

Carol's first day of school with dog Buoy--Fall 1949.

These Pictures Courtesy of former teacher Edna Nelson (later Lackmantz) of Allindale students in 1957.

Norma Luther Grade 7 and Carol Grade 8--note our stylish slacks known as "drapes", and penny loafers!

Front row: l. to r. Maureen Lister, Connie and Noreen Brown with Norma and Carol in back.

Back row: l. to r. Carol, cousins Wayne and Dwight Sexsmith, Norma, Luther and Ross Turpin.
Front: l. to r. Eddy Luther, Noreen Brown, Connie, Ron Brown, Maureen Lister, Gordon Luther, Meredith Lister, Victor Luther and Darcy Livingston.

be borrowed on a regular basis. Miss Railton had the most up-to-date system. I recall borrowing one book in particular, over and over again, in the primary grades called "On Cherry Street". I always wonder what ever happened to all those books when the school was dismantled.

When the teacher was musical and could play and/or sing, we had more singing classes, tonette (recorder) etc. Also, after the gramophone was donated, with records, we also were treated to dancing lessons of a sort, which I loved. One particular dance we learned to do with partners, (boys were usually unwilling partners, but had to participate if the teacher insisted) was the Waltz Promenade:

First couple down centre, and then you divide,
Ladies go right, the gents to the side,
Now honor your partner, and don't be afraid,
To swing your corner lady, in the waltz promenade.

It seems to me, the record for this came with the donated gramophone. We used this machine a lot, playing the records over and over; it was a welcome addition to most students' school experience. For me, it was to be an introduction to a pleasurable pass time, I have continued to enjoy all my life.

Art was always a favorite period also, although, as with music, we only had time for it two or three times a week, and usually at the end of the day. I loved the beautiful white, heavy art paper (heavy bond), as opposed to the creamier colored, thinner paper, that was more "all purpose". The sheets and sheets of construction paper, with its many vivid colors held a special fascination, probably because of the "endless" things that could be made from it, or that it could be used for. I loved our reading workbooks, especially when there were little cut-out booklets we could fold, make and color. Foolscap was more boring, as it reminded me of tests and essays—did any child ever enjoy those? Several times during Miss Railton's term at Allindale, our art work was entered, in competition, at the Regina Exhibition. What a thrill it was to have a finger painting of a bridge, made with the outer edge of my fist, over water, made with my flattened hand, moved up and down all around the bridge, win first prize in its category! The prestige would have been enough, however it even came with prize money too!

Spelling Bees were a particular favorite event for me, probably because I was very good at spelling, both oral and written, and even in the younger grades, often won, or was one of the last to be seated on a missed spelling.

French, as a second language, was unheard of and not taken until Grade IX, at high school, probably because up to that point, it wasn't considered a priority to know another language, and more than likely, none of our teachers were qualified to teach it. Consequently, English was the only language spoken and written by most of us in that area. However, in Gordon's area, the German language was given priority in the home, and English was not learned until closer to school age or even until the child started school. The reasoning behind this rather antiquated theory, was to preserve the German language heritage—English could and would always be learned, as a second language, when the child was older, and in school. This often put the little child at a disadvantage for a while, a situation Gordon remembers sadly and well, when he began school!

The Red Cross Society was active in many schools, in that era, gathering small donations at monthly meetings, and small fund-raising projects etc., to help less-fortunate and war-torn areas all over the world, much as it does today. An executive was formed each year; I seem to recall being secretary of this Society at some point, preparing me a little, to hold this same position, two years in high school for SRC and later secretary of LWML at church, for several terms.

One of the only traumatic incidents to happen to me while attending Allindale was a severe bump to my head, occurring early one spring morning in about Grade V, when I accidentally fell on a small patch of ice at the north east corner of the barn, striking the back of my head a cracking blow. I was momentarily unconscious, and saw stars. By mid-morning, I had developed an excruciating headache, black spots before my eyes, and totally lacked concentration. I recall trying over and over again to make sense of a play about Robin Hood that I was to read to myself as my Literature assignment for the morning, but I was unable to function at all. I now recognize these symptoms as those of a moderate to severe concussion, and today, I would have had x-rays or a CT scan and been admitted to hospital for 24 hours for observation! However, at the time, it never occurred to me or anyone else to report the incident to the teacher, and I remained at school the rest of the day, feeling some improvement by the end of the day, and back to normal the next day, without any lasting ill effects, ever! The other traumatic event occurred to me in Grade VIII, while practicing high jump for field day, I landed at the edge of the pit and sprained my left ankle badly. No medical care was required, except cold soaks with Epsom salts, and several days rest. My pride was hurt as much as my ankle, for being such a klutz!

Several other memorable events stand out in my mind, during these years at Allindale. A contest all students seemed to take part in where we all drew an activity from a hat or some other container, mine being to sing a song in front of class each day for a week. At the end of the week having fulfilled this obligation faithfully, I recall receiving a large bag of peppermints, with true peppermint centers, (not sugary), much to my satisfaction, as they were a favorite at our house, especially for my Mom. A project on cocoa in Grade III or IV, got me writing to the Neilson chocolate company, for information; they obligingly sent all kinds of pamphlets and booklets, that turned me into a life-time Neilson chocolate bar fan! I also recall having to dress a doll in traditional costume, as part of a Social Studies project, in Grade V or so. As we were studying European countries at the time, I chose to dress a Dutch doll for Holland, having a great deal of help with the project from my mother. She had pictures of a Dutch boy and girl hanging on the wall at home, and we used these to pattern my doll's costume. We sewed a long, blue skirt, white blouse, puffy, winged hat, black velvet vest, and of course the traditional, authentic, wooden clog shoes, souvenirs of Dad's overseas wartime experience, completed the doll's outfit. Little did I know, later in life, I would have the wonderful opportunity to visit this beautiful country, and actually see these clog shoes being made, as part of Gordon's company trip - 1990. Adding to these special times and memories of Allindale, was Saskatchewan's Celebration in 1955, of belonging to Canada for 50 years. A special banner was constructed (our teacher Miss Nelson doing most of the work at her boarding place at the time, Uncle Herb and Aunt Ruby Sexsmith's home). Gold numbers proudly displayed 1905-1955, as well as the Saskatchewan Insignia of sheaves, lion and wheat on a red and green background. Each school in the area took part, making their own banner, to carry proudly as we marched in a parade in both nearby towns serving the area, Wolseley and Sintaluta, at their individual celebrations over that summer of 1955. I'm sure there were many other celebrations that marked this occasion for Saskatchewan, but these are the only ones I recall.

Two major events marked each school year all the time I attended Allindale, and for many years previous, and after, and in all country schools across the province, I'm sure—The Annual Field Day and yearly Christmas Concert. Because both were so noteworthy, in their own way, I will devote special time, attention and space to each.

Field Days (a track meet of sorts), were held each Spring, at the end of May. The weather was usually hot and sunny, and it was rarely cancelled over the years, due to bad weather. Taking part took lots of preparation, both individually and collectively, as our school name and reputation had to upheld. A silver cup was awarded at the end of each Field Day, to the school with the highest aggregate points, being engraved for that particular year, with the winning school's name, and passed from school to school, depending on those points. A shield, with little engraved name/year plates was also awarded to the winning ball team of the event. It was a proud moment, at the end of the day's activities, usually in late afternoon, when all the schools represented, lined up collectively on the race track in front of the grandstand, to learn the results tabulated by score-keeper teachers and parent volunteers, who would win these coveted prizes. Parents and friends cheered us on throughout the day, and were seated in the grandstand for this special moment.

For several years, individual gold plastic cup trophies were awarded to a boy and girl from all the students taking part, with the highest individual aggregate points obtained over the day.

It was everyone's desire to earn this individual recognition and prize. I recall having this honor bestowed on me one year, which made my gloriously happy and proud of myself and for my school, as it was through our collective efforts that Allindale earned the above mentioned large trophy cup for our school that particular year as well. I still have and treasure my little gold cup trophy won so many years ago, and all the red (1st prize) ribbons.

Several schools were involved in this competition over the years, namely Durham, Red Fox, Spring Coulee, Allindale and sometimes Sintaluta public school. It was most often held at the Sintaluta sports grounds, but was also held at the Sintaluta school grounds on several occasions. A great deal of enthusiasm went into preparing for the annual event, and as soon as was feasible, in spring, practicing began, for soft ball and relay (used the road by the school), which were team events as well as for individual events, which were as follows: High Jump (my favorite), Broad Jump, Running Broad Jump (one year when Dad was assisting I jumped 13'8", winning this event, by a wide margin). Hop, Step and Jump, Ball Throw and Races for each age group; even Skipping was a competition several years, our school doing well in this category from all the skipping done each day at recess, etc. A sandy pit and graduated measurements on two wooden standards with an adjustable pole across, (dug and made by Mr. A. Luther) served as our jump-practice area at Allindale. (This parent-farmer seemed to take a very active part, in making and providing extra items to help our school function just a bit better—no doubt he was paid for his materials and labor, and he did have more children attend our school than most families, still he always did a great job of all he undertook to make for our school ie. library/map cupboards, ping pong table and outdoor equipment, and looking back, we should have appreciated his efforts more for those items provided on our behalf!)

Four-inch lengths of satin ribbon of red for first, blue for second and white for third place in each individual event were presented to each student, as to standing at completion of each event, and points awarded accordingly. These were kept and given out by each teacher/parent scorekeeper, and attached to students' shirts with a little gold pin. By the end of the day, a colorful display of ribbons, especially red ones, on a student's shirt was the envy of those having a less successful day! Individual competitions filled up the mornings and early afternoon, while soft ball competitions went on until later afternoon, when one team was declared winner. These gave me least enjoyment, as my only forte was speed, but were a necessary part of belonging to each school, and since enrollment was usually only nine or ten students, everyone had to play. I rarely connected with the ball, and if and when I ever did, became so excited, I would throw my bat (to the disgust and danger of those standing anywhere in the vicinity of home plate), and run like heck towards first base, running being my only forte for the game. However, I was usually declared "out" before ever arriving at the base, because my hit had been so feeble! The loud razzing and cheering from opposing teams and their parents, really used to be upsetting to me, I recall, and I always felt, not necessary.

However for the most part, I always looked forward to Field Days as a source of challenge and pride…even the sunburns most of us usually got, couldn't mar the joy of the day! I remember white shorts being an absolute MUST one year; I had a perfectly good pair of blue shorts that fitted me fine, but they wouldn't do of course, as the other girls were wearing WHITE shorts! I recall crying and carrying on in the back seat of our car one Saturday night in town, trying to get my Mom and Dad to listen to reason—I had to have white shorts for the field day! Finally in desperation (as time was too short, to send an order to the catalogue for some, and none could be found to suit me in the one and only Store that would have carried such an item (Robinsons), Mom bought a piece of white cotton fabric, used my blue shorts (taken apart) as a pattern, and sewed me a pair of white shorts by the field day deadline. I remember being very pleased with them and Mom's efforts, as sewing quite often frustrated her, lack of time probably being the biggest factor!

Several other recollections come to mind, with regard to the Field Day. As mentioned previously, it was most often held at Sports Grounds in Sintaluta, and the grandstand beside the race track was used by spectators to view events of the day. Well under the back of this grandstand, a concession booth was run, by local patrons, for the purpose of providing snacks and refreshments for tired, thirsty competitors. It was a big part of the day, to take our meager bit of spending money, and decide which tantalizing treat to indulge in, over several visits, throughout the day. Since there was no refrigeration, in this booth, soft drinks were kept cool with blocks of ice (towns had power before rural folks on farms), in washtubs of cold water. Towards the end of the day, the ice melted and all that was available was "warm" soft drinks! Ice cream would last for a while in insulated type of barrels, but also became melted later in the heat of the day. However, jaw breakers were a favorite, hard, candy of the day, round and covered with a black outer coating, and concentric layers of every other marbled color, flavored with a caraway kind of taste, and finally a small seed in the centre, that had an extra strong caraway taste, wouldn't melt, and could literally break your teeth and/or jaw if bitten—they had to be sucked, resulting in blackest tongue and mouth ever! Black licorice in little pipe shapes, complete with red colored candy bowls, were also popular. I remember loving to buy Double Bubble Gum with a little comic wrapped around inside, and the great bubbles one could learn to blow with it! Miniature, Neilson chocolate bars were also a favorite, as well as Cracker Jack popcorn that always contained a small prize.

We always came home from this annual event, dog-tired, dirty and sweaty, but also happy and contented at having represented our school as best we could, and given all the competitions our "best shot", often with trophies and ribbons to show for our efforts, and the promise in our little hearts to do still better next year! Track meets in later years at high school, just never had the same appeal as did these Field Days of our public school years.

Christmas concerts hold a special memory for any child who was fortunate enough to attend a country school, as they were an individual and group effort that brought all of us closer together, at a blessed time of year.

About the middle to end of November each year, at Allindale, students and our teacher began to work on the concert. Plays were picked from play booklets that could be bought in Regina, or were brought along from school to school by successive teachers. Characters were "chosen" or volunteered for the various parts the play called for (usually from the older-grades—the younger students serving as children, if the play called for them). Props and clothing were often brought from home to add "the right touch" for the stage. Individual parts were written out and copies made, sometimes by carbon paper if it was available, or on a copying type of material teachers sometimes employed. A rubbery sort of material was poured onto a cookie sheet, and a special ink employed to do the writing. I do not know what this material was called, but several teachers used it over the years, to copy concert and school work, tests, etc. as well. In high school, a Gestetner copier was employed for such work—special paper that could be typed or written on had to be used for it also.

With copies in hand, the serious work of learning our parts began, and several hours a week were allotted to practicing together, until each character had memorized their lines well enough to discard their copies and put more effort into "acting". Songs with a Christmas Theme were chosen for choruses that all the students took part in, usually the opening and closing numbers. Of course, a teacher who was musical and could play piano, was a real blessings or an older boy or girl who played, was also of great assistance.

A Nativity was always part of the program, with Mary, Joseph, Baby Jesus (doll), Shepherds, Wise Men and Angels; carols were sung, and a "star" provided by a hand-held flashlight or spotlight for Silent Night, on a darkened stage. Drills were very popular, and usually fell to the girls, as they were a form of dance, and farm boys did not care to dance, at that age anyway! The older girls and mothers helped assemble the costumes, with crepe paper, of various colors, being the material of choice, and could be readily bought in those days. Hours and hours of work went into cutting these costumes from patterns, and then sewing them for each girl involved. Often flowers were fashioned to add to the costumes, or for our hair, or little parasols and wands were made in colors to complement each costume. I recall a particularly pretty drill we chose to present, when I was in Grade VIII. Each girl wore a white crepe paper frock, with ruffled tiered skirt (sewn onto cotton backing). The edge of each ruffle was hand painted with silver gilt paint. Graduated sizes of hand made daisies were attached to each skirt ruffle, as well as each hand-held parasol. These dance/drills were set to music, either played on the piano or gramophone record, with a series of intricate steps that had to be learned. Precision changes of parasol or wand positions added to the over all pretty effect. Practice made perfect, and practice we did, time after time, until we got it just right! Older girls helped younger ones, and of course being girls, we didn't mind all the effort involved, to achieve an attractive and pretty drill, for our parents and friends to see on concert night! Sometimes square dances were performed, with jeans, checkered shirts and dresses being worn, and even the boys helped out then sometimes!

The day before the concert, trustees and some parents came to prepare the school for the big event we had been planning for weeks. Desks were pushed along the sides of the school, and alternate seating was arranged, usually planks over chairs or empty five gallon pails (farm folks always had lots of these saved up from grease, fertilizer, etc.), that would then be covered with blankets brought along from home on concert night, for a bit softer seating!! The portable stage was brought into the school and placed at the north end on the floor by the blackboards. The rest of the year, this sectioned stage leaned against the east side of the barn, outdoors, becoming more silvery grey, warped and splintery with each successive year, as the boards were never painted, and there didn't seem to be any other place to store them. The platforms were about 6 inches high and covered about one/third of the classroom, when installed. Boxes in the school attic housed wine colored felt curtains which were suspended from wires running the width of the school across the front of the stage. White cotton sheets brought from home, provided back wall coverings and side dividers suspended on additional wires. (The globe had to be taken down). The same gilt edged winter scene pictures were pinned to these white "sheet" walls annually, to add a bit of atmosphere. Stored with these pictures were the Christmas tree ornaments, the tree also being brought and decorated that day. It was usually an 8 foot fir, held upright by a pail of wet sand. (This same tree was sometimes taken home by any parent who wanted it, as after the concert, it had served its purpose at the school). We students got to help with the tree decorating part, using the stored ornaments, as well as construction paper rings, and other ornaments we had lovingly fashioned previously for the occasion, in art class. Gold or silver letters of "Welcome" or "Merry Christmas" were often pinned to the front curtains.

The "transformation" of our one room school by all these preparations was MAGICAL… we all loved it! Naturally, regular classes were on hold for several days prior to this and until after Christmas holidays, which most students looked forward to, especially the boys! Family, friends and relatives came for miles around to different school concerts, and all seating on benches, desks, cupboards, etc., was usually taken, with many standing at the back of the room in order to see.

The excitement prior to the evening concert's beginning was electric and keeping everyone quiet behind stage was a major task for the teacher, parent helpers and older students. Lists of order of performance were posted on each side of the stage for everyone to keep track of when to be ready. An older student, chosen or who volunteered beforehand was mistress or master of ceremonies, announced each successive performance, throwing in a few jokes on the side, as additional entertainment. Some were better at this job than others, depending on personality and ability of the student—several years a top hat and tails added to the overall effect of this announcer. Prompting was done as discreetly at possible from backstage by the teacher or other helpers, especially for the plays, etc. A balance of songs, the Nativity, plays, skits and the drill or square dance made for a varied program, that always met with enthusiastic approval from the assembled crowd out front, and helped buoy our spirits and kept things going at a lively clip, the program usually lasting an hour. All too soon, the final chorus was being sung and all our efforts to present the best concert ever, were history for another year. The singing of "Here Comes Santa Claus" by all students assembled on stage, joined by the audience, hailed the arrival of Santa Claus, bounding through the door, dressed in his handsome red suit calling Ho! Ho! Ho! Merry Christmas! The concert ended and everyone went out to sit by the tree for the annual gift exchange. The teacher was usually presented a Christmas gift at this time, bought with money collected from each family beforehand, and presented by a designated student, with our thanks. Then the head of the school board thanked the teacher and students for their fine performance and everyone clapped again. I suspect the role of Santa was performed each year by different volunteers from the district, with Raymond Sexsmith doing it most often, also Albert Luther and Ed Thompson on other occasions.

In this manner, gifts were exchanged between students, family and friends in the community and a general feeling of Good Will prevailed. Treat bags and a mandarin orange were always given out from the School Board to each child present. It was during Santa's visit when I was in Grade V, that I received my very first gift from a boy…a childhood sweetheart. It was a little crown-shaped bottle of perfume and a pretty handkerchief with mauve edges and yellow flowers, with a card. The following year, he gave me a box of chocolates with a blue wrapper and another card. There was no end to the teasing each received because of these gifts, but we remained friends until he went off to attend High School, ending our puppy-love affair and sadly, we have never seen or heard from each other since.

The school building in each farming community, served as a kind of community hall for lots of gatherings over the years. Social evenings, dances, plays and meetings all took place at the school, as it was usually the largest unoccupied building in each community. When the

Happy Memories of Christmas Concerts at Allindale

Drill costumes made of Crepe paper
l. to r. The Spanier twins Sharon and Shirley
Audrey, Norma and Carol in background.

Connie and Carol singing the song "Mamma"
(picture couresty Mrs. O'Neill)

Nursery Rhymn Characters in crepe paper costumes
l. to r. Thelma, Audrey and Carol dressed as Bo-Peep.

Norma and Carol singing the song Silver Bells
Norma's dress was pale mauve silk and mine white
organza (formerly worn to Confirmation)

Note raised platform "stage" with plywood sheets on top.
Juice cans were cut to form stage light deflectors.

Daisy drill complete with parasols and gloves--white
costumes were dotted with yellow daisies all made of
crepe paper. Ruffles and other trim I hand-painted
with silver gilt paint. Alot of work and intricate steps
to this drill, but one of the prettiest ones we ever did!

government decided it would be more feasible, economical and superior, to consolidate education to larger centers and towns and bus farm children to these centers, virtually all of these country schools closed their doors forever. Many were torn down, as was the fate of Allindale. Some were moved to farm yards and used for other purposes. I treasure bricks saved by the Brown brothers, Orval and Ivan, when Allindale was dismantled, as my husband, Gordon was able to incorporate them into several walkways in our back yard. With the schools gone, a valuable "hub" of activity was removed from each district, and sadly, life in farming communities throughout southern Saskatchewan, would never be quite the same ever again. Times changed, families "moved to town" in record numbers, so their children wouldn't have to spend most of their waking hours riding on a school bus. Many farm properties began to be "farmed from town" or on weekends, and many farm yards and buildings were left to weather and wear—a very sad sight. Young couples, disillusioned with poor prices for grain and the exorbitant cost of new machinery and maintenance costs of farming, sought urban jobs and sadly, other ways of life. Nowadays, several sections of land acquired through inheritance or through government Land Bank or private sale are more the norm of farming in Saskatchewan. While both of our families retain ownership of our respective properties at Neudorf and Wolseley, both are rented out to big-business farmers, such as just mentioned previously.

Having collected these thoughts and recollections about attendance at Allindale, and putting them down in writing, has served to help me realize just why school was such an important part of my young life. I can now see that it filled a void. It provided more than an education to most of us—school was where we learned more about our culture, mores and social standards, it provided us with a measuring stick to our progress as related to our peers, and even a peer group, of our own and various other age groups. Nowadays children have organized sports, band, dancing, music, gymnastics, swimming and all manner of extra-curricular activities and learning experiences. For us, school was IT—there wasn't much else besides chores and maybe a pet or two at our farm homes. By today's standards, we would have been deprived Big Time, however, we never really felt deprived at the time. Our needs seemed simpler, and we were contented with less... after all we were just kids, and farm kids at that...town kids seemed to be a bit more sophisticated and more aware of what to expect of the world around them. However, I have found "where" a person grew up hasn't made a whole lot of difference over the long haul of life! Rather, it is experiencing the love and caring of close family life that ultimately results in lasting happiness, contentment and peace in the end. This is the kind of home Gordon and I were both fortunate enough to have grown up in, and the kind we are now endeavoring to provide for our children.

The fall of 1949, when I began school, Mom was expecting a new arrival to our family.

Probably this period involved way more details than I recall, but I remember not too many people outside the immediate family were aware of her condition, because she always wore a full, long cerise red coat, when she went out, that fell from the shoulders, concealing her enlarging size. Walking home from school one day that fall, I recall running to meet her as she worked out in the potato patch beside our lane. Just then a bee flew out of no where and bit me on the neck. I became really upset, and was crying, very glad Mom was so close by to comfort me and put soda on it to make it feel better, when we got back to the house. I remember she was wearing pants, at the time, (something Mom hardly ever wore), and that her tummy was unusually large then. I must have been aware then that a new sister or brother was being planned for, and would arrive shortly.

In spite of this knowledge, no single event of my childhood altered the course of my history as much as the birth of my sister Constance Dianne, on December 5, 1949. I guess no longer being "an only child" was the most traumatic to me, and I still recall feeling literally "threatened" by her arrival! Looking back, and knowing what I know now, this would not have been an unusual reaction in me at all, given my long-standing, single child status in the immediate and extended family unit, for so many years prior to her birth. The six year age gap between us was always a barrier to our closeness, as we seldom had common interests while growing up. (Connie and I are probably closer now since we are grown up with families of our own than we ever were back then). Of course, looking back, many events led to this six year hiatus between siblings, the main one being the war, and the unsettled life-style of our parents because of it.

Having to "share" everything was the absolute worst, especially Mom and Dad's attention and love. I couldn't know then that the addition of another child to the family, doesn't alter the love the parents feel for the first child, but at the time, everything seemed so different and changed for me, and I recall not caring for it one bit! In fact, my first reaction to my new sister's crying and fussing, as all babies normally do, was to want to take her back to the hospital immediately, not realizing then she was ours and would be staying with us always.

Connie decided to arrive in the middle of the night, and I recall being rudely awakened, hurriedly dressed by Dad, who didn't usually assist with my dressing, scurrying to town, being dropped off at Gran Teasdale's house for the rest of the night, while Mom went to hospital to deliver the new babe. Gran Sexsmith came to stay with Dad and I to look after us, during this period. This was really a special experience for me, as I felt really close to Gran, and was very fond of her. Audrey came to visit every day after school, and we would have special snacks and a play. During one of these visits, Gran accidentally fell downstairs, trying to reach something from the shelf over the stairs. I recall Audrey and I being petrified that she had killed herself or at least maimed herself or broken some bones, as of course she screamed as she fell. We were both crying and carrying on at the top of the stairs, not knowing what to do next, when we heard her calling to us that she was O.K. but could we please come down and help her find her glasses, that had fallen off during the flight! She was up and away without a scratch—imagine, and she wouldn't have been a young woman then either! That was our Gran Sexsmith, always agile and on the go, all her life! I was truly glad of her loving presence during this major adjustment in all of our lives.

Gradually, with seemingly no choice but to accept this little scrap of humanity into our lives, I recall finally coming to grips with the situation of sharing life with my new sister. I did enjoy helping Mom and Dad care for her, and finally she could even play with me a little. As Connie grew, I recall getting the spanking of my life from Dad, after I supposedly failed to latch the side of her crib properly, and she inadvertently fell out, luckily without any injury! Needless to say, I was very careful to properly latch the crib side after that!

I was guilty of teasing Connie a lot, as she grew up. Looking back, I think it was my child-like way of "getting back at her" for being born! Her arrival had made my life somewhat miserable, and I intended to return the favor. I recall this causing a lot of strife for our parents and a rather bad reputation for myself! Sibling rivalry has and always will exist in families, and I guess ours was no exception. Being so much older, I had the opportunity to observe Connie, and enjoy her childishness. We loved each other in spite of this age difference, and our squabbles from time to time, and looking back, lots of fond memories come to mind. Connie used to love to dress up and wear lots of lipstick—she was quite the little doll! When we weren't playing together, she always had her imaginary "cousin" she called Stuart (seemingly an older brother-type of person), that she included in all her play—it was cute! Apparently she still gets gifts from him on special occasions (under Barry's guise). She also loved to play with her "real" cousin Bob Morton on their frequent Sunday visits from Regina as we grew up. (The Wilson children Judy, Pat and David visited less often because they always lived farther away in various towns around Saskatchewan through Clippie's work with Beaver Lumber).

One of my earliest recollections of Connie's young life occurred at Bob Morton's christening held at St. Paul's Anglican Church in Regina, when she would have been about 2 years old. She was wearing a darling little pink coat and peaked bonnet set for the occasion. Sometime during the service around the font, with all the family assembled, and the minister droning on in usual Anglican protocol, she became too warm in her bonnet, and in keeping with the reverence of the occasion, and not wanting to disturb the proceedings, she gently took her little hat off and ever so quietly went up and laid it on the base of the font. A subdued murmur went up from all, at witnessing such reverence from such a small person! I guess she knew from attending enough church services by then, not to be noisy or make a fuss during the service, especially in such a big, fancy church! Another memory comes to mind, also involving a minister, Reverend Christmas. He and his family had come to visit us at our farm when Connie would have been about this same age. After a tour of the farm, she noticed he had inadvertently stepped in some poop in the barn yard. Upon noticing this, Connie piped up to Mom that the minister had "chicken chit" on his shoes! We all roared with laughter, and poor wee girlie didn't realize she had said anything out of the ordinary, as the S-word was used quite frequently around the farm back then. I recall Connie called herself "Constance Dinnan Sefum", as she was learning to talk, with a great deal of authority in her little voice, and no amount of coaxing or coaching on our part, could get her to change her idea of how to say her name properly, for some time—she was a determined little sprout, even back then!

Connie loved the many litters of kittens that were born to our faithful mother Tabby cat. "Mamma" over the years. She literally spent hours in the barn playing with them in the mangers where they lived in straw beds. As Mom never allowed cats or the dog in the house, as we would today, the kittens were also "off limits" in the house! This didn't seem to bother Connie though, she just loved them so much, she didn't care that she ended up smelling all "manurey" when she finally emerged from her play with those precious kitties. It was always a very sad day when finally (out of necessity for their sheer numbers and feeding problems this created as they became bigger) that Dad had to put them down, by drowning, all except one favorite one she got to choose. Of course she cried, as she had become so attached to them by then, and we always felt extra sad for her. I know it was also hard on Mom and Dad to seemingly be so mean, however, in the absence of neutering, what choice did they have? Cats would be cats, and would procreate as was their nature—there would be more kittens in due course, and she did have Mamma and her favorite kitten she had chosen to keep. One such kitten grew up to be the male Poodey cat, Tabby and white markings, that also became my friend as he grew up, and we both played with him.

At some point, while we were growing up, Connie and I began calling each other Barney and Fred, in fun, after the popular Flintstone characters. To this day, Connie will still sometimes greet me as "Fred"! It is a little private joke we still share, after all these years, although, somewhere along the line, I ceased calling her Barney—she's probably just as glad, although I don't mind the "Fred" nick-name! It brings back memories of our childhood together.

As Connie grew up, we used to play school, house, dolls and even had some pretend church services from time to time. Living in such a small house as ours, Mom's hope to have us "share" sleeping arrangements together in our one and only other bedroom besides our parent's bedroom, was dashed, when it came to Connie and I sleeping together in the one double bed! Having been used to sleeping alone all my life, up to this point, sharing, especially with my little brat sister, was a difficult pill to swallow. Since the small room intended to be a bathroom was not being used as one, in the absence then of modern plumbing, it was turned into Connie's cozy bedroom, and we parted sleeping company, much to my relief!

By mutual agreement, one time we turned Connie's room into a little hospital, where we played nurse and doctor to real or imagined patients, loving every minute of it! We filled numerous sized and shaped bottles with "potions" of colored water (food coloring was employed) and stored them on Connie's white book shelf. We used our little nurse kit that contained all the essentials for healing, like a thermometer, stethoscope, a deadly red plastic hypodermic needle, an imaginary box of pills, and of course a plastic sling with a red cross stamped on it. We treated each other, our dollies, teddies, our parents, and any unsuspecting company we could "lure" in. I wonder now, if this was our "training ground" for the eventual "helping" careers we would both pursue in nursing and dental hygiene? At any rate, we both wear uniforms and duty booties to work, and both even have caps, that neither of us is required to wear any longer.

Our fondest childhood dream was to have a play house of our very own. While we were growing up, we would wish for it every time an opportunity presented itself. We had a little "ritual" as young girls will, of making a wish by locking little fifth fingers, each time we would say something together, which, as I recall, was quite often! I would always say "Wish we had a play house!" and Connie would always say "Wish we had a bone!" Why she wished for a bone of all things, or what meaning it had in her little mind, I don't know to this day, and she never seemed able to explain it then either! No thanks to her then, that one summer when I was about 10 and she was about 4, Dad built a brand new wheat bin on skids in our yard, that we turned into our first, long-awaited play house! Dad agreed we could use it until harvest, but when he needed it, rather, before he needed it for grain, we had to be prepared to have it cleaned out, to be used for the purpose it was originally built! Of course, it was easy to agree to this arrangement, then—we had our coveted "space" to call our own for the rest of the summer—harvest was a long way off, or so we thought! We relished in the bin's wonderful new lumber smell, and the sticky resin oozing from the new wood. With a bit of help from Mom, we were able to hang a few wires, to suspend old blankets and sheets that acted as room dividers. We drew whatever we felt we needed to add to the decor, on the walls, and colored it, such as windows, lamps, etc.

All manner of "creepy-crawlies" wanted to join us to play, such as spiders, smelly black beetles, etc.! We employed a 2 X 2 piece of wood, our "bonker", to help us with swift extermination, being careful never to touch the end with the "bug juice" on it! Neither of us were very fond of bugs, grasshoppers being our utmost dreaded insect! (If snakes had lived anywhere on the farm, I know they would have been dreaded much more.) However, if an unsuspecting grasshopper hopped within a few feet of either Connie or myself, while riding in the car for instance, we both went berserk, complete with shrieks of terror and fright! Mom and Dad were never able to understand this unrealistic behavior we exhibited! I recall miller moths having almost the same effect on both of us—probably because we grew up hearing about the moth that flew in Aunt Martha's (Dad's sister) ear, and all the trouble there was getting it out, years before.

The bin's auger opening near the roof served to let light in to our bin play house during the day and we would keep the door closed to make it more private. For night-time play, Dad even suspended his trouble light from the garage for us. All of our collective childhood toys that could be utilized to make our "play house" more home-like were carted from the house to this bin. Red table and chairs, rocker, play stove, cupboards, dolls, carriage, stroller, doll clothes, dishes and all the paraphernalia two girls could muster up for a make-believe dream come true. We had wonderful times playing there, even staging "opera shows", taking turns performing, complete with dress-up, make up and exotic sounding names! Connie could bring her beloved kittens there without any problem, and we were completely happy.

However, harvest did come and Dad's warning to be out of our beloved place before then, had to be honored. We were heart-broken to give it up and would not be satisfied until we had a "real" play house, one that we wouldn't be pre-empted from! Harvest must have yielded a little more grain that year, and the price was better, or else Mom and Dad went without something else they needed, we never, ever knew, but later that fall, Dad bought the lumber and built us our much-desired play house—we were giddy with excitement! Dad staked it to the ground on all sides, for stability, and it was painted white with green trim to match the other farm buildings. A doorway faced south, that we could latch from inside with a hook or outside with a wooden latch. A window, with hinged closure door, a half-spool knob, and a screen faced west. I even made us a "couch" out of several wooden boxes, the cushion being filled with dried grass clippings and "a back" of matching fabric, attached to the wall with thumb tacks. Two wooden peach boxes covered with the same fabric, served as "arms". None of our guests ever thought it was too comfortable, but Connie and I (and her imaginary cousin) never seemed to mind it! A room divider curtain on a wire rod hung at the ceiling.

Even the flat roof that leaked when it rained in summer, or from having melted snow on it in winter, couldn't dampen our spirits and we were generally happy in our new abode. We immediately set up house in it, much like our bin house, except Mom had to help us put in a floor to get our stuff off the ground. We used old boards and wood, whatever we could find, and covered it with old linoleum. It had humps and hollows, but served the purpose of a floor, and was certainly better than the make-shift tents made with a ladder or saw horses and blankets or tarps, I had "made-do" with for years before. One day while we were cleaning up, as all good little home-makers did from time to time, Connie found a needle and thread I must have been using to sew doll clothes, furniture fabric, or something. I was up at the house on an errand at the time and Connie came running with the news "Carol, Carol see what I found—a need and threadel!" We sure laughed at how her exciting news came out backwards!

During this time, hula hoops became popular; I recall Connie being very good at slipping this circular tube of plastic (ours was blue) around her waist, and doing the "twist" to keep it rotating for hundreds of revolutions. I, on the other hand, was not very good at it at all, and always marveled at her finesse with the thing! She just seemed to have the right gyrations!

In winter, we loved to play with our sleigh on the many lovely, big snow banks that formed after snow storms, around our big yard and even in the bloughs. I recall, one winter we had oodles of snow, and after one particular heavy snow fall, we discovered a wonderful slope in the large blough surrounded by-willows, just west of our yard, behind the barn. We spent many glorious hours that winter sliding down those slopes on our sleigh and on our bums, only stopping when our ski pants and parkas, mitts and boots became sodden wet from the snow, or darkness fell. One particular favorite hill we called "Slider-down Slope" (very original)! No other snow bank, before or since, has held the same magic as did that particular one, that winter. It seemed there was a sense of mystery and suspense, being surrounded by all those willow bushes, in our own little "winter wonderland". We also spent many happy hours skating on the icy surface of the slough just northeast of the barn, as Dad kept it shoveled off for us. We would hobble down from the house on our tube skates (figure skates with picks were only for town kids that could use the rink and take skating lessons). It used to freeze to the bottom, as was a shallow slough, and then develop cracks in the surface, that were a young skaters worst bug-a-boo. I recall pleading with Dad, to please think of a way to close up those cracks so we wouldn't fall so often, as our skates caught in the edge, but of course he was never able to fix them, as there wasn't a way. Very occasionally, we would join in the free skate on Saturday afternoons, at the rink in town.

Another winter pass-time we loved, was riding on our sleigh, being pulled along behind the stone boat, as Dad hauled water from the dug out, to the barn, to water the cows, etc. with our faithful old horse Babe doing all the pulling. On one occasion, we even took our dolls along, in their doll sleigh, (a wooden orange box) that we had attached to the back of our sleigh by a slender rope of some sort. Much to our dismay, the doll sleigh inadvertently came un-attached from ours, on our return trip around the blough, and was left behind in the pasture. Before we noticed, the cows had come along, and began licking our dolls heads, probably out of curiosity, more than anything else! Poor little mothers, I can still recall our horror and dismay, as we stopped and rescued our precious babies, and had to give them baths, and their clothes had to be laundered, after this incident, with those dirty cows!

I vaguely recall a winter tobogganing party, held in the valley at Ed Thompson's farm one winter when Connie and I would have been quite young. Even Mom and Dad joined in the fun that day, with Mom screaming with glee and/or fright all the way down the hill, much as both of us, now we are mothers would do today! At the time though, it seemed a little embarrassing, for us.

The day Connie began school at Allindale, in the fall of 1955, turned out rainy and muddy, and since we never got rides to school, even when it rained, because Dad didn't care to get the car muddy, and the fact that our lane wasn't graveled, we had to walk there. I recall being totally annoyed with her that she couldn't walk faster, because of her rubbers being loaded down with mud! I was way ahead of her, yelling at her to hurry up, and she was crying and saying she couldn't hurry any faster. My biggest concern was arriving late, on the first day of school (heaven forbid), as I had never been late before, and I wasn't taking too kindly to her making me late now! Looking back, I don't know why I just didn't have her slip off her rubbers, and I could have carried her there, so we wouldn't be late, however, I didn't have much compassion back then, I'm afraid.

Actually, I'm surprised Connie didn't grow up hating me, as mean as I was to her sometimes! However, she seemed to take it all in her stride, and didn't seem to resent me for my bullying. Probably because I was so much older wiser and stronger than her, she felt, it was in her best interests to be tolerant and compliant, traits still very apparent in her nature today.

I recall other childhood experiences and memories made with my sister. After I mastered the art of playing his guitar, from Dad, we often sang together, especially at home, with Mom and Dad often chiming in too. We learned a song Patti Page (popular songstress at the time) sang on the radio, called simply "Mamma". It was about a doll she had owned as a child, and the memories it brought back each time she heard her doll say "Mamma", even after she was grown up. We sang it together, with me playing accompaniment on the guitar, at a concert at Allindale one year. Connie wore a cute little blue velvet dress Gran Sexsmith had made her, and I wore my brown/orange pleated jumper and white blouse Uncle Wilfred had bought me on one of his visits. Connie stood beside me, holding her dolly and we sang away for all to enjoy. We didn't notice at the time, but while we were singing the chorus part, one time between the several verses comprising the song, we sang a sequence of five "Mammas", instead of four, as it was supposed to be. Several commented on how "cute" it sounded afterwards!

I recall Mrs. O'Neill, (Eileen Sexsmith's mother), who was present in the audience, at the above mentioned concert, got a picture of us performing that night, and made sure we had a copy, which 1 treasure having today. Up to that point, it was unheard of to be able to take pictures indoors, especially at night, with the cameras available to most of us at the time. However,

Mrs. O'Neill had acquired a new-fangled "flash camera" that used batteries and a flash bulb for light! I recall it being a source of awe, especially for us kids at the concert that night. Since the bulbs sometimes shattered at the time of the flash, a little plastic shield had to be pulled over the unit each time. Now it is nothing for a family, to own several cameras, with flash, Polaroid's for "instant" pictures, camcorders to record audio and video, etc., but back then all we had was a black box-type of camera that could only take black and white still pictures outside, using natural light. It seems to me Dad bought it overseas during the War and it served us well over the years, although, several attempts made to take still pictures indoors with it were disastrous, as one had to hold a pose over several minutes, while the shutter was s-l-o-w-l-y clicked, and by the time the picture was finally recorded, our smiles were all "distorted"!

Connie and I both enjoyed taking piano lessons, after we finally bought a long-awaited piano, on which to play. We felt we were fortunate to be able to acquire this desired instrument from a family who were retiring and moving away from Wolseley. We even fell heir to the many, various music books their several children had acquired over the years, when they took lessons, and we were most anxious to try our musical talents when lessons began on a weekly basis, in Fall. I will never forget the dismay and frustration experienced, especially by Mom, when we discovered the precious piano had come with an added "bonus"! Tiny golden moths began to flutter out of everything we took from the closet beside the piano, and it was only then that we realized we had inherited an infestation of pesky moths with the piano! Mom went into a tail-spin, treating the piano's felts with moth repellent as well as the closet, a very time-consuming and smelly job! She finally got rid of them, but not without a fight!

Piano lessons were taught by several teachers, who came from Regina, and stayed with local Wolseley families over the years, utilizing the piano in their home, on which to teach students their lessons, for several days each week, namely the Wm. Conns and the Scrivers, while we took lessons. Our first teacher was Miss Mercier, a tall dark beauty, who seemed Italian, wore beautiful clothes and hair-styles, wore silk slippers on her feet, while she taught us (they were long days and evenings), and really knew her music. She followed a very liberal approach to our lessons, allowing us to utilize the music books we had acquired with the piano, so we wouldn't, have to purchase so many new ones. She was so skilled, she could teach you what she knew you needed to know at a certain grade level, from any music book available. Since I could play the piano a little by ear, and was older when I began, Miss Mercier let me begin playing at a more advanced level than Connie.

By recital time, the following Spring, we had mastered several duets, that we played together, with a very pleasing sound. The one we played at the recital was called "Little Birdie", but we also played several other duets that were equally as pretty, namely "The Cuckoo", "Creep

Mousie", "The Whippoorwill", and "The Monkey". Recitals were always held in St. James United Church, and were a joy to play in and attend, (especially after your turn to play was over). It was always an occasion to get a pretty new dress and shoes, too! I recall having a pretty yellow sheer flocked dress and Connie's was pink, with dotted flocking, for this particular recital, when we played the duet. Each spring we took part in these recitals over the years, under the capable direction of other teachers, Mrs. Charlotte Carbno, (whose husband Cliff taught high school in Wolseley at the time), and later Mr. Dan Brown, again from Regina. I really had to practice a lot at the weekends on our piano at home, to get my lesson assignment up to standard. By then, I was attending high school and lived with Gran Teasdale in town during the week (where there was no piano), although it was on her piano, originally, when I was about age 5 or 6, that I sounded out "Kitty, My Pretty White Kitty" and played it by ear, with one finger. (Little did I know then, that we would have two pretty white kitties for pets, eventually, in later life) Mom arranged with a neighbor, who just lived up the hill from Gran, and paid her a nominal fee, to let me practice on the piano in her home, after school each week day. It was by no means ideal, and I always felt I could have excelled much more in piano, if I would have had the opportunity to begin lessons at an earlier age, when most children begin. Connie had this advantage, and continued on for several years after I had to discontinue, because of this awkward practice arrangement, and my advancing high school studies.

Connie enjoyed other advantages, being the second child in the family that I felt I did not. She seemed to enjoy the more lenient upbringing of the two of us; I have learned since, this is not unusual, for parents to have very high, almost unrealistic hopes for the first child, that become more modified with each successive child (we have found this to be true in our own parenting experience, also), Such was the case in Connie's and my upbringing as well! Although, first children, are also known for the high aspirations and goals they set themselves, it is probably because of the parent's input initially.

I recall Connie having said to Dad once, as we were growing up, that compared to other homes, we didn't seem to have very many rules around our house—to which Dad was quick to reply "You just try breaking a few of the rules around here, and you'll soon find out how many we have!" Apparently, we were always well behaved, especially when we were out, but looking back, I think that was because we were both basically shy by nature. Also, as I look back, we were made "to mind" our manners and behavior at home also, but our reprimands were made in a sensible, caring manner, with seldom a spanking, perhaps a light cuff on the ear, or a raised voice, was all that was required, for the most part.

Because of the school consolidation mentioned previously, Connie had the privilege of living at home, even throughout her high school years, a situation I would dearly have loved to have had, even though it meant a boring, daily, school bus ride, on her part. Although I did enjoy those years living with Gran Teasdale, it still wasn't like living at home. Connie and I had very different dental histories because of my being first-born. I have had dental problems ongoing to this day, because of my early dental care, whereas our parents learned from this and took Connie elsewhere for her dental work, and her dental history, needless to say, has been positively affected over the years, by this decision.

Connie and I visited at our Aunt Alice and Aunt Elsie's homes over the summer holidays from school. Before she was old enough to come along, I recall going for a visit by myself at Aunt Elsie and Clippie's farm, called "Sunny Hill" in the Candiac area south of Wolseley. I expected it would be nice to "get away" from my sister, for a while, but I was so homesick, at first, I would have died to have her present for comfort. Aunt Elsie and Clippie were wonderful to me, and had no children of their own as yet. They had a glorious attic in that lovely farm home, that I still recall today, as kind of a magical place, filled with all of Aunt Elsie's childhood treasures, which were many and varied. She had a miniature doll house, with tiny furniture, and a pretty, wind-up merry-go-round, that really worked and played music. Connie and I both visited the Wilsons as she became older, and also spent several summer holidays at Aunt Alice and Uncle Don Morton's in their Claire apartment on Hamilton Street. They were also very nice to us, took us shopping and to see the many and varied attractions of the city, but we were still homesick, and clung to each other for support, especially the first time, as we had agreed to stay TWO WHOLE WEEKS, a bit much for two little farm girls on their first city-stay!!

I had always longed for a big swing, (like we had at school), as we were growing up, made with big poles. However, all we had when I was younger, was a small-version of a swing, that was only as tall as a fence post, Dad made at the corner of the garage, beside a barbed wire fence, that on occasion scratched us as we whizzed by on the tiny arc it was only capable of, because of its short height. I still have a nasty scar on my right leg to prove this point! When I was in high school, Connie got to have the long-awaited swing, erected on the west side of our play house, made with regular poles, that made a wonderful big arc, when swung upon, I even enjoyed it then, after I was older.

Probably, because of Connie's and my age difference, I stayed "younger" in my play and ideas, for longer, because she was still in this mode. I recall receiving my last doll when I was twelve, and making clothes for her. Also, I made a set of clothes for Connie's doll; I recall being especially proud of a little orange suit, made of fine-wale corduroy, and a green plaid skirt and stole, as well as several other items. I had mastered the art of using the sewing machine then, but also did a lot of hand-sewing, a talent I probably inherited from both Grandmothers, especially Gran Sexsmith, who could look at a picture and cut a pattern to make an outfit! I recall she made me a pink, cotton jumper once using a picture in a coloring book as a guide. She also made all of us other outfits, dresses and coats over the years, that will be discussed later under a different topic.

I recall Connie always accompanying Mom and Dad to my high school dances, several times a year. Back then, it was not an uncommon practice for parents to come to these dances, and since Dad especially loved to dance, they hardly ever missed one! She used to become so tired and pale over the course of the evening, and I used to feel sorry for her. She wasn't old enough yet, to stay by herself, and no one got baby-sitters for their kids back then. Although she was always welcome to stay at Gran Teasdale's for the night, she never would, as finally when the dance was over, we would call for her, and wake both she and Gran up in the process—coming along was the lesser of the two evils, and she did seem to enjoy the music, and the occasional dance with Dad, Mom or I. She had a favorite dress back then, she often wore; it was brown, trimmed with pink and little pink flowers; also saddle shoes were popular then, which she wore with her white ribbed stockings.

Connie followed her own course of growing up, living at home for the end of her public schooling, and all of her high school years, as mentioned previously. Meanwhile, I was most often living away from home, first at Gran's for high school and then in Regina at Grey Nuns' Nurse's residence while in nurse's training. Our precious "growing up" years together were ending; she would go on to take Dental Hygiene in Winnipeg. Gordon and I married by then, took her there with Mom and Dad, the weekend before her classes were to begin, in Dad's new Galaxy 500 Ford car, with Gordon doing the driving, as Dad never mastered the art of city maneuvering. We found her a place to stay, but the parting was sad, as we left her there. Her high school friend Irene Lutz was also taking the same course, and together, they saw the 2-year course through. She ultimately met her husband, Barry Robins there, lived in Calgary and Penticton, and finally settled here in Regina to live, work and raise their family of two boys, Joshua and Jason. Instead of a kitty for a pet, as one might have imagined, from Connie's childhood love of cats, they have a little dog, Benji, that she seems equally fond of, as she used to be toward those kittens, so many years ago! Ironically, having been referred to Connie's employer, periodontist, Dr. Claude Ibbott, for special dental work, in the late 70's, I became a patient, under Connie's professional care for a number of years following—nice to have a hygienist "in the family" when needed!

Although we weren't keenly "aware" of growing up in a Christian home, looking back I can now see that in our everyday life, by the morals and values that were taught, fairly regular church attendance, grace being said at all meals, etc., that we did in fact have quite a religious upbringing after all. However, daily Bible readings as a family, around the kitchen table, and the "no swearing" rule followed in some homes, namely Gordon's while he was growing up, were not part of ours. (I recall being so impressed with the Bible readings together, when I first visited Gordon's home, and wished to implement it in our own home, when we had it established, which we did, especially when the children were smaller). "Little Visits with God" & "More Little Visits with God" as well as Advent Bible readings with stamps were used. Michelle's pat answer "Jesus died on the cross for our sins", often being the right answer to so many of the questions. Looking back, my two grandmothers probably proved to have the greatest religious influence over my life, for which I am eternally grateful. I think it had to do with the way both of them conducted their lives, in God-fearing and God-pleasing ways, while they spent time with us, as we were growing up. Gran Sexsmith had me enrolled in Mission Band with the Alexander United Church as soon as I was born, and used to teach Audrey and I to say Grace. She sang/whistled hymns like "Down at the Cross, Where Jesus Died, Glory to His Name", "Precious Jewels", "Jesus Bids Us Shine" and "Trust and Obey" as we helped her with her chores, feeding the baby chicks, etc., and I still recall most of the words to those hymns she taught us, to this day. Gran Teasdale's religious influence probably affected me more, in my teen years, while I lived with her to attend high school. She helped me with my Confirmation, especially learning the 23rd Psalm from memory. Her love of Church and faithful attendance there, humming hymns now and then as she went quietly about her house and garden work, all affected me in a positive way. Both Grans loved God's creations and beauty, and had a reverence for life and God's people, that was part of their nature. They were kind and caring Grans, and all of us were blessed by this.

The home church we knew and loved was St. George's Anglican in Wolseley. (Dad, once United Church, was now confirmed Anglican, since marrying Mom). St. George's, still in active use today, is a smallish grey building, with bell tower, white cross (later lighted pink fluorescent, which we didn't like), stained glass windows and altar at the front (east) end, entered through a small porch/cloak room and then padded maroon colored doors. There was always an air of reverence and peace, bordering on awe in the church proper. It had a certain, burning candles, oldish kind of smell, and was always filled with a kind of soft, filtered light from the colored glass windows, with north, east and west exposures, and south, until the hall was built on that side, and then those windows were unfortunately darkened. Even the walls of pale pink, and the altar area in pale blue always seemed restful and quieting.

A great deal of highly polished, well-cared for brass accented the altar area, including the Cross, ornate sliding communion rail and side supports, Bible stand, Communion goblets. Baptismal pitcher, etc. The ornately carved wooden altar, with little candle-like shapes, always attracted me as a child, as we sat in our pews, trying to grasp the meaning of what was being said in the lessons, liturgy and sermon, etc. A gloriously high, also ornately carved wooden pulpit stood in the northeast corner of the church; well-used, shiny wooden pews, wooden wainscoting all around the interior of the church, baptismal font and remainder of furniture in wood, all added to the overall affect of this cozy house of God.

A small organ stood beside the pulpit, and was expertly played for a number of years by an elderly English gentleman, (also the town shoemaker), Mr. Wm. Hudson. His musical talent introduced us to truly beautiful organ music played exquisitely and well. Mr. Hudson and his wife, were also gifted singers in their younger years; they loved to share their talents and love of music with any and all who were interested, and I recall going to their home after Evensong one Sunday evening, to hear them sing and to visit. When Mr. Hudson was no longer able to play, due to age, several other organists, helped out over the years, namely the Hextall girls, Mrs. Hextall and also Ethel McMain, for a number of years.

We learned not to dare speak loudly in the church (only whispers) and couldn't run or be disrespectful in any way, for this was God's House. For the longest time, as a child, I thought Church was the only place God really was present, and it wasn't until much later, I realized God was in fact everywhere in the hearts of all believers, in Nature's beauty, our gardens, and we could pray to him anywhere, even at the bus stop, as dear Pastor Ruf once said!

In winter, we weren't always able to attend St. George's worship services on a regular basis, because of snow-bound roads and/or weather. In summer, when we could have gone more regularly, Saturday nights of shopping and visiting in town, were a definite deterrent to attendance! Realizing the need for Connie and I to have regular Sunday School instruction, during our young years, Mom enrolled us in Sunday School by Post. These lessons were sent out from Regina on a regular monthly basis under the capable direction, over the years, of Olive Farnden, Superintendent. A Bible-based story, related questions, suggested daily Bible readings, as well as stories appropriate for age and that week's particular message, were all part of each weekly instruction booklet; completed lessons were mailed in to Regina on a monthly basis, and returned with appropriate markings and corrections, if needed. As students progressed in age, so did the degree of difficulty of lessons; Mom often came to our rescue and helped us with these questions. I recall Connie and I faithfully taking part in this Sunday School by Post instruction throughout public and high school.

On one occasion, during public school, two ladies in a Sunday School by Post van called to visit us, staying overnight in our yard, and having meals with us, I suppose because of our long-standing association with this service. I remember the van was quite big and grey in color, with Sunday School by Post written on the sides in blue letters. Dad was so impressed that these two middle-aged ladies would be going about the country in this van, quite capable of maneuvering it, changing a tire, or whatever else was needed to aid in these visitations, (sort of like missionaries). I recall them coming to Allindale, to conduct a morning devotion with the student body and I remember feeling a little scared, embarrassed and proud all at once, of my religion that day!

By the time I was in Grade XI, I wrote my final Senior examination, receiving top marks in it and ultimately receiving a prize of a new Anglican Book of Prayer, inscribed on the first page, by none other than faithful Olive Farnden, with a congratulatory message from the Board of Religious Education, Diocese of Ou'Appelle, May 1960. I used this book regularly during church attendance, over the years, and even since becoming Lutheran in 1968, I still refer to it from time to time, recalling many of the beautiful prayers and liturgy from memory still. This ended a very long and pleasant association with this postal Sunday School, as my school studies took up much of my time by then.

Probably one of my first associations with St. George's that I remember, was on the occasion of Aunt Elsie and Uncle Clippie (my pet name for Clifford) Wilson's wedding day in October of 1948, when I was five. I had the pleasure of being asked to be flower girl in the wedding party. Apparently, I was to scatter rose petals from a little basket I was carrying, down the aisle, so the bride and groom could walk on rose petals as they came down the aisle. Aunt Alice was maid of honor, and I was in her charge for the day. She claims I wouldn't "scatter" the rose petals, as I was supposed to, but rather was "planting" each one separately and too close to the floor! How much does a little five-year old girl know about "scattering" anyway? Somehow, though, with Aunt Alice's help, we did get the job done, and came out smiling—I have the picture to prove it! Poor Clippie had a swollen gland in his neck (right side) for the day, and had to turn his head just so, so it wouldn't show in the wedding pictures, poor fellow!

Other recollections I have of this wedding day were how beautiful Aunt Elsie looked in her long satin gown; how much I loved my own little long, pink gown, with white flocked daisies on it. It was fashioned for me out of organza by Gran Sexsmith, the fabric smelled fresh and new, and was "crispy" to touch. A matching long, pink silky slip was made to wear underneath the sheer dress, and felt all cool and nice on my skin. White strap-over shoes and pink socks completed my outfit. My headpiece was my least favorite part of the whole day, and I would have loved to be rid of it! It was pink sheer fabric, to match my dress, on a plastic band that had to be pinned to my head so it would sit upright. Achieving the ringlets for my hair was the absolute worst of all! My medium length blond hair had to be coiled up all the night before in strips of flannelette fabric (Gran Sexsmith knew how to do it), and I recall, was the devil to sleep on. I remember Aunt Alice's gown was blue. Gran Teasdale wore a grey suit with a high hat, and Mom's outfit for the day was a pretty sea-foam green dress with a lacy peplum, and grey felt hat with a satin band and lace veil. Grey high-heeled suede shoes with a bow at the toe and ankle strap completed her outfit. I don't, ever recall Mom looking so attractive before, as she did that day in all her wedding finery.

Over the years, I recall many other memories that took place at St. George's. On the occasions when we attended Sunday School, my class had Miss Hemming as a teacher; she was also a nurse and matron of the Wolseley Memorial Hospital. Besides being an excellent teacher, she was also fun. On one occasion, she took her class up to the hospital, gave us a tour, and treated us to oatmeal/date cookies, made fresh in the hospital kitchen! They were still warm and delicious.

Confirmation classes taken for a year while in Grade IX, culminated in a confirmation service the following spring with Bishop Coleman presiding over this rite of passage at St George's Church. Five girls met at Reverend Ken Vickers rectory each Monday after school for instruction in the Anglican Doctrine. He made it as pleasant as possible, having a teenaged daughter of his own, Joan, he related quite well to us. Linda Hextall, Georgina Logan, Judy Lewthwaite, Lynn Tubman and myself were in this class. Mom made me a white dress of organza nylon for the occasion, with a crinoline slip, as they were in style then. Unfortunately, mine had red trim on each flounce, that showed through the sheer fabric of my dress—however no one seemed to mind except me. I must have had a white veil, but I have no recollection of whether I borrowed one or had my own. It was a big occasion, but happy and meaningful to all of us, especially with the Bishop present. (Thank goodness public questioning was not part of the service, as it was for our children, when they joined the Lutheran Church—I never would have survived this, with a microphone for all the congregation to hear each answer!)

I remember helping teach Vacation Bible School one summer while in high school, at my Mom and Gran's insistence, and then I did enjoy doing it after all. Also during my early high school years, all of the above mentioned girls and myself were members of the Anglican Girl's Auxiliary, or G.A. During the several years we attended this group was very capably led by Ethel McMain and later by Sharon Lewthwaite. We met for Bible Study, fellowship, crafts and attended several rallies in Regina. I still remember one particular rally we attended at St. Matthew's Church, Regina, that was a lot of fun; we played lawn games with a really fun leader, with lots of fellowship and sharing with other groups from Regina and surrounding area.

Earning badges was one of the facets of Girl's Auxiliary, to generate interest in skills considered appropriate for good Christian girls to learn—crafts was one such badge. I recall working on this badge gave me special pleasure, as I was really fond of any/all crafts even back then, and any opportunity to take part in or learn a new one was of particular interest to me. Mrs. McMain arranged for us to learn copper tooling, a very popular craft back then. My picture was of a deer by a stream, with a blue background. I really enjoyed making it, but the frustration of fashioning a plywood frame with an outline of quarter-round with mitered corners was quite a challenge, with my limited carpentry skills! In any event, I got it completed, and it still hangs proudly in our home today! Another project we undertook was to dress a doll, in traditional costume, in one of our mission countries, for our mission badge. I chose to dress a Japanese doll, with green/white striped silk kimono, with deep pocket sleeves, colorful cumberband, black silk slippers, and similar black trim on the neck of kimono, with pink embroidered oriental design on all. The doll's under slip was of pale peach silk, and I fashioned her hair into a bun with pale peach flowers in it, (the closest I could come to their traditional bouffant hair-style.) I recall being quite proud of this effort, and still have the doll tucked away in a special box. It seems to me all of these traditional dolls were sent to one of the above mentioned rallies for display, when completed, and all of us earned our mission badge through our efforts with these dolls.

When Sharon Lewthwaite was our leader, she thought it would be fun to do an outdoor kind of project, for our campfire badge. We undertook to hike to Mount Witness, one of the higher-hills in the valley north east of Wolseley. We took along provisions for a cook-out supper, that was the highlight of the trip! Being physically exhausted by the hike itself, a distance of probably seven miles along country roads, and then through valley hills, we barely had enough energy to gather kindling and wood for lighting our camp-fire—the real purpose of the whole exercise! However, Sharon was quite a task-master, and with the threat of rain hanging over us, we scurried a little faster.

Soon our suppers were sizzling merrily, and with a few songs to pass the time, we were able to eat in no time. (I guess this was probably my first barbeque meal ever—the first of many I was to enjoy over the years, cooked by master chef of barbeque, husband Gordon.) We were instructed to prepare raw hamburger meat, salt and pepper, layers of onion, carrot and potato slices, in a double wrapping of aluminum foil, (this foil being quite a new invention to most, of us). In another double wrapping of this same magical foil, we were to place a layer of graham crackers, a milk chocolate bar, a layer of marshmallows and topping of more graham crackers. This delicious dessert was also heated up over the burning coals, melting together to make "shmores" (as our kids now call them), although we had no name for them like this at the time. I think we must have brought along utensils and something to drink, and after partaking of this delicious feast, we sang a few more songs, put out our camp-fire, and began the long trek back to town—all before the rain storm. Needless to say, we were tired drowned rats on arrival back to Wolseley, but we felt we had really earned our campfire badge!

Although this next little segment does not really fit in with my recollections of St. George's Church, it has to do with a group that I became a member of during high school years in association with the St. James United Church. There was a Young People's group there, under the very capable leadership of a dear-minister Reverend Harvey Clark. Many of the kids that attended high school belonged to this group, that met for fellowship, Bible Study, guidance with common teen concerns, lunch and the occasional Social. Since no mixed peer group of this nature existed in the Anglican Church, several of us Anglican girls joined it during this time. I recall Gran Teasdale and I had differing opinions about belonging to this group, and it was the only point we really disagreed on all the time I stayed with her during high school. (her main concern being that it was not Anglican). However, I had my parent's support, and in the end was able to attend for several years, which I did enjoy. The beautiful hymn "Abide With Me" was always sung at the close of each meeting, where we stood in a circle and held hands. Because of many fond memories of belonging to this group, this hymn has always been very dear to me ever since.

Since I liked to sing a lot, belonging to the Junior Choir at St. George's Church, while I was a girl, gave me special pleasure. The girls mentioned previously from Confirmation, also belonged to this choir, as well as several other girls older than ourselves. Our gowns were kind of cute, and I will endeavor to describe them as best as I can remember. We wore a little black-velvet four-pointed hat with a little matching button on top. A snowy white surplus of starched cotton, went over a long under dress of black cotton, that consisted of a long skirt and separate vest that tied at the waist and had a lacy collar. Our Moms kept the surpluses washed and freshly ironed, as well as took turns doing the pastor's gown and altar linens. I suppose we enhanced the services more by our presence, than by our little voices, however, we felt we were doing our best to God's glory.

Adult, choir members had similar surpluses over black under- dresses, but they were short-skirted with a white pointed collar, for the ladies, and men wore the surplus over their pants, shirt and tie, without a hat. The ladies wore enviable hats compared to ours—they were called mortar-boards, and had a solid square top, fitted with a head cap and glorious tassel, that was worn over the side, attached by a top button. It seems to me the adult choir only became active after a lady by the name of Betty MacDonald came to town and joined our church, her husband Len being the new station agent at the time. She had a good voice, and had come from a parish that had an active adult choir that was learning Marbeck chanting, a new concept in the Anglican liturgy then. Reverend Thistle was the minister at this time, and he was also very anxious to incorporate this new mode into our little St. Georges. So, with Rev. Thistle's and Betty's enthusiasm and direction, both choirs began the arduous task of learning Marbeck, so we in turn could lead the congregation in becoming familiar with it. Gradually it became reality, and once mastered was very melodious and pretty sounding, and is still used in Anglican

The "Growing Up" Years

Christmas 1956 taken by Audrey with her new camera

We always went to church on Christmas Eve--had stopped in for a visit at Uncle Herb & Aunt Ruby's house.

Connie with two of her lovely kittens--she loved them all!

With New Sister Constance Dianne--first studio picture taken of us both by Stan Biram/Jack Biram (Reliable Studio) in Wolseley. Connie would have been about 6 months old here and I age 6 or 7. (Connie wore a white silk dress and I my favourite pink checkered suit, and white blouse trimmed in blue embroidery Gran made me. (Note "Owey" scratch on left knee).

services to this day, I believe. Previous to this, the adult choir only sang on Festival occasions, and I recall we all learned the perennially popular hymn Praise To The Lord, The Almighty, The King of Creation, during Reverend Morrow's tenure. Whenever we sing it now, I still think back to those girl-hood days, as I have known it from memory since then.

When both choirs were active, the Senior group sat in the choir pews the Junior choir once occupied, behind the minister's kneeling areas then the junior members had chairs in front of the organ, and knelt on the wooden floor, for praying, my knees remember, with excruciating clarity!! Mom and Dad sang in this choir for a few years, as well as other parents and members that had good voices and liked to sing. I recall liking it a lot that, we were all in the choir together. I think Connie must have been too little yet to take part, and sat with Gran Teasdale in the pew during services.

All female heads had to be covered while attending services back then, and a lady was never too young to begin wearing a hat! Little girls wore cute little straw or felt ones, in white or pastel shades, trimmed with flowers and lace, etc., while ladies wore ones made of similar materials, but in more varieties of color, to match outfits, and often with veils of varied openness, from fine mesh-like net to that with bigger spaces. Feathers, sequins, marabou, lace and all manner of ornamentation was featured on hats over the years. I recall one particular hat that Mom wore frequently back then that seemed to be a favorite. It was fashioned in a pretty bright green, (her favorite color being green), in a kind of velvet fabric, but with a solid base, that just kind of perched on her head, over her short, wavy hair. It was trimmed with a little matching green veil in medium-sized mesh, and decorated on both sides with gold sequins. Also I recall having a little green felt hat, with a fitted back and little brim that had brown gross-grain ribbon trim and a little nosegay of flowers on one side, that I wore as a small girl. Later on I wore a brown felt hat in a very similar style, except that it has an upright feather trim. I recall once during a service, while I sang in choir and was wearing my four-point hat as part of my choir outfit, the same Betty MacDonald (mentioned above) borrowed my hat, and wore it to the service, as she had somehow come without one, and couldn't attend without her head being covered (she wasn't singing in choir that day). I thought it was a bit presumptuous of her to borrow my hat that I had left safely with my coat in the cloak room, but also was a little proud that this grown-up lady would think my girlish hat was appropriate enough for her to wear during church service. Over the years, we all owned and wore many hats, the cost of them becoming more exorbitant along with all manner of clothing. However, since it was an acceptable and appropriate form of dress and fashion, and necessary for church attendance no one seemed to mind. They could be bought in any fabric, color and form and often matched shoes, purse, gloves and scarf, to go with a certain outfit. I think Women's Lib and fashion had something to do with the decline

Memories of St. George's Anglican Church at Wolseley.

St. George's Anglican Church.

Recent picture of St. George's Anglican Church and Parish Hall.

Aunt Elsie & Uncle Clifford (Clippie) Wilson with little Carol (age 5) as flower girl

Clergy, (Rev. Morrow), Bishop Coleman with adult and junior choir and Confirmation class outside Parish Hall.

Junior choir members(l to r.)Linda Hextall, Lynn Tubman, Georgina Logan Judy Lewthwaite and myself in foreground--the Coles behind me.

Inside St. George's Church as I recall it as a child, showing Altar and Chancel area.

in popularity of wearing hats, in the mid to late sixties and by the seventies they were not even required for church attendance. The occasional one still surfaces, as part of an outfit, or if the woman feels inclined, but now hats and scarves are mostly worn for warmth in winter or as sunshades in summer.

St. George's church was built on its present site in 1902, with a seating capacity of approximately 100. The addition of the Parish Hall on the south side of the church was built in 1952. It can be accessed from the west outer door, or through the church, and has served its purpose well over the years, for meetings, overflow church attendance, etc. Our confirmation reception, as well as our high school graduation dinner, and my bridal shower were all held in this hall, to name a few fond memories of special occasions.

Ministers serving St. George's over the years that I recall were the Reverends' Howell (I don't remember him, but he is remembered fondly by family members during the War, and apparently I played with his daughter Janie, later killed in an auto accident), Christmas, Morrow, Ragg, Thistle (came to us as a bachelor, but married a widow with twins-boy and girl during his tenure in Wolseley), Ken Vickers (confirmed us), J. Major (married Gordon and I, and was also my patient at Grey Nuns').

Families in attendance at St. George's during the years I recall were: Mellors, Coles, Hudsons, Tillers, Mrs. Kenny, Nettie Poulson, Walter Chapman, Olives, Logans, Peaches, Flemings, Lemckes, Tubmans, Lewthwaites, Hextalls, Smallpieces and Peagams (Summerberry), Jack Biram, Jim Hood, Willises, MacDonalds, Mary Adames, Gardens, McMains, Olivers, Boyces, Holowells, Merricks, Audrey Chatterson, Gran Teasdale and Sexsmiths, Wilsons and Mortons on special occasions while visiting. I recall elderly Granny Olive always sat by herself on a wine colored felt pillow, in the front left pew, and none of her family ever sat with her, although they all attended regularly; we never seemed to know why—perhaps hard of hearing?

I recall always liking to attend church, I think a trait learned from the love and devotion Gran Teasdale had for church and the importance attendance there held for her. I especially liked to take Communion, once confirmed, learning to hold the chalice just so, and the significance of this Covenant, both spiritual and as a rite of passage on the way to adult-hood. Harvest Festival with little sheaves of wheat and garden bounty gracing the church and altar, and Christmas midnight service, as well as our wedding service, bring back special memories. To this day I still enjoy attending services at St. George's.

The Alexander United Church in our farm district, conducted Vacation Bible School over several summers while we were growing up. We were Mission Band members from birth, at this church, thanks to Gran Sexsmith enrolling us. Aunt Ruby, being a member there also, invited us to attend this Vacation Bible School, and we gladly accepted, as summers were long and boring on the farm.

I recall a pleasant male pastor/church-worker coming to conduct the sessions of Bible Teachings, Songs, Crafts and Games. We took our bag lunches and stayed all day. We made vases one year, with a bottle brought from home, swirled in a tub of several colors of house paint, floated on top of water. As each bottle was dipped in slowly and carefully, some of the paint adhered to it in a swirled pattern with a pretty result. Aunt Ruby and several other United Church district ladies helped us with some of the teaching, crafts and lunch supervision. I recall having Kool-Aid there for the first time, (a delicious new drink made by dissolving envelopes of flavored crystals into water and adding sugar—Voila! Instant thirst-quenching drink that could be made anywhere). I remember a little scroll made with local tree branches, cut into foot-long sticks, and wound with long strips of brown paper, tacked to the branch with thumb tacks. We stuck Bible stories on the paper and unwound it as the story unfolded. I still have it saved all these years, thanks to Mom keeping it for me.

At the end of the week, we presented a program for parents and friends. I remember Joyce Malo and I had been chums over the week, as we were ages with each other. We were asked to light candles during the evening service at an appropriate time during the minister's sermonette to coincide with "light a candle in the darkness", in relation to Christians lighting the darkness of the world, an easy enough task for two responsible girls at about age 9 or 10, (or so he thought). However, since we were always made very aware of the dangers of playing with matches, at home, and the subsequent disasters that lighting and playing with them could result in, (Dad always said "A good servant, and a poor master") I was literally petrified to light a match, even when asked as part of this meaningful service. I was so nervous about lighting this horrible match, and candle, that I inadvertently lit my match at the wrong spot in the sermonette, thus somewhat spoiling the effect and purpose. I wanted to die of embarrassment, however, the minister quietly waited, until Joyce whispered to me to put my match out, and then we both finally lit our candles at the appropriate time. Otherwise, apart from this minor faux pas, these summer interludes at Alexander Church were a pleasant chance to spend time with other children our own age in a Christian atmosphere. Unfortunately, this dear little church was closed soon after this, and moved away, parishioners then having to attend church in Wolseley or Sintaluta. Over the years it had served the community well, with humble beginnings by the early settlers, namely Aunty Martin, a staunch and God-fearing lady in the district at the time. Grandparents Dave and Agnes Sexsmith were founding members of this humble prairie church, as well as many other early district families, all anxious to have a place of worship within closer proximity than Sintaluta or Wolseley.

Visits to the Wolseley Cemetery always held special meaning for our family, probably because many loved ones rested there, especially Grandad Teasdale. Over the years many more family and friends were laid to rest in this place, always well-maintained over the years, with mowed lawns, clipped Caragana (Caraganda as the long-standing old custodian Mr. Tom Poulsen used to call them) hedges and all manner of marble tombstones. The serenity of the cemetery, located on the edge of the coulee at the north-east corner of Wolseley, was always apparent, and even a slight breeze could always be heard whispering through the many large fir trees that grow along the perimeter and as dividers of the sections. In summer, garden flowers were always taken to the graves in memory of departed loved-ones, Gladiolus and Sweet Peas with Baby's Breath being perennial favorites. A little quiet time and a pause or a tear at each grave in remembrance usually completed the visit. In winter, visits could still be maintained, as the main pathways were kept open, however flowers weren't usually so readily available.

Years later, Dad Schroeder gave us a new way to look at cemetery visiting. We were viewing Mom Schroeder's new grave-site at Melville cemetery in November 1988, when he mentioned that it didn't help him to visit her grave, because she wasn't really there anyway. And of course he was right, her spiritual living soul had departed for heaven. However our family had always held that a person's mortal remains were still here on earth, and that was why we felt the need to visit the graves of our loved ones—sort of a last connection to the departed one. A personal thing really, and we are all entitled to our own thoughts and feelings in this regard, I suppose.

Although death did not mar our immediate family during our childhoods, we were aware of its sometime harshness, cruelty and untimeliness. Farm children grow up with birth and death situations as related to animals, chickens, kittens, etc., and probably cope overall with it better than city children. It was just the way things were; no one back then ever really took the time to explain death, as is done nowadays, even with small children. Then, children rarely went to funerals, and death was kind of hushed-up and not talked about too much. It wasn't questioned, just accepted as a part of life.

While our parents were growing up, it was an accepted procedure to keep the body of a deceased relative at home prior to the funeral. Undertakers looked after the funeral, but funeral homes as we know them, weren't in existence yet. I suppose this practice eased the departure of the loved one somewhat, for the family, however it must also have been a bit of a trial, with everyone coming to pay their last respects to the departed, right in the family home, especially in summer, without the benefit of modern embalming practices. Back then, things were often done out of necessity rather than design, as was the case here. The establishment of the Tubman Funeral Home and Ambulance Service in Wolseley in 1946, was therefore of vital importance to the community, remaining in place to the present day, although the original founder Garnett, passed away in the 1980's.

We grew up with Mom's constant referrals to her father's early and sad demise at the age of 52 of heart failure, and even though we didn't have the privilege of meeting him, we felt we knew him quite well by her many references to him. She always felt she would follow in his footsteps, as she was very like him everyone said, and also die at an early age. We always felt threatened by this prediction, that she wouldn't be around much longer—I remember this making me very sad thinking of the prospect of being without a mother, and not knowing quite when it would happen. Consequently, I feel I always distanced myself somewhat from Mom, emotionally at least, while growing up, depending more on Dad for emotional support, in preparation for this eventuality that never came. Instead, the reverse happened. Dad passed away suddenly at age 58 from a massive myocardial infarction, without even time for a good-bye, which was devastating to say the least. Mom on the other hand, seems to be following in her mother's footsteps of longevity—so much for predictions—our allotted time on earth is in God's hands, as always.

It has been my experience, a person never really recovers from the death of a parent, life goes on but is changed forever—with a constant sense of loss in all of life's situations that follow, especially those involving family. Gran Sexsmith's death in 1961, affected me with a similar sense of loss, as well as Gran Teasdale's in 1982, although they were elderly ladies at the time of their passing. I have no remembrance of Grandad Sexsmith's passing in 1948, but have scant memories of cousin Patsy Wilson's death as a newborn baby in 1952. The darling white flocked coffin, lined with satin, the little form, as if asleep, dressed in the knitted sweater and hat Gran Teasdale had knitted—Clippie carrying the coffin, and all the family filled with much sadness, especially Aunt Elsie. Their family was also touched with sadness about that time again when Vera, Clippie's sister and her son Kenny drowned in their farm dugout. We were always warned about the dangers of going near this man-made body of water, common in every farm pasture, as a source of water for livestock.

The Heebner house fire claimed the life of his wife and children one winter in that era—I recall this because I met this nice lady, Mrs. Heebner, one day while Dad did some business with Mr. Heebner at their farm, north of us somewhere. She and I walked to fetch their cows from a far pasture, visiting all the while. I recall she had pretty long, dark curly hair and wore wire-rimmed glasses like Gran. She was nice to me, and as I remember they had no family of their own as yet, at the time of our visit. I remember the death of this nice lady really saddened me then.

There was no doubt about the finality of death—even to child-like minds. Loved ones were buried and no longer with us, but it wasn't until much later that I was cognizant of the concept of everlasting life afforded to all Christian believers, with eventual reunion with our loved ones in Heaven. This realization came much later, after association with the teachings of the Church and with maturity. A person almost begins to look forward to Heaven, to be reunited with so many of our loved ones now departed—if only we wouldn't have to die first!

A deep and abiding faith was nurtured during those girlhood years associated with St. George's church that sustains me still. I feel I would be remiss not to mention it, so have chosen to do so here. The beautiful Anglican liturgy, so proper and reverent, is still tucked in my memory, and can be recalled easily, whenever we have the opportunity to attend an Anglican service. The service of Evensong with its beautiful Nunc Dimittis, brings back special memories, as we often attended that service on Sunday evenings as a family. The numerous hymns with melodious tunes have special significance, because as I recall them, I can hear Dad's, Mom's and Gran's voices singing them, and learning from them. Probably, as a child, one doesn't realize the significance of certain happenings until much later, looking back. So it is now, as I recall this association with the Church of my youth, and the many fond and beautiful memories it imparts.

As mentioned previously, grace was always said prior to our meals at home, and we never started a meal until everyone present, and the blessing had been said. Connie and I always seemed to be the ones to provide the family with grace, saying it in unison. At first we learned the blessing Gran Teasdale always used:

> For what we are about to receive may the Lord make us truly thankful,
> Bless it to our use, and our souls to thy service
> (And make us ever mindful of the needs of others—a line Gran sometimes inserted when someone in particular needed prayers),
> ending For Christ's sake, Amen.

The second grace we learned from a traveling fellow, selling Christian literature, pictures, etc. (We bought the red velveteen plaque with white lettering, "Christ Is The Head of This House" that always hung above the south window in the living room all the years we were growing up, from this man). He stayed for lunch with us, and knew the following table prayer that he suggested might be more appropriate for children to say:

> Bless this food that we partake,
> And make us good for Jesus sake. Amen.

We thought so too, and so we proceeded to learn it, after he wrote it down for us; we said it for a long time following. Connie was just a little girl at the time, and when she learned it, she thought the words in the second line were make "it" good, instead of make "us" good, referring of course to the food in her little mind! We sure thought it was cute one day when she said grace by herself for some reason, and we picked up on it! We sure teased her, praying all those times to make the food good, instead of us!

Other graces learned over the years and said at home and then in our own home were:

Come Lord Jesus, be our guest,
And let these gifts to us be blest. Amen

As well as:

God is great, God is good
let us thank him for our food.

which was learned by our children in Sunday School, and said a lot at home. The Table Prayer learned at Grace Lutheran Church and sung is a particular favorite, although we don't use it at home

Be present, at our table Lord,
Be here and everywhere adored,
These mercies bless and grant that, we
May feast in Paradise with Thee. Amen.

Evening prayers said kneeling at the bedside, were part of the ritual of going to bed, when we were young, "Jesus Tender Shepherd Hear Me" and "Now I Lay Me Down to Sleep" were both taught to me by Gran Sexsmith, and said by both Connie and I. Also we had our "God Bless" prayers—for family members and others we wished to remember, often closing with the Lord's Prayer. A commendable and God-pleasing habit to grow up with, and one that has endured to this day, although being Lutheran now, I must confess I have gotten away from kneeling to pray, as we learned growing up in the Anglican faith.

Along this same spiritual train of thought, another type of service comes to mind—the November llth, Remembrance Day or Armistice Day interdenominational service held in all towns and cities following World War II to honor the war dead, lost in all wars over time.

I presume we always attended these as a family, just like church, because of Dad's war association. We were always off school for the day, whenever it fell in the week, just as now. Poppies always arrived at all schools each year for us to sell and wear, probably from War Amps or Saskatchewan Handicapped Association (now Abilities Council), the proceeds to help them with funding. Depending on the teacher, we would sometimes have a little service of songs, poems would be read, always "In Flanders Fields", etc. Often we did art work around the white crosses and red poppies theme. I am happy to see children are still encouraged to write poems and essays, and do art work in school, with regard to remembering what November 11 stands for—may they never know the ravages of war, just as we have not thus far, not directly in our country at least.

The Remembrance Day service was always held in the Town Hall, and was always well attended, especially when I was a young child. After all, World War II had just ended, many families were still mourning the loss of a loved-one, and it seemed fitting and appropriate to attend. Winter had often just begun and usually a bitter cold wind prevailed, serving as a reminder of war's misery and chill to those present.

Ministers from all the local churches took turns in conducting these services. Hymns like "0 God Our Help In Ages Past", "Lest We Forget", "Lead Kindly Light" and "Abide With Me", etc. were always sung to piano, the only musical instrument at the Hall, that always sounded so different from the organ at church, to sing hymns to, I thought. A sermon was given, and finally all assembled outside for solemn "Last Post" trumpeting, and laying of wreaths at the cenotaph, directly west of the Hall. For as long as I can remember Garry Moore, local trumpeter lad, always played the Last Post, then two minutes of silence were observed, during which time at least one or two local dogs had to bark and howl, (probably upset by the trumpeting sounds just previous), or else a car horn would peep, somewhere in another part of town.

One particular year, when Connie was just a little girl, it was particularly cold, and so she and Mom went to our parked car to wait for the end of the outside part of the service. When later asked if they could hear this part of the service from the car, Connie piped up and yelped 'No, we couldn't, because the dogs were barking and the horns were blowing and we couldn't hear the Lord"! We sure laughed at her little mind's interpretation of the events, especially that she thought the Lord would speak!

The cenotaph of white marble is of an unknown soldier, clad in war trappings, leaning on a cross, looking down at the names of those fallen comrades that are engraved on the mid-section, with the words "Lest We Forget" on the base. The area surrounding the cenotaph is raised from the sidewalk, fenced with chain link fence, and entered by two cement steps. Pots of pansies always stood at this entrance, and over the years the area has been maintained well.

The Legion—returned soldiers, sailors and pilots, always attended in a body, wearing uniforms, flashing medals, etc., and it was very impressive when they marched as one unit. Dad never joined the local Legion on his return, although he had medals, and his uniform, and I always felt sorry he didn't take part with the other returned people, but honored his personal wishes not to do so. He never ever wished to share his experiences during that period of his life with us at all, wanting to put it in the past somehow. However, we were proud of him for his war-time duty just the same and always treasured the gifts and artifacts he brought back from his travels. (Little wooden case with shells on top, with note enclosed "To my Bonny Fine" from him, a peachy sea shell, the Dutch shoes, thimble and an earthen glass).

The Legion remained active throughout this period, (and to this day, for those veterans that remain) and attended Dad's funeral as a unit on November 12, 1968, filing past his coffin at the graveside to pay their last respects, dropping red poppies on his casket, a most memorable scene, that still saddens me to this d a y, whenever I think of it.

It is commendable that Remembrance Day services are still held at our Nation's Capitol, Ottawa, and throughout the country, as a tribute to the thousands of souls lost, and lives altered and changed forever because of War. May we never forget their sacrifice for our freedom.

Looking back, it seems that the love of music, singing and dancing played a significant part in my young life, a fondness that has endured to this day. Mom records in my Baby Book that even as a baby, I loved to be sung to and danced with and apparently I learned to hum and sing at an early age. Little wonder, with both parents loving music and dancing together the way ours did!

I always had the feeling Dad could have been quite a musician, if he would have had the right chances at the proper age, as he loved to sing, bought himself a Hawaiian guitar with money he had saved and taught himself to play it, cording with a steel bar. He knew how to harmonize well, and also played the mouth organ with skill. To such a musical person, dancing came naturally, and he and Mom danced "many a mile" in their courting days and throughout their lives together, as recreation and as a form of entertainment, in an age when it was very popular to do so. When Connie and I were old enough, Dad also taught us to dance, first at home, and then at dances. His sense of rhythm and skill on the dance floor, especially to a good old time waltz or fox trot tune, were memorable to watch or to be his partner. I've yet to dance with such a great dancer before or since! No wonder our Mom misses those happy times so much—we all still do!

Mom also had her musical talents in singing and especially in piano. She took lessons on this instrument all of her girlhood years, Grandad Teasdale driving her to Wolseley for instruction on a weekly basis. She managed to achieve a high level of expertise in piano and theory, and still plays nicely to this day from music, but not by ear. Mom's musical abilities helped Connie and I a lot with our own piano lessons; she was always willing to help us, especially in learning a new piece, to get the sound of it and the counting, etc.,

There was never a Sexsmith get-together without a sing-song as we were growing up, as both Dave and John Sexsmith clans inherited the ability to be good singers and talented musicians, especially Aunt Gladys on the Dave Sexsmith side and Vic Sexsmith on the John Sexsmith side. They could sit down at the piano any time and play all the old favorite songs in whatever key was required, a wonderful talent indeed, and one we all loved and appreciated. Many fond memories of these sing-songs come to mind, having taken place either at the original Dave or

John Sexsmith large, and beautiful homes, that could accommodate any number of persons around the piano in the parlor, and the overflow in the huge adjoining, rectangular dining rooms at each home. Depending on the occasion and time available, these sing-songs would sometimes go on for several hours, usually always ending with the songs Good Night Ladies, Show Me The Way To Go Home, or There's A Long, Long Trail. These were favorite times for all, and it saddens me to think that most of these relatives, with their wonderful voices and talents are now gone from our midst.

One of only several recollections I have of Grandad Sexsmith', was him singing an old Scottish song (his ancestry) "The Hat Me Father Wore", at some community get-together at Allindale School, before I was old enough to attend school there, sometime prior to 1949. As I recall the words went like this:

She's old but she's beautiful, she's the best I've ever seen, She was worn for over ninety years, 0n that little isle so green Since me father's great ancestors, It's descended into yore. It's the relic of old agency, It's the hat me father wore!

It seems to me he was very old and frail by then, but still maintained some vitality, and a full head of white hair. I seem to recall him being helped back to his seat, perhaps this exertion being almost too much for him. Grandad also used to coax me to eat cooked carrots, (a vegetable I loathed at the time, but have since come to love), as by eating them, my poker straight, hair would "curl", miracle of miracles, according to him. But it never has worked even to this day! The only other memory I have of Grandad was sitting on his knee, as a young child, in his big arm chair in the kitchen of his and Gran's big farm home, and him teaching me to make a sort of "gung" sound in my throat, and him being so proud of me, that I could in fact make an identical sound in my throat at such an early age —an unusual inheritance from your paternal Grandfather, I would say, but I've never forgotten it, or him because of it, and those carrots.

Although Grandad Teasdale passed away long before I was born, I am told he loved to sing as well, and took part in several local musical reviews over the years, while he lived. Golden Slippers., Tip Toe Through The Tulips, Look For the Silver Lining, Long Long Trail, and Rainbow Round My Shoulder were a few of his favorite songs.

No account of my girlhood would be complete without mention being made of participation in Amateur Hours. Looking back, I suppose it could have been considered a very youthful kind of community service of sorts, as it was volunteer work for a worthy cause, a passion still dear to me now (Heart/Cancer canvassing, school library, Block Parent, Neighborhood Watch, etc.).

Amateur Hours were sponsored in local towns by the Associated Canadian Travelers to raise funds to combat the raging affliction of tuberculosis, affecting so many adults and children in Saskatchewan, in the 1940's and early 1950's. Fort San in the Qu'Appelle valley was built as a special care home for treatment and eventual recovery of patients with the disease, much of the building and treatment being funded by the tireless efforts of these Travelers and the volunteer efforts of contestants that took part in these Amateur Hour presentations. Hence the long-handled name. Associated Canadian Travelers Tuberculosis Prevention Fund, going by the call letters A.C.T.T.B.P.F., was coined and used for this very worthwhile effort.

Since 1 had grown up loving to sing with Dad, to his guitar accompaniment, first together and later in harmony, and had learned all the songs of his era, many with complicated verses and words, I guess we were "naturals" as far as amateur talent went, to be asked to take part in several of these amateur hour presentations being sponsored at this time.

These concerts were held in mainline towns, usually in the Town Hall, and were broadcast, over local radio stations, the station donating the sound equipment and the announcer, probably from Regina, the nearest large centre. A program of local and surrounding farm area talent was set up to perform for the evening; a local audience participated with pledges of money for the entertainer of their choice. In addition phone lines were in place, so that radio listeners could also pledge by phone, for their favorite entertainer. The more support a contestant had, the more money was pledged and ultimately collected for the treatment of tuberculosis. At the end of the evening, with most of the audience long since departed, and only a few die-hards still phoning in with pledges, the contestant with the most money pledged was declared the winner, with placement of second and third following. (something along the lines of Telemiracle now, only there is no contest, for winners).

The first Amateur Hour Dad and I took part in was December 11, 1948, when I was five. (I wouldn't have remembered this date, but Mom kept a souvenir program all these years that I was able to refer to). 1 recall getting to stay up very, very late, and becoming awfully tired, and because pledges for our entry had been quite good, as opposed to some of the other contestants, Dad and I found ourselves in "the finals" on that occasion. A farmer we knew from Sintaluta, was in the audience, a bit tipsy, and had taken a real liking to us. His pledge of grain or something, at the end of the program, put Dad's and my entry in the lead, and we won that night. I'm not sure if I realized the significance of helping others through our efforts, at such an young age, however, I remember enjoying doing what I loved most in those early years—singing with my Dad, with him playing the gee-tar, as he sometimes called it!

Dad and I took part in several Amateur Hours during this time. The next one 1 recall better, because I was older—nearly seven, and even have a recording of us singing "Daddy's Little Girl", that was a particular favorite, and still saddens me to hear or sing it now, because of all the fond memories associated with it. Joe Hatcook was the radio announcer assigned to that particular concert, and I can still remember him a little, as blond, young, and he was nice to me

ASSOCIATED CANADIAN TRAVELLERS

T.F. – C.P.

AMATEUR RADIO NIGHT SHOW – WOLSELEY, December 11, 1948

Total	Contestants
..........................1.	Mt. Crescent School, Orchestra
..........................2.	Marlene Brown, Wolseley
..........................3.	Urban Thoroughgood, Wolseley
..........................4.	John White, Deveron
..........................5.	Marion Read, Wolseley
..........................6.	Rose Lane School, Orchestra
..........................7.	Shirley Evans, Glenavon
..........................8.	Emily Grzenda, Glenavon
..........................9.	Veronica McKinnon, Glenavon
..........................10.	Joan Garden, Wolseley
..........................11.	Edna & Pearl Schick, Wolseley
..........................12.	Carol Sexsmith, Wolseley 13 3.50
..........................13.	Ruby Laverdiere, Kathleen Rogers, Verna McLean, accompanied by Opal Jackson, Wolseley
..........................14.	Five Razors & a Strop (Hector Tourigny, Ashley Pow, Henry Rood, Don Gilron, Arthur Miller, Bill McCully, Wolseley).
..........................15.	Garry Moore, Wolseley
..........................16.	Marlene Brown & Marion Read, Wolseley
..........................17.	Della Acton & Donelda Moore, Wolseley
..........................18.	Grades 7 & 8, Wolseley Public School - Choral
..........................19.	Harold Sexsmith, Wolseley
..........................20.	St. James' United Church Junior Choir
..........................21.	Mildred Pearen, Indian Head
..........................22.	Lorraine Moore, Regina
..........................23.	Ruth Mitchell, Wolseley
..........................24.	Mrs. Flora Jeeves, Wolseley
..........................25.	Murray Hurst & Kathleen Rogers, Wolseley
..........................26.	Wolseley Canadian Legion - Trio
..........................27.	Wolseley Canadian Legion - Accordion
..........................28.	Ray Fleming, Elmer Lyke, Ronald Broan, Wolseley
..........................29.	Wolseley Orchestra
..........................30.	Lloyd Pearen, Kenneth Livingstone, Indian Head
..........................31.	Betty Buzash, Regina - Piano

CKRM - 980 on Your Radio Dial

and Dad. His voice is recorded on the record also. It was cute how he termed my age of being past six and closer to seven, as being "on the near side of seven"! Besides Daddy's Little Girl, some of the other songs we sang were: Four Leafed Clover, Carolina Moon, Let Me Call You Sweetheart, Long Way to Tipperary, You Are My Sunshine, and Swing Me In The Moonlight. There were more too numerous to mention. I don't recall our standing at the end of the other concerts, but we did enjoy our participation in them.

We sang together publicly on other occasions too, at Lions concerts, etc., in the Town Hall. As I grew up, I learned to play the guitar, under Dad's careful supervision, according to him, better than he could. So on the last occasion we were to sing together in public, before I no longer wanted to perform with him (because teenagers didn't sing with their dads or something), and he had just volunteered us, without consulting me, I played the guitar, and sang the harmony part, while he sang the main tune. We had chosen to sing "Bless This House" a particular favorite we sang together at the time. He had a bit of a hoarse throat, and decided to take an Aspirin for it, backstage, without any water! Needless to say the pill stuck, the cure was worse than the ailment, and his voice was not it's usual for that performance, although several remarked later, how nicely we sang together, with this new arrangement of me singing the harmony or alto, as one lady described it, and thought I should look more seriously at studying voice as a profession! Although I never seriously considered singing for a living, as I didn't think my voice was that good, it was still nice to hear it.

Thus an era ended, and Dad and I had finished our singing career together, publicly at least, although we did still enjoy sing-songs in the car, especially on the way home from town or church. Just a Closer Walk With Thee, In The Garden, Galway Bay, God Be With You 'Till We Meet Again, etc., being particular favorites for these family times. On occasion, we would sing more recent, popular songs, that Connie and I would know better, but of course the old songs were still best! When we obtained the piano, we had a few jam sessions at home, with guitar and piano and singing, as I played some by ear; the closeness of family sing-songs together could definitely be felt and in memory still endures. The beautiful melodies and lyrics of the hundreds of songs learned from our parents, especially Dad, that had been popular in their younger years and through the War years, will probably live on in our hearts forever, always bringing a smile or tear, as we sing or recall them. Songs like that just aren't written anymore! (The titles of a number of these songs that I can best recall is recorded later). I also remember little piano chording ditties taught to me by my Aunts, including the "courting" song, as well as chopsticks and "Blue Moon" chords.

I recall with fondness, tinged with sadness another event that occurred in our family in the early 1950's. Our cousin Bob Morton came to stay with us for several weeks while Aunt Alice went into hospital for a cholecystectomy. Bob would have been one and a half to two years old at the time and still went by his little boy name Robbie. Try and explain that long of an absence from both parents to a little guy of that age! Needless to say at first he was devastated, and cried himself to sleep saying over and over again "I want my Daddy, I want my Daddy" as he cried into his little hankie (one of his Dad's white handkerchiefs he had brought from home). Connie and I felt so sorry for him and tried our best to make him feel at home; it was kind of neat having a little brother, even for a short while! I recall he had a cute little checkered brown and white coat and peaked cap he wore for good that looked so cute on him.

Gradually, he felt more at home with us and would play a little, especially with Connie. He used to dread Mondays, wash day for Mom, as she spent a good deal of time in the basement where the washer was located, doing the week's washing. Robbie would stand at the top of the stairs, and call down to her "Don't, go down a basum, Aunty!" over and over again in his little sad voice. Connie and I were to entertain him as best we could, as it seems to me it was summer holidays from school, but of course Aunty Margaret was his favorite. I recall he used to think Aunt Ruby's name was "Druby" as we always said Herb and-Ruby, when referring to this couple together, and somehow to Robbie the d and R together made her name into Druby! She sure laughed when we told her and it was a little joke for quite a while, even after Robbie went back home to Regina, after his Mom's recovery,

Looking back, it seems we did the little fellow a very cruel injustice, by thinking it was wiser not to let Uncle Don (his dad) visit him either, just because Aunty couldn't come too, while she was recovering from surgery. We felt he would want to go home with his Dad and the pain of separation would begin all over again. However, the way it was, I think Robbie felt totally abandoned by both parents and perhaps was more deeply affected by this separation than we realized at the time. So much for hind-sight—it is always 20/20!

Another memory comes to mind, involving the Mortons; Aunt Alice had a dear friend Betty Lazurka, that I had met on several visits to Regina; she was always helping Aunt Alice save me "grown up" things like lipstick, purses, old high heeled shoes, (black suede with really high heels, with silver clickers and open toes—I can still picture them!) etc., that all little girls love to fall heir to. Apparently, on one visit, when Aunt Alice had promised to bring me a purse from Betty, I had the audacity to ask her about the purse, before I greeted her "hello". Needless to say, I was reprimanded soundly for this faux pas in etiquette, and my promised purse from Betty was nearly forfeited! I wasn't allowed to forget this for a while either, and whenever Aunt Alice visited after that, I was always careful to greet her first and ask questions later!

Betty had a niece about my age, and this fact seemed to endear me to her. So, when Betty was planning to be married, in Moose Jaw, the summer I would have been about 8 or 9, she asked me to sit at the guest register with her niece. Of course I was delighted to accept, as I liked Betty a lot. Arrangements were made for me to attend, and Gran Sexsmith made me a lovely pink sheer nylon dress with an inverted pleat in the skirt, a satin belt and a matching pink slip. Everything went along fine, until I tried a fancy, dainty rolled sandwich for lunch, that had mushy asparagus in the centre! I had never tasted it before, and it was awful, but somehow, being a little lady, out at a wedding, I made myself swallow it, gagging all the way down! The bride and groom were never aware of my misadventure at their wedding reception. (Small world that it is the groom's brother is now one of our children's favorite teachers at Luther College!)

Another memory comes to mind, this time involving Uncle Don; as mentioned previously, as we were growing up, the Mortons visited us at the farm lots of weekends, especially on a Sunday. Uncle Don had many skills and was a handy fellow. He knew how to whittle a whistle from a poplar branch in spring, when the bark was just right! And it would even make a sound! Try as I might—I was never able to duplicate this skill, even though I seemed to follow his instructions to a tee, on many other tree branches in spring!

I recall sometime after I began school, Gran Sexsmith, who was always sewing or knitting us something, decided to sew me a lambs wool quilt, I think as a birthday gift. I was thrilled at the prospect of having my own quilt, and she proceeded to make it. I can't recall whether or not Gran and Grandad ever raised sheep and she had the lambs wool saved from then or did she buy it from someone, I don't know.

She sent for fabric for a covering, from the catalogue, and when it arrived they had substituted the feminine pink patterned cloth she had ordered for a more masculine white fabric: with blue sailors on it. We were both disappointed, her the most, but I was so anxious to have the quilt, she proceeded with the sailor cloth. It was completed in no time, and felt so great to snuggle under. I loved having it and her for being so kind and making it for me. It is hard to think of this being the same quilt we still use on our bed to this day; it has been recovered twice and carefully washed, fluffed and air-dried over the years, still maintaining its softness, lightness and warmth.

Life was not without its traumatic events while growing up on the farm. I have already related the episode of running out of the house with no outer clothing, right after we moved to the farm, thinking Mom and Dad were going off to town without me, when all they were trying to do was get the car going! I seemed to live in fear of being an orphan back then, as it seemed to me there was no worse plight!

I recall the winter Gran Teasdale was in Wolseley Hospital after having caught her arm in her wringer washer and having to have skin grafts etc. under Dr. Turnbull's care, (later on he became a noted ophthalmologist in the city). Mom and Dad went to town every other day to visit her, and I dreaded those days with a passion! I was petrified they would be run over by a train and be killed, just as the Mellors had a few years earlier, crossing the tracks to come home, and I used to cry and cry with fear and dread after school each day, waiting for their return. Sometimes, when I couldn't bear it any longer, I would walk to Uncle Herb and Aunt Ruby's about a mile away, to the east, and cry there some more. I can see now, I must have seemed like a real wimp, however, at the time, my fears and concerns were very real to me!

Then at about age 9 or 10, I was hospitalized myself in Wolseley Hospital, for a persistent ear infection. This was probably one of the most traumatic experiences of my entire childhood, as I was bundled up one cold winter night, and Dad and Uncle Herb drove me to town, all because I had this bad earache and had also had a nosebleed, and vomited up a bit of blood. Mom panicked, (not knowing about the nosebleed), and thought I was dying of some kind of internal hemorrhaging, so Bingo! I was in the hospital in no time. Probably on looking back, the bleeding was a blessing in disguise, as the ear infection obviously wasn't going to clear without antibiotics, and perhaps I would have had hearing loss if it hadn't been treated properly soon. Dr. Isman came, looked in my ears, prescribed bed rest and intramuscular antibiotics. I ended up in a bed in the Maternity ward, because that was the only available bed, and my room-mate was a kindly, young Indian lady, the only other patient in the four-bed ward.

Gran Teasdale came to visit me every evening, her neighbor Mr. Relf driving her, and bringing me warm celery soup in a little jar with crackers (all transported in her beige shopping bag with wooden handles, a common conveyance carried by ladies back then). To this day warm celery soup is still a particular favorite soup. Mom and Dad came every afternoon, and I used to count every minute until they would come again the next day, as visiting hours were only from 2-3 p.m. and 7-8 p.m. back then. At first, the nurses wouldn't let me out of bed, and yet no one offered me a bed pan or commode on which to relieve myself. I recall finally scampering across the shiny polished linoleum floor the first afternoon, in desperation to find a toilet, and being caught by the cleaning lady, who was kindly and nice, and kept the hospital spotless, especially the floors! After that I was offered the silver saddle (bed pan) more often, and shortly after that could get up to the bathroom.

I swear, I have never seen longer, or felt duller needles with hooks on them, than the ones those nurses found to stick in my little hip with my antibiotics in them! The only bright spot in the entire experience, was all the mail I received each day, namely from Aunt Alice, and the visits from Mom and Dad and Gran. Probably the whole experience only lasted several days, but it seemed like an eternity to me. Thank goodness it was the only hospitalization experience I had as a child.

I recall Connie having her tonsils out in Wolseley Hospital as a small child, and seeing her go by the hospital waiting room, where we were waiting, being carried to the operating room by the matron Miss Hemming. Connie was all drowsy and sedated wearing a little blue and white dress and had bare feet. Mom was crying, and it was then I realized how much we all loved this wee girlie, and the possible complications of this operation, even though I had been through it myself, and it was a common procedure, carried out on most children in those days. Fortunately, Connie came though it just fine as well.

Epistaxis or nosebleeds were a common occurrence for me during my school years, and even though I got one regularly, I still panicked, thinking during one, I would probably bleed to death! Peroxide was commonly used on a piece of cotton batting (before cotton balls became fashionable, the equivalent came in boxed rolls of batting, rolled in navy paper, for home first aid), being inserted in the nostril to quell the bleeding, a home remedy that didn't work well, dissolving any clotting. Pressure on the nose or ice on the head and neck, weren't known then. The worst was the blood running down my throat, and making me feel sick afterwards. We were never able to figure out why I was subject to these nosebleeds then, and still a slight blow to my nose, will start one, even today.

Catching my left foot and leg in the grate at the post office one Saturday night in town was my other childhood misadventure, at about age seven. It happened so fast, probably just the way my small foot wedged beside the cement and the edge of the grate, and zip, I was about to lose my foot and leg to this iron monster: The idea was to keep mud and grit from entering public buildings by having patrons walk over the grate at the doorstep. The grate was over a kind of ditch in the sidewalk that collected all manner of trash and dirt, so losing your foot and leg in this ditch was a scary thing for a small girl! Luckily, several passers-by witnessed the incident, and before Mom had to do anything, and I'd barely started to cry, a gentleman passerby had managed to free me from the nasty grate's grasp without any problem. (Years later, this kind man's daughter, was in nurse's training with me, and I was her big sister).

The only other traumatic incident that occurred during our childhood, involved Mom. She and Gran Sexsmith were going to butcher chickens, a common practice to obtain poultry to eat on the farm. Somehow, Mom inadvertently stuck a sharp butchering knife into her left forearm, in an effort to quiet a fluttering chicken, resulting in a deep stab wound. Since Dad was away, we had no phone, and only Mom could drive the car, it was my job to run for help. (I would have been about 8 at the time). Luckily, that day Raymond Sexsmith was grading our lane with the municipal grader, as part of his road maintenance job for the municipality. With my little heart just pounding, at being so close to this monstrous grader, I hailed Raymond down, quickly telling him of our plight. He was able to arrange for medical help in town, the same Dr. Turnbull securing the laceration with several stitches. Thankfully no lasting ill effects came of this trauma. Connie and I had our share of coughs and colds over the years, and both had chicken pox and mumps during our childhoods and red measles as older children. I had a particular liking for Bassett Lozenges sold over the counter at the time as a sore throat remedy. I recall they were made in England, and came in a skinny blue box. They were linseed tasting, pale brown in color and had squared off corners with a powdery surface. I loved them with a passion, and bought them at the drug store with my allowance, even though the clerks cautioned me they were not candy! (Now 1 see they are only available at candy counters, and I still love their taste just as much)!

Mom and Dad rarely became ill, and when they did fixed themselves up with over-the-counter drugs or the odd aspirin, bought in town at the drug store. Dad was a firm believer in Mentholatum and often rubbed his chest and neck with it, securing it on with one of his woolen work socks, wrapped around his neck (a clean one)! There was another reddish, mustard ointment he would sometimes use, but it was very potent, and burned our skin. Cuticura salve in a small lidded tin, was used for minor skin irritations and cuts, as well as the old favorite Iodine. Ozonol became popular for burns about this time, as opposed to the age-old "butter" treatment, which of course did more harm than good, because of the salt content. Dodds kidney pills (bright red) in a cardboard lidded pillbox and Carter's little liver pills (brown) were common over the counter medications of the time. Covered with fabric, these lids made great doll hats!

Cod Liver Oil and Scott's Emulsion were vitamin supplements taken by children over winter, as well as Neo-Chemical Food (brown syrup). Listerine mouthwash, tasted bad and was strong, so it had to be working, right? We always used plain white, boring Listerine toothpaste, however, I can recall always begging Mom to buy Ipana, in a pretty yellow/orange tube. The paste was creamy yellow in color, and tasted much better than Listerine—however, apparently it was more expensive, and we never got to buy or use it. (Aunt Alice used Ipana)

With regard to personal hygiene, baths were taken only once a week, due to the shortage of soft water and modern plumbing, with sponge baths from a basin in the kitchen sink having to suffice in between. We always used Lux hand soap in a white bar I recall, as they sponsored one of our favorite radio programs Lux Radio Theatre, at the time. Deodorants were almost, unknown, and not worn then, so B.O. was common! Whew! Ban was the first stick deodorant I can recall using in the early 60's; later this same company made deodorant history with the first "roll-on" liquid deodorant. Gradually, more and more people accepted this new-fangled idea of using deodorants, and with the advent of modern plumbing and running water, even on the farm, everyday bathing became the norm.

Female sanitary protection was out of necessity "home-made" from flannelette or other soft cloth filled with cotton batting for absorbency, and sewn into pads, that were washed and re-used, or just thrown away or burned after use when our mothers were young. Commercially made sanitary-protection was more the norm by the 1940's, being marketed under the Kotex name. Since then great positive strides have been made in this regard, with many more companies producing this essential feminine commodity in different absorbencies, etc. Tampons became more commonly used in the late 1960's early 1970's and finally adhesive strip pads became available. Obviously, the security these products now provide, has been a major factor in facilitating women's active role now, in every walk of life. Women are no longer held back because of their femininity or the fact that our nature dictates we bear the children for future generations.

Sex and health education weren't a priority and indeed the whole subject of sex was "hush, hush" and not discussed—quite different from today! Even maternity was considered kind of a private affair, and public displays of pregnancy, especially in the last trimester were thought to be in poor taste. Even when I was expecting Heather in 1970, I was forced to terminate my nursing employment as store nurse, with a major department store downtown at six months, which was quite normal business procedure back then. The paid maternity leave our young women now enjoy, and in some cases even paternity leave being allowed by some employers is a far cry from only twenty-five years ago—but a very positive change, thanks to women's lib., and changing social attitudes.

Very little make up was worn as we were growing up; not much was available, and few women used more than a pat of rouge on their cheeks, a bit of powder to keep the shine off their noses, and a dab of lipstick for going out. Nail polish, if worn at all was clear or pale pink—only ladies of the night wore bright red! Avon or other beauty companies were not yet on the local scene. The massive focus on all manner of beauty and hair care products today, and the phenomenal amounts of money spent on it boggles the mind compared to back then!

Hair care consisted of washing once a week—oily hair or dry being of no consequence (a sore bone of contention between my mother, Gran Teasdale and myself, as I had oily hair, that needed more frequent shampooing). Curls and waves were obtained in straight hair by coiling wet hair into a curl and securing it with crossed bobby pins. Metal curling rods with hinged wire securing fasteners and a little rubber end or silver metal clip wavers could be used to wave wet hair. Later on, curlers were made of mesh-wrapped coils of wire in various sizes, with a bristle brush inside, to hold the wrapped hair around it, and secured with bobby pins in each end. Metal hair clips, with a little hinge, were used to secure pin curls. Curlers of foam rubber and plastic all became available in following years, as these materials became available. Air or towel drying were the only means of drying damp or wet hair back then, except at the beauty parlor, where coned silver hair dryers were available.

Home perms were sometimes given to grown up ladies by each other, marketed under several brand names, and causing the hair to smell to high heaven for days! They must have been very caustic and hard on the hair. Salon perms and hair cuts at a hair dressers in town weren't common, although Gran Teasdale always had her fine white hair permed at Simpson's beauty salon during the years we were growing up, and always looked very prim and proper because of this. Mom or Dad used to cut each others and our hair when it needed it, and trimmed our neck with the clippers. I don't recall having a salon hair cut until my first year of high school in 1957, and never a perm until much later, after marriage. Dad always felt if God had intended women to have curly hair or colored hair, He would have made it that way, and so we girls and women in the family abided by this kind of creed and never permed or colored our hair, even for years after his passing. Mom was fortunate to have been blessed with beautiful curly hair, that has now turned gracefully white, still maintaining its waves and curls to this day, never requiring either perming or coloring.

It was common for women to wear fine mesh hair nets being available for sale in a number of brown colors, black or grey and white, depending on the lady's need. Mom and Gran always wore them. Gran also had several pastel colored nets that tied around her head at the front that she wore to keep her hair tidy while doing her housework, or perhaps to hide her hair when she was in need of a perm, I can't recall, just that I remember seeing her wear them sometimes. She and Mom also had colored turbans they sometimes wore over their hair to go out shopping etc., but never for good, like to church or out visiting. It seems to me the fancy knot that went to the front was permanently sewed into the turban, and then it wound around the head and tucked in the back somehow. (Having never worn one, and only recalling them from memory, I'm no expert on this!) It was common to wear scarves over curlers while the hair being curled was drying, or to keep curled, waved hair in place outdoors in perennially windy Saskatchewan! No hair sprays for holding existed over the counter back then, but I recall Mom using a kind of gel for waving her hair.

Braids or pigtails were common for girls as we were growing up, and I recall Mom French braiding mine on a regular basis when I was in early Grades at school. Linda and Jean Debenham always wore their hair in long braids all the way down their backs, and I recall envying these beautiful braids, but never seemed able to grow my hair long enough, and it was always fine and "fly-away" as Mom put it! Maybe this was a blessing in disguise for apparently, at school, girl's long braids could be dipped (with disastrous results), in ink wells, by boys sitting behind these unfortunate girls, although I was never witness to this. Barrettes and colored satin ribbons were common hair adornments for girls, and later when "pony tails" became common, elastics were employed to draw the hair into place.

Dandruff seemed a common scalp scourge in those days, needless to say encouraged by infrequent, shampooing and passed between family members by sharing common brushes and combs; it didn't seem to be known then that it could be caught in this way. Medications to clear the scalp like Selsun or Head & Shoulders Shampoo were not readily available as they are today, unfortunately.

Dad was a barber of sorts, and haircuts often took place in our kitchen, Uncle Herb and Harold being his most frequent customers, and done as a favor, with no monetary gain on Dad's part. Barber shops, always readily identified by their red/white spiraled pole out front, and pool halls commonly went together back then, where men usually had their hair cut, and female company never entered there in!

Men and boys wore their hair short in length with short sideburns in the late 40's and early 50's, with slicked back hair popular with younger men into the 6O's copying the rock 'n roll stars and Elvis's influence. Brylcream, Vitalis and Score were all common hair dressings back then. Brylcream even had a little ditty that was kind of catchy advertising, and went like this:

Brylcream, a little dab will do ya,
Brylcream, you look so debonair!
Brylcream, the gals will pursue ya,
Simply rub a little in your hair!

Brush cuts were a common boys hair cut, with some men having their hair cut that way too. Clean shaven, achieved with a safety razor, seemed the most popular way to go, however a few men sported mustaches, namely Uncle Don and Ed Poels that I recall. No one had beards, as was the case when our Grandads would have been young men in the early 1900's. Into the 70's with the Beatle's influence, longer hair became fashionable for men, with long, bushy sideburns.

Perfumes for women and colognes for men were worn in moderation, but not to the extent and variation of today, or the exorbitant cost. Lavender was a common scent women wore. Men carried cotton handkerchiefs to blow their noses or wipe their brows, while women carried lace, embroidered hankies. Facial tissues weren't commonly used, but Kleenex with a new "pop-up" method of dispensing seemed to bring them into popularity about this time. To this day, with so many brands on the market, these popular tissues are usually still referred to as "Kleenex"! Color and decorator boxes also became promotional gimmicks for tissues. Toilet tissue has come a long way since those days with a scarcity of this commodity, as we were growing up. Some households utilized old newspapers and catalogues for this purpose, especially in the outdoor outhouses, however we always had white, scratchy Purex rolls of tissue, I recall, probably due to low cost.

Getting back to health care, as we were growing up at home, mustard plasters were a common remedy for chest colds/pneumonia etc. They were made with a paste of flour, dry mustard and water, spread on a piece of flannelette of double thickness, edges secured and laid on the chest or back, for 20 minutes several times/day. I recall having one or two of these as a child, and they felt yucky; hot and cold at the same time and burned tender skin. I guess they worked alright, especially on Dad in his younger years, who was subject to bad chest colds. Apparently the wearer had to protect against a chill by going outside, etc. after mustard plasters had been applied.

A more modern version of mustard plasters was Thermogene. This was a kind of medicated orange-colored pad of batting covered with gauze that was worn on the chest in winter to relieve congestion from colds. I recall Audrey, my cousin, wearing one from time to time to school, under her sweaters, etc., to ward off a cold.

Some of these home remedies for maintaining health and vigor were obtained from traveling salesmen, representing major companies like Watkins and Rawleighs that carried quality products for moderate prices. These men called on the rural communities regularly, carrying commonly ordered items right with them in their vehicles. If they didn't have the items with them, they would bring them on the next trip. Camphor balm, Mentholatum, and other related health care products were common.

I recall a faithful Watkins man, Mr. Pernitzki, who traveled our area for many years, as we were growing up. I think he lived at Fort Qu'Appelle and had a large family. All manner of health care needs, spices, household/cleaning products were available through these traveling merchants and farm wives depended on their regular calls. They also carried veterinary products, that also filled a real need. In the absence of veterinarians back then, farmers had to rely on their own skills and innovations, or on each other for help at calving or illness of animals and these products were often relied upon. Watkins had a yellow medicinal salve in a silver and yellow tin with a lid that was a main-stay cure-all. A tin of it remains in our barn, up on the rafter to this day, as witness to Dad's abiding faith in the stuff!

For lack of a better place to mention it I will relate an incident I recall with regard to the following veterinary illness. Hoof and Mouth Disease killed many cattle during the 50's and cars traveling about the province had to be sprayed with disinfectant if crossing in and out of affected areas. I recall coming home from Regina during this time, and having to stop at a highway spraying station for "disinfecting". We were to allow them to spray our shoes and inside the car also, but Dad told us to lock our doors, and when the outside of the car had been sprayed, we took off out of there! I recall Gran Teasdale was with us, and she was very glad Dad took the stance he did, too. None of our cattle were affected, or any in our district that I recall, thank goodness, as there was little compensation for losses of livestock back then.

With regard to traveling salesmen, others also came, like Fuller Brush, Electrolux and Insurance/Investments, etc. Ed Poels traveled for Investor's Syndicate out of Indian Head and called on all the farms in our district on a regular basis, not so much to promote his company, as just to keep in touch and have a visit. While we were growing up, we always loved to see him; he seemed to lead such a flamboyant life-style compared to our boring farm one, and brightened up the day with his jokes, trivia, and hugs, often staying for a meal or at least a coffee.

Several medical break-throughs during the 1940's-50's affected everyone's health in positive ways. Regular x-ray screening for Tuberculosis was carried out throughout the province in traveling vans, to ensure freedom from this disease that was then so prevalent. Polio had affected and crippled many children, but Salk vaccine soon eradicated this disease. Immunization against whooping cough, small pox and diphtheria was available and administered by public health nurses in all public schools, (also Allindale). The discovery of penicillin and related antibiotics in the 1940's was a literal life-saver; prior to this, many persons died of infections, pneumonia, etc., as was often the case during the days when our parents were children and young people.

Publicly funded health care, or Medicare was legislated into being during our childhoods in the late 50's and early 60's, under the capable leadership of Tommy Douglas of the CCF party. This proved to be a boon to ensuring all people, regardless of financial status, proper hospital care/surgery and treatment whenever required. Gone were the days of huge debts incurred by serious illness requiring long hospitalizations, as was the case with Gran Teasdale in the 1930's. She required surgery for cholelithiasis, now considered routine surgery, mostly with few complications, but back then she was hospitalized for months at the Regina General Hospital under Dr. W. Alport's care. The monumental debt that resulted had to be paid, but Grandad Teasdale, a poor farmer, on rented land with limited resources was plagued by this debt, unable to pay it. Mom has often said she thought this worry may have partly led to Grandad's early demise in 1939 at the young age of 52.

Many persons in those days were left in similar straits by an unexpected illness; it was not uncommon for doctor's bills to be paid in the form of a commodity readily available, on the farm namely livestock, poultry, etc., rather than money. Often these bills just went unpaid—few had very much money or wealth back then.

Home births were common prior to the mid-1940's and mid-wifery was practiced out of necessity, in the patient's home, or at the mid-wife's home, commonly called a nursing home. The building of the Wolseley Memorial Hospital in 1947 was a wonderful addition to the community and surrounding farm area, and with more extensive health benefits in place, it became more common to utilize modern health care services in hospitals and institutions, rather than rely on care and treatment at home.

Saskatchewan's health care system was second to none back then; it was admired, studied and similar versions of it were implemented in other provinces, and indeed even other parts of the world. It has worked well and served all the people of this province for over forty years. However at the time of writing, things are about to change—the cost of health care now has become phenomenal; the present government is implementing major cut-backs, health care is once again becoming home-based, with a trend away from hospitalization and institutionalization. The emphasis is on wellness, rather than illness. Individuals are again bearing more cost for their own prescriptions, and specialized therapy like oxygen, chiropractic care, dental and eye care. We have come full circle—from the heady days of all health care being covered, and now seem to be going backwards, towards where we were some forty years ago! Who knows at this point where the province's health care will end up?

Modes of transportation went through quite a transition during the years we were growing up, 40's to the 60's, so I will endeavor to relate some of my recollections in this regard.

Of course, automobiles and trucks were common conveyances by then, but looked quite a bit different to the sleek, aero-dynamic vehicles we know now, and the speed limit was more moderate, because of road conditions common then.

Even as a small girl, I was always fascinated by cars, and longed for a toy one with a passion; each year when a new catalogue would arrive from Simpsons or Eatons, they would show a newer version of a toy peddle car in the toy section, and I would beg and plead, to no avail, to my parents to buy me one. They probably cost only twenty dollars, or so, but back then that was a lot of money to spend frivolously!

My first memory of actually riding "in a vehicle" is when we moved our belongings to our farm home from Gran Teasdale's house, as mentioned previously in Ted Lewthwaite's red box truck, and becoming stuck in winter snow drifts, when I would have been about age 4. I would have had a long train ride from Fort William to Wolseley by then and many car rides, but have no recollection of these of course, because of my younger age.

The other "ride" I recall (I would have been pre-school at this time), was returning from Regina with Gran Teasdale by Grey Hound bus after a visit with Aunt Alice and Betty Lazurka, to see the Barbara Ann Scott (popular skater at the time) Carnival, featuring Teddy Bear's Picnic. I had enjoyed the performance a lot. The morning we were to come home to Wolseley, I ate a huge breakfast, even though I didn't usually eat breakfast at all, and at everyone's persuasion even had coffee, of all things! Well, on the bus ride home, I became so terribly ill, and wanted to throw up, but because it was in the days prior to washroom services on buses, I had to wait. Gran tried to divert my attention by having me trace a yellow rose on some writing paper she had along, however, it didn't work very well. I thought I would be O.K. if I got some air on arrival, while Gran went into the bus station to phone Mr. Relf for a ride for us. However, this just proved the final straw in my gastric upset, and my first bus ride ended in disaster! I remember being very embarrassed, but also terribly relieved—and had learned a good lesson. When traveling on the bus eat lightly! This was to be the first of many trips I would take on Grey Hound buses over the years.

As a small child, when we first went to the farm to live, I have vague recollections, (corroborated with Mom) of threatening to "run away" from home, when things weren't going my way! This involved running a little ways out our lane, towards the main road. However, a scary-looking, well-treed blough then existed in the field on the right side at the end of the lane. I always felt wolves or robbers would be lurking there (vivid imagination)! This thought always frightened me enough to force me to run back home as fast as my legs would carry me; my threat to run away evaporating for that day!

Apparently, I always explained to Mom that I didn't leave that day because "it was so f-a-r away!" I guess meaning leaving the security of the farm and ending up in "the middle of no where" only half way out our lane, was a pretty scary prospect, to a small person aged 4 or 5. I must have abandoned this idea altogether after I began school, and realized that I could in fact leave my home, and return by walking on my own. Probably the fact that I had somewhere to go then—school, made the prospect of running away less appealing, I don't recall. However, that blough always remained scary to me, until Dad had it cleared and leveled a few years later, and was able to use it as additional arable land.

The first family car that I recall was an old Chevy, that had knobby tires, wooden spokes in the wheels, and chains that could be put on the back tires, for driving in mud and snow. It had a very squarish looking box-type of body with running boards. It had to be "cranked" with a crank to start it, as it had no starter. (Gordon says these cars had no battery and no key, either). I don't recall actually "riding" in it, but I guess I must have. It seems to me Mom and Dad painted it themselves, quite a medium, bright blue color, during the coarse of our ownership, and they felt quite proud of how it looked following.

Our next car was a metallic green "humpy-backed" Mercury car that seems to me Dad bought second-hand through trade-in, etc., at Tom Allen's, his favorite garage in town. I recall an incident involving Connie and this car. Dad had left it parked by the house, and Connie, age 2 or so was playing in the car by herself. Somehow, she put it into gear "and drove" it down to the garage! (actually it had just "rolled" down there as there was a slight grade down from the house!) We sure laughed, and she thought it was funny too, once she realized Mom and Dad weren't mad at her. We referred to this car as "The old Merc".

The Merc was followed by a green & white sedan-type of Ford—our first "modern" looking car; this was bought second-hand sometime in the late 50's. I remember feeling we had finally joined the ranks of civilized living with this car!

I recall another incident involving Connie and this green and white car as it sat out after washing. She would have been about 5 or 6 at the time and was again playing in the car with her beloved kitten. In her play she had somehow managed to get a bobby pin twisted around the cat's tail. Of course it started screeching and attempting to get the offending pin off its tail, running about wildly in the car. Connie must have jumped out of the car to get help, and inadvertently locked the cat in the car! Dad must have had an extra set of keys, and freed the hapless kitten from its bondage, in a short time, but poor Connie felt so bad to have put her little pet through this ordeal. Needless to say, she learned a lesson regarding kittens, bobby pins and car locks that day!

Dad's last car was a brand new maroon/white Ford V8 that seemed like a rocket at that time, with so much obvious power and speed! It had plastic bubbled seat covers, (still in place today) and I recall I sure liked riding in it on weekends when Dad brought me back and forth from town while I attended high school. It was his pride and joy, and he cared for it in the usual protective manner he maintained with all of his cars and tractors. Regular washes, waxes with Turtle wax and polishes as often as needed with a soft, oiled cloth, he kept in garage just for this purpose. Looking back, it was a blessing he was able to enjoy at least one "new" car in his short life time, as he did treasure it so. Since his passing, Mom has maintained this caring vigil over it also.

I recall being "in awe" of kids in my peer group, like my cousin Audrey who got their driver's licenses practicing with their Dad in their Dad's cars, and then being tested by the R.C.M.P. in Indian Head. Our dad, in his customary protective manner in dealing with his cars, said there would be no use in Connie or I getting our licenses, as we wouldn't have anything to drive anyway—meaning we would never get to take the family car anywhere, so there would be no use trying for our license. Kind of an "ostrich" attitude for a parent to have, now as I think of it! However, recalling what a nervous teenager I was, almost totally lacking in self-confidence and esteem, I think I was almost relieved that he took this stand, thus sparing me having to go through this "ordeal", judged now-a-days as a right of passage or a status of growing up! Then, it didn't seem very important to me, until after being married, and living in suburbia, and I needed it—at which time I took a few driver lessons and obtained my license on the first try! As I recall, Connie obtained her license sometime after leaving home as well.

Strangely enough, and much to my Mom and Gran Sexsmith's horror, Dad let me drive his John Deere tractor and a small disker, around the field on my own, when I was only 7 or 8 years old, while he did some stubble burning in another part of the field. All I had to do was follow the previous round's furrow with the front wheel and the pup-pup (sound the John Deere engine made at the time) tractor did the rest! If anything went wrong, Dad taught me I could stop the tractor with the big gear shift knob. Our faithful brown and white mongrel pet dog came along, running in the furrow behind the disker, and Dad's old pet crow Jack, flew overhead. I loved every minute of it, and couldn't understand why Mom and Gran were so concerned. I loved riding on the big wide fenders over the large back rubber wheels, and was really disappointed as the newer tractors were built with almost no fender, especially the Case tractors of later years.

I was Dad's helper of sorts, out in the yard. As he filled his tractor's gas tank from barrels of fuel Vicky Tapma (nick name for Sexsmith) of Sintaluta Co-op, delivered regularly to our yard, behind the garage, it was my job to watch for the little red gas gauge to come up on the hand-turned gas pump, and signal for him to quickly turn the handle backwards, to reverse the flow, so the gas wouldn't run over! I remember seeing the wavy fumes rising over the tractor's fuel tank on a hot summer's day, and can almost still smell the fuel! Dad also did his grease-ups at this fuel stop behind the garage, using his maroon colored portable grease gun, containing yucky clear yellowy-brown grease. Sometimes I got to press the handles to release the grease, but I usually wasn't strong enough. Perhaps that's about the time Dad wished he'd had a son, although he never said. There was always an oiled rag to wipe the tractor's shiny green surface of the day's dust, as with the car. It was a happy day when the two-door garage was built for both vehicles, and they were "safe" from the elements.

The stone boat was utilized as a conveyance on most farms; it consisted of a set 4 x 4 wooden runners set on steel, with planks boarded over top, that could be attached to a single harness to be drawn by a horse, or tractor. I rode on it often, inside an old trunk box Dad would throw on top of this stone boat to provide protection from cold winter winds as he drove me "cross-country" to Allindale school, being pulled along, at a speedy clip, by our faithful old Clydesdale horse Babe. I recall in about Grade III, I had to keep a weather chart as part of a science project, and record the direction of the wind. This always proved a mystery to me back then, and without Dad's input, my weather chart would not have been very accurate!

Gordon says the word "stone boat" was coined because this common farm vehicle was often used to haul large stones from fields to a stone pile, after they had been removed with crow bars, etc. Our stone boat was utilized mostly for daily removal of manure from the barn, to the manure pile in the pasture. Dad also used it to haul water from the dug out in barrels, to water the animals in winter, or to water the garden in summer. Naturally it slid along much easier over the snow in winter, than the dirt in summer, and was harder then for Babe to pull, so Dad used the tractor for summer hauling. It was to this same stone boat Connie and I attached our sleigh, and then our dolly's sleigh to ours, for many, happy winter rides, as mentioned previously.

Other winter conveyances in common use on the farm while we were growing up were open cutters, closed cutters, box-type sleighs with runners, all pulled with horses. To have a matched team of horses back then was a real joy to own, as they pulled evenly and well together, and provided a means of transportation when country roads were closed to motor vehicles. To many farmers it was a status symbol to have one or more nice teams; it could be equated to owning a nice car these days! Matched harnesses, collars, jingling bells and other decorative finery often went along with owning these teams. Livery barns in towns provided shelter, food and water to horses belonging to surrounding area farmers for a nominal fee, while they were in town for supplies, visits, etc. Much like today, horses were also owned just for riding or as race horses (Joe Sanderson, the Conns, Dr.Isman, and Merricks being some race horse owners I recall at the time).

The two horses that I remember us having were Prince, a red/brown horse with light mane and tail, standing quite tall, and Babe, a huge dark chestnut brown Clydesdale. I have no idea of either one's heritage or history, but Prince was sold shortly after we began farming, when we had no more need of two horses. Babe remained on our farm until the early 60's performing the chores mentioned previously, as well as any other job that required heavy pulling. Dad used to hitch him to a small cultivator, to work the rows between our new trees planted around the west and south sides of our yard, with Mom leading Babe and Dad pushing on the implement. Mom always remarked how gentle Babe was, always compliant with commands, and never once stepping on her little feet, with his generous hooves! He was also called upon from time to time to pull some car out of the ditch, when rain had made the main road running by our lane muddy, even sometimes at night! Babe always got the job done, without fuss or fanfare, plodding along, strong and steady. We never rode horseback on him, as he was too tall to mount from the ground, and Dad had no saddle for him. We girls didn't have anything to do with him, as his size made him so intimidating. Later after I left home, and Babe was no longer on our farm, I recall Dad bought a smaller horse, of Palomino breed, that he could ride to get the cows from far pastures, etc.

Nowadays, at the Exhibition parades, it brings back a bit of nostalgia when we see the clowns gathering coins for the Sunshine fund in mesh wire basket nose-guards that in days gone by were attached to some horse bridles to prevent them from stopping to feed/nibble when they were supposed to be working!

Our cousin Audrey had a tame, gentle and faithful old horse named Nelly, that she rode bareback to school each day. On occasion Audrey would persuade me to ride Nelly with her, however, I never did enjoy those rides! I seemed to ride in direct opposition to the movements of the horse, especially if she trotted, and always ended up with a stomach ache after dismounting! Other children also brought horses to school (Allindale) namely the Balfours and Spaniers, the latter using their horse to pull a red cart that all five children rode in.

On one or two occasions in winter, we used an open sleigh box attached to a set of red runners (that doubled as a wagon in summer when attached to a set of steel-rimmed wheels), to make trips to town. This was a true "adventure" to us as children, and I recall one Christmas making this trip with Aunt Ruby & Uncle Herb—the men standing up front to drive the team while the Moms and kids snuggled under buffalo robes. Probably Dad made these trips to town on his own over several winters in those days, for groceries, mail and supplies, when the roads weren't open. I guess probably snow plows weren't too readily available back then, for constant clearing of country roads, and we seemed to have many more blizzards then than we experience now in Saskatchewan! It seems to me someone in those days owned a bombardier, a kind of home-made closed in vehicle with caterpillar tracks, powered like a car, that they used to travel about the country in winter, but it wasn't anyone in our district; something like our modern-day ski-doos, only closed in and larger. Gordon recalls seeing one in their Neudorf area of similar design, but with a propeller in front for added thrust.

Although we did not have our own closed in cutter, I often got to ride in one during my public school years; Raymond's hired hand Bill used to drive our cousins Elaine and Wayne to Allindale in winter, traveling across our land in a diagonal "shortest distance" (as the crow flies) path, and would often stop to pick me up as they crossed over our lane, if I was walking in the vicinity. This conveyance was the neatest thing, equipped with a small wood burning stove, complete with little stove pipe that stuck up out of the slanted roof. There was a small window in the front for the driver to see out, and holes for the horses reins to go through, to drive the horses. Hinged doors that latched on the inside, opened on each side of the cutter. Bench seats covered with old blankets or a buffalo rug, and straw on the floor added warmth and insulation. Although I wasn't familiar with them, Gordon says he recalls foot warmers were sometimes employed in winter for warmth when riding in cutters and sleighs. Briquette-like blocks were heated before the trip on the kitchen stove, and placed in a drawer of a metal warmer with handles on each side. Apparently these blocks stayed warm for quite a while, warding off winter's chill, during long trips in these conveyances.

Angling up and down over the hard, crusty crests of drifted snow that covered the usually flat prairie fields made for a "joyous" ride, but could also result in a tipped-over cutter, that could prove quite disastrous, especially with the burning stove on board! Thank goodness Bill, the driver, was skillful or lucky or a combination of both, as there were never any upsets while I was "on board" or ever that I can recall.

The summer conveyance still used a little when I was a young girl was the buggy, although they had been very popular in our parent's day, before cars came on the scene. My only experience riding in one was when my cousin Elaine was in grade VIII and still attending Allindale. She would drive herself and Wayne to school with their horse and buggy, and I would sometimes get a ride with them, sitting in the little back shelf, that served as extra room for horse feed, lunch kits or baggage, etc. There was only one bench seat in a buggy, facing forward, that could only accommodate two or three riders. The buggy itself was made of wood, painted black; it had wooden spoke wheels, rimmed with steel bands, and wooden shafts that hitched up on each side of the horse, one horse being sufficient to pull it.

Horses were used to pull racks, when gathering sheaves from the fields in fall, or hay that was mown in summer, that grew wild in bloughs, or was planted in Alfalfa or Brome grass just for that purpose. Racks were large, rectangular conveyances made of wood, and ran on wooden spoked wheels, rimmed with steel. There was nothing more glorious, as a child, than riding in the rack on top of the hay or sheaves, being pulled along by the plodding horses, switching their tails to keep off the flies, (a modern-day "hay-ride"!) The horse's reins were loosely wrapped around the centre post of the rack, and just a slight command of "giddy-up" or a cluck of the tongue was all that was needed to get the rack moving again for the next pick-up of sheaves or hay. I am now aware that our Dad and neighbor helpers were laboring rather heartily with their pitch forks to get the rack loaded, however, we were not aware of this then. (Gordon recalls as a young lad, helping with this work, and falling asleep on the loads of hay on the way in from the field, because he was so tired from the hard work). Hay was usually hauled to the barn, and pitched up into the loft, from the rack through an outer, upper doorway in the barn, and sheaves were made into stacks, the latter of which will be discussed with harvest. Tractors were used later on to do this gathering, but somehow that just wasn't the same as riding on a "horse-drawn" rack!

All the tractors I recall Dad owning were rubber-tired, however previous to this, tractors had steel wheels. He was always partial to John Deere models, green with yellow-gold decals, and as mentioned previously, large fenders that completely covered the back wheel, and were just right for young girls to sit and ride on, a favorite pass-time for me, as Dad worked the land. Later models had less and less fender, until finally the wheel showed altogether! The familiar pupp-pupp sound of Dad's John Deere was later replaced by the unfamiliar "whine" of Case tractors, orange and yellow-beige colored, the tractors Dad bought after I left home. They became more and more sophisticated with hydraulic lift attachments to raise and lower implements into and from the soil, working on an oil-pressure system of hoses. In later years, tractors came equipped with a power-take off that was run from the motor, and served to provide the power to run combines, swathers and any other implements without their own motor. Tractors were a farmer's vehicle of labor, their "right-hand man", so to speak, gradually replacing horses altogether. Further modernizing has taken place since those days, with cabs and air-conditioning replacing umbrellas to protect from the hot summer sun, although Dad never did have an umbrella for any of his tractors. (We borrowed one from neighbor Orval Brown on our wedding day, to help me get from our house to the car and church without getting wet in the torrents of rain that fell that day!)

In the country, roads were only graded and graveled and paving was unheard of except on city streets. Grid roads were maintained by the municipality with a pull-type grader with huge up-right wheels on the back that were turned to adjust the blade. It seems to me Harold Sexsmith did this job, and Uncle Herb drove the tractor to pull the grader. Later on a modern-type grader was utilized, usually driven by Raymond Sexsmith. The lane into our farm from the main road consistently became impassible during rains and in spring, so we either stayed put or walked out to the road and got a ride with someone else. Don't know why Dad never had the lane graveled—whether it was related to cost, or he didn't feel the need was that great. (I have a suspicion it had a lot to do with not wanting to get his car muddy, going out the lane when it was rainy or in spring!) At any rate, it was graveled in later years, and to this day this lane remains a favorite part of our farm property, whenever we visit, even though Mom moved the house to town in 1969, the year after Dad passed away. We have spent many pleasant hours at the farm taking Michael there to ride his dirt bike, in his early teen years.

There were two dirt/gravel led roadways "into town" as we were growing up, and still in common use today. The trip to town was approximately 7 miles, but it seemed a "major trip" to us as children, and literally the only way we kept in touch with the outside world, except for the radio and school. The Main Road ran north and south from the valley, and was accessed by the "mile-and-a-half" down past Uncle Herb and Harold's farmsteads. The Church road past Alexander country church, was a quick route to town, but was more like a country trail, and only used in summer. The School Road, past Allindale School also running north and south from the valley, was our closest roadway leading to the highway, and the one we used most often. Even the highway (commonly called the #1) was only graded and graveled back then; Clouds of dust were generated by each vehicle, making travel a bit of a dirty experience. Thinking back, life as a traveling salesman or trucker must have been quite a bit different compared to now!

Paving or "black-topping" was reserved for city streets only back then, and it wasn't until the early to mid-1950's that a new paved Number One highway was built, running parallel to the old graveled "wash-board" one, as it was commonly called. This new highway revolutionized road travel for everyone in the vicinity; we were fortunate to live as close to it as we did (about 5 miles), as it was "clear sailing" to Wolseley, once this highway could be reached. It was and still is referred to by many rural people as "the black top", rather than any other name.

Sidewalks of cement were also mainly part of city-life, or immediate downtown areas of towns. Board walks were more common, along the streets of Wolseley or even just, dirt walkways, in some parts. Cement (or cigarment, as I preferred to call it as a child), was gradually put into place in all areas, replacing the more nostalgic "older-era" boardwalks. Wolseley's swinging bridge over the dam has been a unique landmark since 1906.

Besides cars, trucks and farm vehicles used for travel, buses and trains were the next most frequently used modes of transportation, when we were growing up. The Grey Hound bus line served our area, providing economical, reliable service to all the main line towns back then, just as it does now. Gordon and I both used it frequently for getting back and forth to Regina from our respective homes. Mom was also a frequent traveler, when she was able, coming to visit "her girls" and their families, living in Regina, in the 1970's and 1980's.

With regard to train travel, the first major trip of my life was taken on a train, as a baby, traveling back to Wolseley from my birth place, Fort William, when Dad went overseas during the War. It would be the first of many trips taken by train, as next to the bus, train travel was a common means of public transport while we were growing in the 1940's to 1960's. Regular freight and passenger service was provided to all mainline towns between major cities all across Canada, with the Canadian Pacific Rail (commonly known as C.P.R.) serving southern areas of the province, and Canadian National Rail (commonly known as C.N.R.) serving the north. Train stations were a regular feature of all small towns, and I recall as a child being "in awe" of this bustling place, where people began and ended journeys—it always seemed exciting. Station agents were employed full time, to conduct the business generated by the train service, such as ticket sales, mail and parcel service, cream shipment. A telegraph service received and dispatched important messages by Morse code from the train station, in the form of telegrams, before the days of computers and fax machines, so the station agent provided many services to the community from his train station vantage point!

Some of my earliest recollections centre around the Wolseley train station, either meeting or sending off Aunt Alice and Uncle Don, on their many weekend visits from Regina, staying at Gran's house with Gran, Mom and I. The trains back then were commonly called Puff n' Billies, as they were steam powered, burning booker coal, Gordon recalls. The engines were huge black iron "monsters", with equally huge spoked steel wheels; the size was overwhelming to me as a small child. A large clanging bell on the outside of the engine, always signaled the arrival and departure of each train at the station. The jets of steam that had to be let off by the engine while the train was idling at the station were really scary; one couldn't stand too close! Huge billows of smoke erupted from the engine's smoke stack when the train was getting into motion again on departure from the station, and it made great "puffing" sounds I still recall vividly, that were slow at first, becoming faster as the train sped up.

Passenger cars were maroon colored on the C.P.R. line back then, with many windows at each seat for people to see out and enjoy the passing scenery. Berths or sleeping compartments could be reserved for passengers traveling long distances; I recall Gran Sexsmith always getting a berth when she went by train to visit Uncle Lloyds family every few years, as we were growing up. A dining car for meals, baggage car and of course the caboose at the end was the usual design of a passenger train. The dome car was introduced much later than this along with diesel powered engines that "droned" rather than "puffed". Freight trains looked much like those of today, except the familiar caboose has been eliminated now. It was a common occurrence to have the engineer in the engine of the train wave from his window, or the conductor from his caboose window also wave, especially to kids as the train passed by.

On board, the conductor took tickets, announced the stations as the train sped along and called "all aboard" as the train was departing. They wore navy blue uniforms with gold trim and jaunty caps. It seems to me they wore white gloves, and always seemed to be elderly, kindly and male. The conductor seemed to keep everything running smoothly on the train, and had a neat set of stair steps he put out at each station for passengers to enter or leave the train.

Lonna Geister and I were frequent train travelers on trips back and forth to Regina from Wolseley while we were nurses in training in the early 1960's. Her father was employed as a C.P.R. repairman then (I recall him telling Dad he had "worked by the track for thirty years" in his heavy German accent). These repairmen used little yellow vehicles called "jiggers" to do their work on the rails, that had wheels that fitted on the tracks, like a train, and were powered by hand-driven pumps that propelled them along. They were a common sight back then, scooting along from job to job. (Now trucks fitted with regular and train wheels transport these repairmen from place to place, replacing the little jiggers). By virtue of her Dad's employment, Lonna enjoyed reduced fare tickets that she shared with me also, very much appreciated by student nurses with meager means to travel! We enjoyed those rides together and getting home!

The Peanut, a local running train was a common sight in Wolseley, running from Reston, Manitoba, serving the mainline towns until 1961. It was a kind of work train, carrying some passengers, freight, cans of cream from local farmers to ship to dairies for processing. The station was always one of our first stops when we went to town for groceries, etc. To deliver a 5 gallon can of cream for shipment, and pick up an empty can. Payment came by mail, and often helped supplement Mom's grocery allowance, together with her egg cheque from the local candling station, which was located behind the locker plant at the time.

Several other remembrances Gordon and I have with regard to trains. He recalls "turn-abouts" the train engines were driven onto, with a huge pit under, containing a swivel apparatus, used to turn the engines around, as they couldn't reverse as diesel engines do now, in order to operate in an opposite direction. This would have been a necessity for local running trains like the Peanut, etc. at that time. Then, as now, the sound of a train whistle especially at night, has such a forlorn, mournful sound to me, and always saddens me, making me think of the past, and home, and all that has been. I recall Dad having similar feelings about train whistles when he lived.

Needless to say, train travel played a vital role in the days of early Canadian history, and will forever be a vital part of our heritage. It is unfortunate that the day has now come when train travel has largely been replaced by other modes of transportation that are quicker, faster and more reliable.

I have failed, thus far, to make mention of the most often used means of transportation, that required no vehicle at all—God-given to all species—that of walking! We did plenty of walking to Allindale most school days, except, occasionally as mentioned previously, when we got rides during inclement weather. While in high school, I walked back and forth several miles each day to school, while living with Gran Teasdale, never thinking anything of it, as most in attendance there also walked. Walking was a common means of getting from place to place then.

However, after that time, into the 1960's and 1970's, walking lost serious favor, and people preferred to drive everywhere in their vehicles. The trend of thought was "why walk when you can drive there?" Lately, though, with health and fitness in mind, people walk and/or jog for miles (not going anywhere in particular), along walking/bicycle paths or on sidewalks in cities and towns everywhere! Whole lines of track equipment such as jogging runners, sweat suits, sweat bands for foreheads and wrists, and of course portable headphone radios to listen to while jogging, have sprung up to meet public demand to walk and jog "in style", while we improve our cardio-vascular systems, tone muscles, lose weight and improve our self-esteem and well being! Wouldn't our ancestors have been surprised by our present thinking regarding this age-old manner of transport!

Next to walking, probably bicycles were the next most common means of conveyance used on an individual or tandem basis. I can recall Dad saying he owned a bike, so they must have been in common use when he was young. Also that Mom never learned to ride, even after practicing for hours on end on the Chew farm verandah where her family lived when she was a girl. I always felt I may never ride either, just like her, as never was able to "master the art" of it as a child growing up, practicing on cousin Audrey's bike, and her patiently coaching me. At home, I had a blue tricycle that I literally rode the wheels off of. I found that if I sat on the back step plate and pedaled really fast, I could tip the bike over just enough so only the big front wheel and one back wheel made contact with the ground—creating a two-wheeled bike of sorts! I was that desperate to have one! However, Mom and Dad never seemed to think in terms of getting me one, whether because of cost, or because I couldn't ride Audreys, I never knew for sure. My need to have a two-wheeler was right, up there with having a pedal car of my own, as mentioned previously, neither of which became realities in my childhood.

However, I am happy to report, as an adult, I finally mastered two-wheeled bike riding, thanks to son Michael's patient coaching, encouragement and moral support, when he was about eight years old, and Gordon's birthday gift of a shiny new blue bike! I cried I was so happy—a child-hood dream had become a reality! Since that time we have spent many happy hours riding on the Devonian bike trail in A.E.Wilson park in our area, and/or riding in the neighborhood in the evenings for exercise and pleasure. I suppose because of my thwarted childhood memories of bike-riding, I always got such a thrill out of watching our own children learn to ride their bikes, with Gordon running behind to steady them, especially after their training wheels came off. Also seeing them all ride to school together always brought a tear. Then, when Michael got his pedal car at age 3, how happy I was to see him enjoy it so much—my dream as a child.

Gordon recalls always owning second-hand bikes as a boy, as he was the second child in the family, while his older brother, Helmuth had the new bikes. He also recalls a cute incident that occurred when he was about 8 years old. He and Helmuth had ridden out to the field on their bikes to meet their Dad on his tractor. For some reason, the boys brought the tractor home, and Dad brought both bikes, riding one and bringing the other one by the handle bars. Gordon remembers bring so surprised to learn that day that his Dad could even ride a two-wheeler let alone bring a second bike along! Dad was a "hero" in the little lad's eyes that day—cute! Gordon doesn't recall his Mom ever riding a bike, but perhaps she did know how.

Air travel wasn't very common as we grew up, although we heard of Uncles Wilfred and Harry both being flyers with the Air Force in WW II, piloting propeller planes. I have no recollection of this or their experiences at that time. The nearest planes flew overhead, and we saw then only at a distance.

Small propeller planes sometimes flew over farmsteads taking pictures from several angles, during those years, with the intent of visiting the farm people several weeks later, with those same pictures for sale. Nearly everyone who farmed lived right on the land (not like today, where many farm operations are run by town or even city dwellers), and they were proud of their property and yards. Of course, to see an actual aerial view of one's farm home was quite

Some Modes of Transportation

Newly constructed garage on farm with Chevy car beside it (note the baby calf lying down on East side!)

Dad with one of his many John Deere tractors with baby Connie on board and me at front (wearing my "butterfly" dress).
Note Dad standing in a pose he often assumed--with one foot resting on the other. (I note Michael stands like this sometimes now!)

The first car I remember--our Chevy with running boards! Mom & Dad painted it a pretty bright blue.

Our metallic green Mercury car
1950's

Dad with his pride and joy 1964 Ford Galaxy 500 Maroon and White on the way to CB'ers Picnic

A "One Horse Open Sleigh"

Carol on Nelly + Gan 1949

S/S Ile De France (French Line)
The ship Dad went overseas on during WWII

impressive, back then, even in black and white photography. Needless to say, most farmers in our area, bought at least one or several of this type of picture over the years—a good business to be in for the photographer and possibly the plane operator as well. We have several of our farm home, we treasure to this day. (Dad had one regret that always nagged at him—the garage door was open just a little, when one of the first pictures was taken—we thought it was cute; it also showed him weeding the newly planted trees west of the house). Several more aerial pictures were taken of our farmstead over the years, but we didn't always buy one.

Crop spraying planes were the only other planes we saw—also small propeller ones, that could be hired to spray-kill unwanted weeds/insect pests in fields planted with crop, as opposed to spraying with wheeled implements on the ground, that trampled a certain amount of the crop. These sprayers always worked in pairs—one man "marked" on the ground, wearing white coveralls and held a flag, while the partner did the flying/spraying. They could only work when it was still, so the poisonous spray wouldn't "drift" in the wind—in windy Saskatchewan, a rare occurrence! They often sprayed in the early morning or at dusk to avoid this ever present "wind-threat". On several occasions Dad hired these crop sprayers to help achieve a good crop and eventual harvest, free of weed seeds and/or insects. It was always a big event to us as children, but an expensive one for Dad; we always worried the marker man would be hit by the plane—the pilot always seemed to fly so close to him, but it never seemed to happen, in our area, thank goodness!

Although we weren't keenly aware of it, I suppose sometime in the 1950-1960 era, commercial air travel became more common, with Trans Canada Airlines and later Air Canada and Pacific Western serving Regina and area from larger centers. Propeller planes gave way to jet propelled ones, and the by mid-60's and later, people took planes more regularly for business and pleasure. Little did we realize, as we saw planes flying overhead as children, the time would come when we would all travel on them fairly regularly, especially Gordon in his work. It still fills me with awe and wonder, that a vehicle of such size, loaded with people, their baggage, and all manner of freight, can in fact, take off from the ground and fly through the air to its destination, even across oceans and continents. I recall a little incident related to me by Gran Teasdale with regard to air travel. Apparently her father had predicted that in the future, planes in the air would be as common as cars on ground, to which one of the children questioned "But where will the traffic policeman stand Daddy?" Indeed, air-traffic controllers do this job expertly from their airport control towers today!

With regard to boat travel, we were never very familiar with this mode of transportation. We learned of Gran and Grandad coming to Canada from England on a boat, Clippie being in the Navy during the War and Dad being transported with his Army unit on the Ile de France overseas for duty. We heard and read about the ill-fated Titanic, even seeing the movie about it. However growing up in land-locked Saskatchewan, the only boats we saw were at Katepwa Lake, being used for pleasure. Back then, we didn't know anyone with a boat, so didn't have the opportunity of ever riding in one. The only little boats we knew we fashioned ourselves out of half a walnut shell with a tiny paper sail glued to a toothpick anchored in the bottom with plastersene. We floated them in little rivulets the melting snow made in the ditches and fields each spring. We even had races with these little boats, and shared many happy hours playing with them.

Little did we know then, annual visits to Lake Katepwa each summer to the Rein and Hill cottages there, would result in many pleasurable boat rides for us now. Also Gordon's company trip to Egypt in 1984, in the form of a cruise down the Nile River past pyramids and desert, was an unexpected thrill two farm children growing up on the prairies would not have dreamed possible back then.

Farming and hard work seem to be synonymous. Since Gordon's and my childhoods both were spent growing upon farms, we were very familiar with the daily tasks and chores involved in the farm's operation. Fun and entertainment weren't a priority, and holidays away from the farm consisted of a day or evening trip somewhere at most. Cattle had to fed, watered and milked, while other farm animals had to be fed and watered, eggs gathered, etc., either before leaving or on return. No farm operation was without animals back then, as in addition to the fields of crop planted each year, livestock provided ongoing provisions needed in many cases for survival.

Thus, the "all-encompassing" work ethic evolved primarily through necessity—to obtain and secure the many necessities of everyday life such as food, clothing, water, heat, light and shelter, and were mostly procured through the efforts of the farmer and his wife and family, right on the farm or near-by land. Therefore, many of the following pages will be devoted to describing remembrances of this bond common to all farmers—that of hard work.

The division of labor varied from farmstead to farmstead; usually the farmer and sons were in charge of all outdoor operations, like crop planting, livestock, and general maintenance of the farm. Farm wives and daughters were in charge of the home, garden, food preparation, provision of clothing, etc. There was understandably a lot of "crossing over" of chores between husband and wife, as they were each other's helpmates in every sense of the word. Each farm family seemed to have a work-ethic that suited their particular interests and needs best.

It seems work didn't figure very highly in our everyday lives as children growing up on the farm. We were often aware of all the work going on around us to provide a home, and necessities of life, but we weren't much "a part" of it, as in some farm families. On the other hand,

Gordon's experience was much different, growing up on their farm. A lot was expected of both boys by their parents, in the day to day farm operation. On questioning Gordon regarding what he would have wanted or liked with regard to this, he says it never occurred to them to rebel or refuse to do their chores, as children of today would. They didn't seem to feel they had a choice—everyone worked to help his Mother in the house, or his Dad in the barn yard or fields and each parent helped the other in either place, so the boys grew up knowing their way around the kitchen, although Gordon being younger, tended to help his Mom more and Helmuth being older helped his Dad. A feeling of "sharing the load" seemed to prevail, of being part of a job well-done—a feeling not present in some farm families, sadly enough, not really in ours.

Looking back, I can see reason for this to some extent, and now understand why there wasn't more sharing of tasks in our farm operation as we grew up. Mom was used to managing her own household, as from quite a young age, she was often called on to help out as she grew up, due to Gran Teasdale's poor health. She was always an independent worker, preferring to "get the job done" as expediently as possible, as time was of the essence, and she never seemed to have enough of it to accomplish all she had set out to do each day. So, stopping to teach a none-too-willing girl to do a task she could easily accomplish quicker herself, didn't happen very often. Also, the fact that Dad grew up in a home with very distinct divisions of labor, with a very able mother, sisters and hired girls to perform cooking and other household tasks, while his father, he and his brothers and hired hands took care of tasks in the yard, livestock and land, etc., that this attitude also prevailed in our household. Old habits die hard, and by Dad's own admission, he "couldn't boil water-without burning it". The kitchen was therefore off limits to him, however, he did help Mom a lot with jobs outside, like hauling water for the garden watering, weeding the trees, picking raspberries, etc., and she in turn helped him with many outside jobs, although she drew the line at milking cows! Consequently, neither Connie or I learned to milk either.

There were certain jobs I liked to help Mom with as I grew older, and because I was a quick and efficient worker, it seemed to help her quite a lot. In summer, the produce from the garden, like peas, beans, strawberries and raspberries had to be prepared for the Locker Plant, and I recall helping with this (probably because I liked their taste so much in winter). Once in a while I'd sweep floors, set table and always dried dishes after meals. I remember enjoying the baby chicks, and recall digging them clumps of earthworms from the garden beside their chicken pen—they sure used to love this little treat!

As mentioned previously, cooking wasn't something we learned while growing up, but since Connie and I both love food and eating, we have since become relatively good cooks and bakers in our own right. We were basically "self-taught" with advisement from Mom, and in my case

Aunt Alice and Mom Schroeder, probably learning the most from the latter. She loved to share her cooking knowledge with Joyce (sister-in-law) and I, having no girls of her own, I suppose. I am eternally grateful to her that she chose to show her boys "their way around the kitchen" from an early age, as if required, Gordon can whip up a great meal, barbequing being his specialty (even in winter sometimes!)

I recall helping Dad with several little jobs while growing up. Each summer, before harvest, we would go fixing bins. I was his "gopher" fetching hammer, nails, holding brown butcher paper in place while he nailed it down with lathes. Fence fixing also required my "gopher" skills, adding bits of water as he dug a new hole in the ground with a crow bar, getting "slupped" with water in the process, holding reinforcing posts in place, while he attached staples to the barbed wire, etc. The other job was stone-picking, which I hated with a passion. It was always hot, dirty work, but we often worked as a family at this, clearing the land of pesky stones, and when we all helped, it seemed to go faster and better, and was one of the jobs we all shared. One summer we shingled the roof of the hen house together. I'm not sure how much help we all were up there, but we have had many a laugh since about when it came time to get Mom down onto the ladder off the roof—all she could think of was the possibility of falling, saying "I might fall, I might fall". Somehow, she managed to get down safely, but not without quite a lot of trepidation on her part, and I don't think she ventured up there ever again!

Connie and I often took turns taking Dad a cold drink to quench his thirst in mid-morning and afternoon when he was working on the fields. He seemed to appreciate it lot, and it was a little job we could do; also waving him in with a tea towel in hand, from the field when lunch or supper was ready.

I remember during my high school years, while home at the farm on summer vacation, I took quite an interest in helping keep the yard looking nice. I often mowed all the lawns with our push-type lawn mower, clipping the edges with hand clippers, to help Mom, who always seemed busy with many other jobs. Gardening/weeding was not my specialty back then, but since that time, with both Gordon and I finding our "green thumbs", we have derived much pleasure and satisfaction from our own yard and garden, sharing many happy hours there. I plant as many flowers as is feasible each season, telling Gordon when he comments about not being able to eat flowers, that they are food for my soul! Pressing glorious blooms and preserving their beauty in pictures, cards and bookmarks has become an enjoyable consignment business for me with local gift shops.

In those days, the produce procured from vegetable gardens during the summer months, provided farm families with a variety of fresh food in season and during winter as well. Back then, fresh produce in the stores was very expensive in winter, if available at all, so a great deal of time and effort went into home preserving as much garden produce as possible. Before the days of electricity and home freezers, homemakers had to can vegetables, fruit, meat, poultry and fish, or else cure, smoke or dry it. Canner after canner of mason jars filled with all manner of food, were sealed in boiling water baths, then stored in cool basement cupboards in preparation for the winter months ahead. Needless to say, this was hot, hard work for our grandmothers and mothers, using coal and wood stoves, in addition to their many other farm tasks.

I recall Gran Sexsmith having an ice house or root cellar in the Sexsmith home farm yard. Sometimes when I was visiting to play with cousin Audrey, Gran would take us down into this cool, underground "cellar" that kept cream, eggs and vegetables cool and from spoiling during summer. An 8 to 10 foot deep hole was dug in the ground approximately 10 feet square. It was entered from an above ground hatch door, on a wooden enclosure, down vertical wooden steps attached along one side. Straw lined the walls and floor, covering blocks of ice, cut in winter from dams and sloughs, and placed in the cellar in late winter. This ice would last, until late summer, providing a cold storage unit all those months. Gordon recalls this type of cellar at his farm as well, and even recalls cutting ice blocks for it as a lad. I suspect mice, lizards and snakes also sometimes lived in such ice houses, although none were ever apparent on our visits there with Gran!

Some farm homes, with cement basements, had built-in cold storage units, with separate stairway entrances from outside, whereby garden produce could be taken directly into storage from outside. Other older farm homes had wooden or even just earth walls and floors that were also used for storage. Food and produce was kept from freezing during winter, because usually the furnace was located there also. Gordon recalls potatoes and other root crop vegetables being stored in their dirt basement. Our basement at home was cemented, and always kept cool enough to store eggs and milk for a day or so. A square of dirt was left uncemented in the southwest corner, and squared in with boards, with the eventual intention of growing mushrooms, as Mom loved them so much. Spawn after spawn failed to produce any, so Dad finally dug a deep, round hole in this dirt, which lined with newspapers, would accommodate and keep a can of cream sweet for a week, even in summer!

Safes or cupboards with several shelves and a screened, latched door were sometimes placed in basements to keep food-stuffs cool, and yet protected from mice, etc. Gran Teasdale had this type of safe in her cement basement, where she kept her canned jars of fruit, and vegetables. The safe could keep out mice, but not an invasion of ants! Somehow these pesky fellows had managed to enter one of the sealers of canned grapes. What a laugh Gran and Mom had when they realized they had eaten more than just canned grapes from that jar of preserved fruit; (this story was told and re-told many times) following the War years, when Gran, Mom and I lived together, in Gran's house at Wolseley, while Dad was overseas. Such were the joys of those days, when preserving, storing and eating food-stuffs at home was the norm.

Besides canning, other methods of food preservation employed during that time were curing, pickling or smoking. Meat and poultry was especially vulnerable to spoiling and once butchered had to be cooked and eaten immediately or else canned. Chicken was especially good canned, chilled and then served on hot summer evenings for supper. Also, this same canned chicken could be heated with vegetables and served with dumplings as stew. Sections of pork were cured into hams by placing them in mason crocks in a strong, salt brine. Bacon was also made in this manner and then smoked and stored by being hung in cool basements. Gordon recalls having a smoke house on their farm that was utilized in this meat-smoking process—a smudge of sawdust over several hours was usually sufficient to smoke sausage and bacon. A pickling process was utilized in much the same way as today for food preservation. All manner of cucumber, tomato and other vegetables were pickled as well as hard-boiled eggs, pigs feet and fish such as herring, when they were available.

Livestock born and raised on farms were always a ready source of meat for farm families. Although it was often difficult to butcher familiar farm animals for this purpose, they were often grown with this intention out of the need for meat or the instant cash the sale of such animals could bring if necessary.

Year old beef steers were usually butchered in late Fall (as it was cooler then), after being stall-fed for fattening and little or no exercise, so the meat would be well-marbled but not tough. Animals were usually shot in the head, throat slashed and then hoisted up on a block and tackle at loft level of the barn to bleed and be skinned. Several neighbors usually got together to help each other in butchering, often sharing meat back and forth, in an effort to use up as much fresh, before it could spoil, before butchering another animal at a neighboring farm, repeating this "good-neighbor" process again. The animal was skinned first, the hide being sold later in town for profit. Then it was gutted, cut in quarters and hung in cool basements for 4-5 days, or cut up, cooked and eaten or canned. Some areas were fortunate enough to have a local locker plant that would cut, wrap and store meat and vegetables. (This valuable service will be discussed later). The heart, liver, kidneys, tongue and sweetbread (of younger animals) was saved and cooked to enjoy as special culinary delights in our household. Suet or animal fat was saved and stored in tin pails, chilled and later used in mincemeat and Christmas puddings. Wild birds also enjoyed suet pieces being hung in outside trees as a winter treat for them.

Pigs were butchered in much the same manner as steers, but were not skinned, but scalded in very hot water, after which the bristles and hair could be scraped off. Gordon recalls the intestine of pigs being saved, turned inside out, scraped, washed, and kept in salt water, to be used as sausage casings. His family always ground pork and combined it with special spices, etc., and made their own sausage. It was quite a big job, but a family operation, and the delicious taste well worth the effort he remembers. Sausages were smoked and canned as well. Pork fat could be rendered, or cooked at high temperatures, allowed to harden into lard for baking or for lye soap-making. Although pioneers often made all their soap for washing purposes in this manner, our family never did. Gordon recalls his Grandma and Mom making soap from this lard when he was a small child.

Sheep were sometimes grown as a source of meat or wool for farm families, or sold for profit, for these same two reasons. Gordon's family raised them as pets and sheared them for their fine wool, or sold them. He often recalls how cute the lambs were, and also remembers helping wash and card the wool his Mom used in quilts, or sent to mills in Winnipeg to be made into blankets.

Poultry and water fowl were often raised by farm families as a source of food on the farm or for sale. Chickens especially, were usually present in every farm yard, as a source of food, as well as for their fresh eggs. Gordon and I recall both of our mothers ordering day-old chicks from the Hatcheries in Regina and Melville, respectively, in lots of one or two hundred each spring, as we were growing up. It was quite "an event" when the chicks arrived in a huge, flat square-lidded box, with four compartments, each containing about 25 yellow balls of fluff, peeping loudly. Several days of preparation had gone into getting the back compartment of the chicken house ready for their arrival and occupancy. More than once, the outside temperature was too cool for the chicks to be put out into the hen house, and they spent their first night in the house, in our portable galvanized, aluminum bath tub, if you please!

In view of the cool, early spring weather, heat was provided to the young chicks by brooder lights—red, high intensity heat lamps, that were lowered over a round metal enclosure by a pulley fashioned for the purpose on a piece of plywood suspended from above. Water was supplied to them by several quart sealers inverted into special fluted pans, to accommodate little heads and beaks; as the sealer was tipped to allow air in, water flowed into the pan for drinking. I recall this water being a pinkish color, because Mom placed tablets in it for extra nutrient and to avoid against cannibalism.

Special pellets were fed to the baby chicks, and later chop soaked in milk. A mixture of oatmeal and mashed hard-boiled egg was sometimes offered to them as a treat. As the chicks matured and the weather became warmer, they were allowed out of the metal enclosure into the main area, and finally down the chick run into the small yard fenced with chicken wire for them. They loved earth worms from the garden, and as mentioned previously, I often dug for them as a girl, being careful not to hit any chicks with the accompanying clumps of garden earth.

Cannibalism was sometimes a problem in the flock and weaklings were often culled out in this manner. It only took a drop of blood to get this started and in no time the unfortunate chick was dead—pecked to death by the others. Mom used to become so cross and sad at this unnecessary loss and had a rust-red, foul smelling Watkin's ointment she rubbed on the heads of any likely weaklings, in the hope of preventing this occurrence, however we usually lost a few in each flock annually.

The young chickens were allowed into the main hen yard a few at a time, and eventually all were amalgamated with the main flock. Colored leg rings were used to band the legs of the chickens that belonged to each year's flock, so their age could be determined at butchering time in Fall. Year old hens that didn't lay as well anymore, were often butchered and canned, as their meat tended to tougher, and the processing tenderized them. Referring back to the colored rings, these made excellent fashion rings for little girls fingers, as they were always brightly colored green, yellow or pink and were often used in our play, whenever we could squirrel a few away from Mom's main box!

Laying mash and an oyster-shell mixture were fed to encourage the young poulets to lay eggs. Apart from fresh eggs for family use and baking, great numbers were sold in Wolseley at the candling station, located then in the northeast corner of the locker plant. Dad built a double egg crate, that would hold 24 dozen eggs, which when full was heavy and fragile, needless to say! Eggs had to be gathered each day from "nesting boxes" in the hen house. Long double rows of these 18 x 18 inch cubicles lined the east and west walls of our henhouse, and a small perching shelf allowed the hen wanting to lay her egg to flutter up to a nest for this purpose. Each box had to be kept lined with straw, that had to be ruffled down every so often out of the corners, as the chickens tended to scratch hollows or "nests" in the straw before laying their eggs—the center of the nest would eventually be quite near the wooden base, and could result in broken eggs.

After gathering, never a favorite job for Connie or I, although we did help with it on occasion, the eggs had to be brought to the house for cleaning. Although we sometimes helped with this job, it was one that usually fell to Dad. A soft cloth with a water and vinegar mixture was employed for this cleansing process—many eggs requiring no cleaning at all, but none could be put in the crates for sale, unless checked. Cardboard egg trays separated the eggs in layers, that were then placed one on top of the other in crates of 12 or 24 dozen, and kept cool on the basement cement floor.

The price for the sale of eggs varied according to size, freshness, blood spots, uncracked shells, etc., and was never very much, but did supplement the family income, along with the sale of cream each week, and those two meager cheques most often bought the groceries Mom needed from the stores in town. I recall payment for eggs especially being at an all time low on one occasion, and Dad wrote to Mr. Alvin Hamilton, the MLA for Qu'Appelle-Wolseley at the time. Dad wrote the poor price for the sale of farm eggs was not worth the "wear and tear on the hen's patusch" (bottom) to which Mr. Hamilton replied in some appeasing way, and they corresponded on several other occasions about farm concerns Dad had, even after Mr. Hamilton went on to Federal politics. Dad took a stand in the only way he could or knew how to, and I always felt kind of proud of him for that! It is probably why I have sent off so many letters over the years to praise or defame a product or cause I felt strongly about as well, not usually accomplishing that much, but having the satisfaction of knowing that I tried. (I can't do everything—but I can do something to make a difference).

Some farm families also raised turkeys and water fowl for family use or for sale. These birds could be ordered from the hatcheries or raised right on the farm, if male and female birds were kept and their fertilized eggs "set" with clucking female birds. This of course was the natural order of things in the minds of all poultry that laid eggs in the first place—to reproduce their own kind. After laying many eggs in nests and having them taken away each day, a laying hen would eventually cease to lay eggs and turn into a "clucker", because she wanted to sit on the eggs and hatch them! To "cure" her of this natural urge, she was segregated from the flock and placed in a "punishing coop" with an open slatted bottom and no straw, with other hens in her same situation. After several days of this, the hen was released into the flock, and would resume her laying patterns again.

Gordon reports he and his Mom had much success setting clucking hens on eggs and having chicks produced, thus increasing the flock with new poulets and roosters. Turkeys were also hatched in this manner, by keeping back a few turkey eggs from a clucking turkey hen and giving them to a clucking chicken to sit on and hatch. The turkey hen would thus be forced to lay more eggs to hatch, sometimes being "fooled" in this manner into laying as many as 20 some eggs, some of which she hatched and some hatched by her chicken cousin. All of this was achieved up in the barn hay loft, away from the flock. Much success was also realized with tame, white ducks, or occasionally geese, and a clucking chicken. The chicken would raise the little ducklings, or goslings as her own, but was really frustrated when they grew a little bigger and could go swimming (quite natural for them), and she as a chicken could not! Besides providing variety in the family diet, some of these birds were also grown for sale, and for feathers and down. Feet were washed and heads wrapped in brown paper for sale to the town butcher or to private customers.

Gordon's Mom also had an incubator that she used on occasion to hatch poultry. He seems to recall it was warmed by lanterns, but not used very much. I don't recall Mom ever raising poultry in this way, however as a young girl I recall Gran Sexsmith raising chicks from clucks in a similar manner, using little A-shaped wooden coops she kept on the grassy area south of the main yard. Gran never seemed "too busy" to let Audrey and I share in their care; we fed them mashed egg/mashed potato and oatmeal, and really enjoyed helping with them I remember. They were so cute and fluffy, especially when first hatched.

It seems farm women had their preferences when it came to the type of chickens they would raise, and usually always kept to the same breed. Mom always ordered White Sussex, white feathers with a black, fringed ruff, wings and tail feathers. I recall Aunt Ruby usually raised rust colored chickens with black ruff and tails; I think they were called Rhode Island Reds. Barred Rocks were also a common type raised being grey and white like bed pillow feathers. Leg Horns were great laying hens, small and compact, all white, with very red "combs" on top of their heads, and very yellow/orange feet and legs, but they weren't very good poultry to eat. Light feathered hens laid white-colored eggs and darker feathered laid brown as I recall. At least one male bird or rooster was usually kept with each flock, as a protector against small predators like weasels, etc. Besides providing fertilization services to the hens, the rooster's familiar crowing or cock-a-doodle-doo was often the first sound heard on the farm each morning, issuing forth another dawn!

There were always a number of roosters in each flock of chickens ordered from the hatcheries. It was the usual custom to grow them over the spring and summer season and butcher them in the late fall, (as they were in their prime for eating, and their new pin feathers were all grown out by then for the coming winter, making them easier to pluck and clean). Prior to locker plants or home freezers, poultry could then be frozen for winter, (if it was cold enough), preserved by canning or sold, often to customers in town, whose names were kept from year to year, much as we now buy our poultry from the Hutterites. Laying female chickens or poulets were kept into the winter and following spring for their eggs, and then butchered the next fall as stewing hens or canned, (as previously mentioned). With the new batch of chicks from the hatchery the annual farm poultry cycle would begin again.

One adult rooster usually became dominant over the others and kept the rest in submission by pecking or out and out "rooster fights" with each other. Occasionally these dominant roosters became so cocky they developed a mean-streak, and would chase other barnyard animals, like cats, young calves of even people, inflicting a nasty wound with their talons, or back claw, if possible. More often than not, these hapless fellows ended up on the Sunday dinner table, and caused no more harm, in such cases. Gordon recalls his Dad swinging a pitch fork at a rooster that was chasing him as a young lad—needless to say it was killed and never bothered anyone again!

Each hen house had laying nests, as mentioned previously, as well as "roosts" for the birds to perch on during the night. The roosts in our particular hen house were angled along the north wall at about a 45 degree angle, at 18 inch intervals, about a foot off the floor to the ceiling. It was up to each chicken where it chose to roost, some preferring to stay on the lower roosts and some hopping up to the higher ones. Once in their desired spot for the night, they would squat down on their bent legs and feet and actually close their eyes and sleep in this position, as is peculiar to a bird's nature! It was always kind of cute to see each member of the flock hop up into the hen house each evening about dusk, until all were inside, and take their places for their nightly roost, and then to see them all dropping off to sleep, after a bit of twittering to each other. It was wise at this point to close the hen house door for the night, so predators like skunks, weasles or the like couldn't get in for a quick meal of chicken!

Poultry flocks were subject to infestations of lice that seemed to thrive on their bodies, under their feathers. Black-Leaf 40 was a common disinfectant solution that could be used in hen houses, particularly on the roosts, to help eliminate this problem. However, a few usually remained on each bird, and never failed to creep onto Mom especially during egg gathering or butchering. I recall always hating to have to help her find them on her neck or in her hair, if any got on her, however, they could be promptly and easily squeezed into oblivion.

Chicken butchering, as with other farm butchering, was not a job anyone relished, but out of necessity had to be carried out each fall, as a means of procuring additional food for the farm family and to supplement income in some cases. After fasting overnight, each bird had to be individually hung up by its feet, usually in the barn, and had to be put to death by having its throat slit with a sharp knife, then allowed to hang and "bleed" while the feathers were quickly plucked away. Evisceration was done later, in the house or shed if available. It was not a job for the faint-hearted, and one we never cared to watch or be any part of as children, while we were growing up.

Occasionally, we would help remove pin feathers that remained on each bird, as we hated the thought of eating any of them, and it helped Mom quite a lot, as was a tedious job, requiring a lot of time. The birds were then washed in mild vinegar baths and put to freeze or canned or eaten as quickly as possible, as the danger of spoilage was great. Some farm families scalded their chickens, before plucking, in very hot water, to aid removal of feathers. This process yellowed and thickened the skin, and our family never did process ours this way, but Gordon reports this was a usual chicken butchering procedure at his farm.

In a "pinch" to obtain fresh poultry for dinner, it was occasionally necessary to butcher a chicken, by methods other than discussed above, especially in the absence of Dad, who usually performed the procedure. I recall assisting Mom on several occasions when we had to do the honors, either by wringing the chicken's neck or by chopping its head off with a sharp axe on a large block of wood. In the latter instance, and for some reason, unknown to us to this day, the chicken was not killed by the chopping procedure, but jumped up and ran away from us towards a slough of water behind the barn, with Mom and I in hot pursuit! It must have been some kind of "flight" reaction, and it soon toppled over, where we were able to retrieve it at the water's edge! What an experience! Did we ever laugh when it was over, and many times since about this unusual incident. On another occasion, when Mom and Gran were butchering chickens alone, Mom ended up with a nasty laceration to her arm, no laughing matter, (as previously discussed on previous pages under traumatic incidents).

For as long as I can remember, Barn Swallows came each spring and built their nests in the rafters of our hen house. Their cheeky chatter, and brilliant navy blue/rust colored breast feathers that flashed in the sunlight during their constant aerial acrobatics in and out of the hen house and around the barn yard, was a constant joy each summer. Their nests were never accessible, but we could see the dabs of mud and straw they carefully built it from, and finally the little hatchlings would emerge, and be taught by the adults to swoop and soar by fall, when they migrated south, to return as usual the following spring.

For lack of a better place to discuss it, I will mention now the other wild birds that flitted about our yard and fields as we grew up, and looking back, provided us with a certain "backdrop" of nature, that was so common then we didn't notice it much, but has since, in remembering, become more dear. Red-winged blackbirds always spent each summer season in the large blough north and west of the pasture. Their radiant song and flashing orange breast made their stay enjoyable, and remains a favorite to see and hear, when we are visiting in the country, or even in some park areas of the city (Grassick—where Michael played soccer as a boy). Meadow larks always heralded the Spring season, and were always a welcome sound—their song "Here I am, sitting on a post" being familiar to all. Kildeers, with their song sounding just like their name, swooped for food in our fields. One dog we had called Tippy, used to chase these birds for miles, as they swooped for insects, calling their lilting "kildeer, kildeer" song to each other. Tippy always seemed to think they were calling his name, Tippy, Tippy—hence the fascination we felt he had for these birds!

Prairie Chickens were quite a common sight along road allowances and in the fields, especially in the fall season. Their ability to blend perfectly into their surroundings because of their many-shaded brown/rust feathers, was always distressing to me as a child walking to and from school, I recall. A flock of several would flutter up, seemingly from nowhere, and scare me half to death! They never seemed to fly and soar like other birds, but rather fluttered, just above the ground, their wings beating furiously, but never seeming to get them far. It seems to me they winter on the prairies also, not migrating, probably because of their limited flying abilities. Back then, since they were quite abundant, they were hunted and enjoyed as a special fowl treat to roast and eat.

Wild ducks were also hunted in Fall for their great taste, and were always abundant and fattened then, as they would feed on the swaths of grain, lying in the fields, waiting for harvest. Uncle Don was the "hunter" in the family, and being quite a master at it, often brought Mom these birds that we would then all enjoy for Sunday dinners together. He always maintained it was the Sunlight bar soap he used to wash the dirt from their oily skin, that caused them to taste so~o—o good! Male Mallards were the best ducks, followed by the female Mallard, this breed being the largest birds in the area, and most prevalent of the migrating ducks that had summered in the North, and were on their way South for the winter. Dad always maintained any and all ducks were the bane of the farmer, especially at harvest, as they could make quite a mess of the swaths in the fields, especially if large flocks landed and fed over a large area for several days. However, he was never able to convince us ducks were all bad, and even today, the memory of the taste of those delicious roasted birds stands out in my mind, as a favorite eating experience of the past.

Dad always felt a certain fondness for crows, and even had a pet one he named Jack, that flew with him as he worked his land with the tractor and plow, hopping along in the furrows, etc., for a quick insect meal. I recall him being some mad at the government directive that allowed "open-season" on crows any time of year, and they could be shot, as their numbers were becoming too large. An added incentive of payment of three cents/pair of legs got a lot of farm boys involved in the hunt, as they liked the spending money they could earn from such "adventure". There was a similar incentive payment for gopher tails about this same time, when that rodent became over-abundant, and wolves/coyotes were hunted, supposedly for the same reason, until their numbers dwindled significantly, all by government intervention. Gordon recalls he and his brother Helmuth being involved in this crow-legs/gopher tail venture, as were many boys at Allindale School, I recall. Being natural predators, crows occasionally robbed nests of other birds, etc., and coyotes were blamed for preying on range cattle, especially calves, but Dad always felt the good they accomplished, helping keep the insect/rodent population down, etc., far outweighed any bad either crows or coyotes/wolves were blamed for. The familiar raucous "Caw caw" of the crows was certainly a welcome sound as late winter gave way to spring each year, as these familiar black-feathered birds were always the very first heralds of hope that indeed another winter was behind us, and we could look forward with joy and hope to another spring-summer season. The occasional nocturnal sound of howling wolves/coyotes never failed to send a chill down our spines, as children, and we were always thankful to be safe at home then.

Very occasionally robins visited the farm, but seemed to prefer town-living, probably because of the number of crows and blackbirds on the farm lands. Jenny Wrens, Blue Birds and occasional Cedar Waxwings were sometimes sighted. Gran Teasdale was fortunate to have both a Robin (built a nest right on her milk box by her back door) and a Jenny Wren at the front of her house under the eaves, over several summers, as I lived with her in high school. I suppose because of her quiet and beautiful yard and flowers in summer, they were particularly attracted there. She also seemed to have a special repoire with the Robin especially, and would talk to it with her own little "Eed-a-dee" language, and the silly bird would stay right on her nest as Gran came and went from her back door—it was amazing to see. Everyone in our family was thrilled by the sight of a Hummingbird, and every so often, one would be seen in summer, being especially attracted to deep-throated flowers such as Gladiola and Nicotine etc., where they could easily obtain nectar, with their long beaks.

Sparrows, common everywhere, lived on the farms and in towns and pigeons were often sighted in flocks just as they are today. Chickadees were often apparent in winter, their familiar song, sounding the same as their name, giving away their identity. Magpies, with their tell-tale long black tails, and black and white coloring, were often thought to bear ill (Gran Teasdale's idea, and she always hated to see one), were also quite common in the area. Hawks, another friend to the farmer, for keeping rodents and insects in check, were often seen lazily circling over the fields in search of food, and owls perched now and then on fence or telephone posts, peering with huge, staring eyes, like professors, always all-knowing and wise, as the owls portrayed in our story books, etc.

I recall several summers a heron or similar stork-like bird, lived and waded in the blough northwest of the barn, as we were growing up. We occasionally caught sight of it flying with mighty wing-span and long legs outstretched. It made a kind of phr~u~m-p, ph-r-u-m-p sound, that was kind of eerie and strange, compared to the other birds we were familiar with on the farm, and since the willows and wild grass were rather dense, and that blough was usually filled with water, that bird, whatever it was, was not bothered by anyone on our farm. Many frogs chorused from there each spring evening, and of course, as mentioned previously, each summer, the red-winged blackbirds lived and sang gloriously there.

Pursuant to the procuring of food, another source of meat and other meat/poultry products was the local butcher shop efficiently run for years by Mr. Stanley Knight, assisted by Hughie McCloy. This establishment provided Wolseley and area with delicious, freshly butchered beef, pork, lamb, some poultry (heads and feet tied in brown paper), as well as some processed meats such as wieners, ham, head cheese, some cheeses and delicious sweet breads we still love to this day! I can still recall him slicing ham, just the thickness asked for, from a huge square block of ham, he would place in a silver slicer. Mr. Knight loved kids, always sharing little anecdotes about his own grandchildren (Bacheldors) who lived in Toronto. On occasion, when they visited Wolseley, I sometimes played with these children, in their tent out in the yard, as they lived close by Gran Teasdale.

A peeled, raw wiener was usually given to each child that accompanied their mother to Mr. Knight's shop; we considered this a real treat and it was always free! The white painted shop was always cool and clean, and the floor was covered with fresh saw dust (I presume to be swept out at the end of each day, and replaced with fresh for cleanliness). Carcasses of beef and pork always hung on gigantic steel hooks suspended from the ceiling, at the back of the store, and usually gave us a fright (reminds me of Fuddrucker's window front now). A huge weigh scale used for weighing carcasses for sale, always proved fun to weigh ourselves on, (since we had no access to a weigh scale otherwise), our feather-weight back then, barely making a visible waver on the giant needle!! Mr. Knight did all his own butchering, even to an elderly age, until his well-earned retirement.

The introduction of the Wolseley Locker Plant in the early 1950's under the management of Tony Gruber and later John Baran, proved a wonderful and useful service to the town and community before electricity was available on the farms. The concept provided a meat market (minimal competition for Mr. Knight's shop, until his retirement), as well as a walk-in freezer with numbered, locked drawers that could be rented by customers on a monthly or yearly basis. The idea was to provide frozen storage of meat and garden produce, etc., to customers for a profit—a viable and innovative concept. All keys hung on a large wall board close to the door, our drawer number was 172 I recall.

Meat could be brought in, cut, wrapped and frozen, or could be bought from Mr. Gruber, then cut, wrapped and frozen. I remember being petrified of the place as a child, and always thought it would be awful to be locked in that totally frozen place, with its huge push-round-disc-handled door, clanging shut with an icy thud. A warm winter coat always hung beside the board of keys, as the extreme temperature change from summer to frigid was drastic!

I recall helping Mom shell peas by the pail-full, washing, blanching and packing them in pill-box containers with matching lids, a green/white penguin decal on top, that had to be processed quickly and brought to the Locker plant in a matter of hours after picking. Lines on the lid provided space to mark contents, name, and drawer number. Strawberries were another favorite, done in a syrup pack and placed in similar containers. Mom had a huge, ever-bearing strawberry patch all along the south end of the garden that must have provided bushels of luscious berries over the years. We ate many fresh, but always seemed to have an abundance to take to the Locker too. Very occasionally, tiny wild strawberries could be found in the pasture, down behind the barn, east of the big blough. It had to be a special spring, with just the right amount of rainfall and sun, for them to appear at all—I recall they were extra tasty!

Mom also used to grow peas, yellow and green beans and raspberries that we ate fresh as well as prepared for the Locker. A huge raspberry patch ran north and south at the northwest corner of the garden, all along the hen house/pig pen and pasture area, to the east of the shelter belt of trees. All the family, especially Dad, took turns helping each other pick raspberries; we each had a metal can with a strip of left-over electrical wiring attached to each side that was worn around the waist freeing the hands for the delicate picking procedure. Some beautiful raspberries originated from that patch that were also prepared in a cold pack of syrup for freezing. Our garden raspberry patch began with canes secured from this very patch begun so long ago on our farm.

It must have been a huge hassle running back and forth to town with all this produce, as it was ready for freezing in its season, but those yummy suppers of fresh garden peas, fresh fried sausage, potatoes and those juicy red strawberries for dessert, after a trip to town in winter, remains to this day, one of my favorite memories, and seemed to have made all the effort during summer very worth-while.

The Locker plant concept prevailed well into the 1960's or later because Gordon and I had a locker drawer for our meat at the Co-Op when we were first married, living in our suite at Bert and Ida John's at 1428 Pasqua Street, and had no freezer, except a small one in our refrigerator. Our parents provided us with meat, poultry and produce from the farm whenever possible, and we also bought bulk meat on sale, storing it at the Co-Op Locker, until we moved to our own home, and bought a home freezer. What a wonderful appliance it is, now taken so much for granted, but back in those days could have made farm life so much easier, as with so many of our modern-day luxuries.

B.C. and California fruit such as peaches, pears, cherries, and apricots were bought at local stores as it came into season, often in case lots and was preserved by canning for the winter months into fruit, jellies, jams, etc. Local fruits such as saskatoons and other valley berries were also preserved. Mom used to make a peaches & pears mixture for popular fruit salads she often served, as well as many quarts of each individual fruit, as they were favorites of our whole family. Crabapples from the Brown orchard were also a welcome treat.

Before the days of refrigeration as we know it, ice boxes utilized large blocks of ice in a compartment inside, as a coolant, whereas now Freon is used in modern electrical refrigeration. Of course the ice would melt in several days, and the water, collected in a tray had to be removed and discarded. Ice delivery to homes in cities and towns was common back then, made possible by being able to freeze such blocks in units like the local locker plant, I suppose. It seems to me, Gran Teasdale had an ice box in her kitchen, when I was a child, and also Aunt Alice in her city apartment.

In addition to keeping livestock on the farm for meat, to eat and sell, the dairy products procured from them, like milk, cream, butter and eggs were a vital, useful addition to the farm food supply.

As mentioned previously, eggs were usually in plentiful supply, year-round, because of the annual addition of new birds into the flock, and the surplus of eggs not used or needed by the family were sold to the candling station in Wolseley. The summer diet of the laying chickens, that consisted more of greens etc., caused dark, stronger tasting egg yolks, while the winter diet of chop (ground oats) soaked in milk, as well as straw, potato and other vegetable peels, etc., resulted in lighter yellow yolks which had a mild taste. Oyster shell also supplemented the winter diet, and greatly strengthened the egg shell, while in summer small pebbles, grains, etc., seemed to supply this diet ingredient naturally. It was always a curiosity to us as children, as Mom eviscerated butchered chickens, to look inside the gizzard, the lining of which was removed, if possible, intact, so as not to contaminate the organ, but if opened, contained the partially digested diet last eaten by the chicken, like bits of straw, small pebbles etc. The other thing I recall about this evisceration process was seeing the "egg tract" containing egg yolks of various sizes, from very tiny to medium that the chicken would eventually have laid as eggs. Of course this was only seen in a laying hen, and for that reason, even though their meat was more tender and nicer to eat, only male birds were usually butchered for eating.

I can't help but recall an incident that happened while we were growing up, that brought to light for me, how much farm children take the necessary life and death process of farm animals so much for granted. A Regina cousin was visiting in the district, and being ages with me, we often got together to play either at her Aunt's home or ours. This particular day she had come to play at our house, and was to stay overnight, as I recall, as it was summer holidays. Mom decided to make a treat for supper the next evening of roast chicken, and proceeded to choose a bird, butcher it in the barn, and eviscerate it as usual, on the kitchen table. What was a usual course of events to obtain poultry for a meal on our farm, seemed to our visiting city guest a traumatic, barbaric experience—one she was not about to share with us! She asked to return to her Aunt's home immediately, not able to stay and play another instant, with people that could be so mean to a chicken, and worse yet plan to eat it! I guess she thought chicken originated on trays in the supermarket, like she had always been used to seeing it or had never really given it much thought at all, prior to this. I have never forgotten the impression this incident had on me, but looking back, I'm sure there were many things about city-life back then that would have frightened me half to death, but that this cousin felt completely comfortable about.

Another time when a group of us cousins were playing together in a neighboring farm yard, we somehow decided the hen house roof would be an excellent place to run and play, as it was a fairly low building, and the roof had a gradual slant, especially on the south side. We were cavorting around, running as close to the edge as possible, hoping every second not to be caught by our parents, when this same cousin ran too close to the west peaked-edge, and flew off into space, fluttering to the ground, almost as if planned. We all looked over the edge, aghast to see her lying very still on the soft-packed earth of the chicken yard. Help was summoned from the house, and needless to say we were all soundly reprimanded for ever having decided to play up there in the first place. As for our cousin, she seemed only to have had the wind knocked out of her, and suffered no lasting ill effects, however, we all learned an appreciation for safer play places after that day!

Milk, cream and butter were always in plentiful supply on the farms back then, as nearly all farm families kept livestock, not like now, where some farms are strictly grain or strictly dairy. Usually a herd consisted of milk cows and calves in various stages of growth, depending on when they were born in the Spring. The larger the herd, the more milk and dairy products procured, however it was also more work. On our farm, Dad depended on his two Jersey milk cows named Pat (tan color with darker facial features and tail) and Patsy (fawn colored with similar darker markings), bought from a local dairyman, who had also helped Dad build our farm house, mentioned previously. By nature, Jersey cows are big milk producers, noted especially for the high cream content. This suited our needs perfectly, as part of the reason for maintaining milk cows on our farm, was to sell the cream for profit.

The cow Patsy seemed particularly prone to mastitis after calving, while we owned her, and Dad almost came to dread breeding her for this reason. Treatment for the mastitis involved inserting thin capsules of medication into her teats, needless to say a painful procedure both for the cow and Dad, but he would persevere, and always ended up making her better. In the meantime, the calf could not suckle and her milk could not be used for drinking. Another time, this same cow managed to cut one of her back hooves badly on a discarded tin can that had been dumped in a distant pasture blough along with other refuse from our green tin garbage barrel that always sat to the west side of our porch, by the back door. Treatment for this injury consisted of frequent linseed poulticing to draw the infection out, and then the all-time veterinary cure Watkin's yellow-brown ointment.

It seems to me Patsy gave Dad more than a normal share of farmer's grief over the years, and Mom used to get kind of annoyed over the way he seemed to baby her—who had ever heard of a cow "enjoying poor health"? However, being the caring, kind man he was, Dad never seemed to mind; it was nothing for him to spend the night in the barn when a cow was in labor at calving time, sometimes catching a chill or cold in the process!

Over the years, we had other breeds of cows, namely Hereford, and some Holsteins. In the days before Veterinary services were available, who also provided artificial insemination for breeding purposes, farmers had to depend on neighbors who kept, a mature bull to provide this service. Often a "mongrel" calf resulted, if the heifer or cow was of a different breed than the bull available, however with artificial insemination, the breed could be matched. As I recall, a gentleman by the name of Peter Manners was in charge of this service in the Wolseley area, probably in the mid 1950's; he provided a much-needed service to surrounding farms, working on a fee for service basis, much like today.

As children, we didn't have very much to do with the cattle, and in fact were afraid of them. The young calves were cute, but unpredictable and rambunctious! After birth, they were allowed several days of feeding from their mother, and then had to be taught, to "pail-feed", as we wanted the cow's milk for our use and the cream for shipping. Of course, this was pretty traumatic for a calf, after being used to suckling from its mother's teats, and caused a lot of rebellion! I can recall helping Mom with this task in the calf pen of the barn, while Dad was away at Uncle Herb's working one day. The object was to grasp the calf by the snout and force its head into the pail of milk, to help it learn to drink and feed that way. All went well for a few minutes, and then Bang! The calf butted its head up out of the pail, sending it flying, milk and all, everywhere! All over Mom and I and all over the pen and calf—needless to say, we were some upset, and the poor calf went hungry that noon, after several other foiled attempts to get it to feed properly.

Eventually, all calves on our farm did get the hang of this feeding arrangement, and happily fed from pails of milk, until they graduated up to grass feeding in the pasture in summer, and then hay, chop and oat sheaves in winter. I can still recall seeing one or two calves feeding this way, Dad holding the pails, as they would still butt them, even up over their heads, spilling their milky contents all over, even after they knew better. They would switch their tails rapidly, sometimes stamping their front feet, and their little heads always had short curly hair, especially the Hereford's, were cute with white faces, and one could always see the circular wheal where their hair began on their foreheads as a cow-lick (that must be where this term originated). Cute!

Some farm families were very involved with 4-H Clubs, a group farm children could belong to that promoted more involvement with the farm operation, as well as the fellowship and friendship of other school-aged boys and girls. Emphasis was on raising prize livestock and grains, both readily available on most family farms. The actual logo of a green four-leafed clover on a white background, with the 4-H superimposed on it, had special meaning for this group, but since neither Gordon or I were ever involved in 4-H, we are at a loss what it stood for. It seems to me farm children can still belong to this group, where there is an active interest. In our district, Harold Thompson's family was always very involved in 4-H, as they had a large dairy operation, and children who were interested in taking part in this group, I recall.

Milking the cows twice a day, morning and evening, was a daily ritual on most farms, unless the calves were allowed to "milk-feed", meaning left to nurse until they were almost grown, fattening up on the whole milk their mother provided, rather than the skim milk they would be fed from pails after it was separated. Usually these milk-fed animals were intended for butchering for home use or for sale, as would bring a good price. In a larger herd of cattle, the farmer could easily let several calves feed in this way, and still have enough milk and cream for family use and for sale. However, on our farm, we seldom went this route, preferring to milk our several cows by hand. This job always fell to Dad, as Mom refused to milk, and consequently neither Connie nor I ever learned either. It was always there to do, and "tied" us to the farm on a daily basis, always waiting to be done morning and evening, with no holiday from it. Very occasionally, a neighbor would help out with milking, if a farmer just had to be away from his duties, especially in the evening, and then the favor would be returned if needed, on another occasion. Gordon reports that all four of his family helped with the milking, his mother and the boys often doing it alone at harvest, etc., when Dad was too busy. Those were the times when I wished at least one of us could have helped our Dad with this task, as the cows weren't too good at waiting to be milked until late evening, often bawling loudly, as their udders over-filled with milk. (Having been a nursing mother, I can vouch for the actual pain experienced by this milk build-up, and know something of what those cows must have experienced at such times!)

In later years, after our Jersey cow era, Dad went into Holstein cows on a larger basis, even installing a second-hand milking machine set-up in the barn, to help him with the extra work. Having left home by then, I don't recall much about this particular segment of life on our farm, except that it took a lot of struggle to set up and maintain.

Milk obtained from the cows, no matter how, whether by hand or machine, had to be separated into milk and cream content, by a hand-driven machine logically called a separator. Ours was bolted to the basement floor, in front of the cistern, in the central part of the basement. Milk was carried in pails from the barn, downstairs, and poured into the bowl of the separator through a stainless steel strainer, held over the bowl in a triangular-shaped wooden holder. This strainer had a very fine mesh sieve that filtered out any impurities that may have floated into the milk after milking, such as fine hair, specks of dirt, straw, etc.

After the milk had all been strained, and the large silver bowl of the separator was full, the operator, usually Dad, began to turn a large wooden handle, attached to a gear box on the separator. This turning had to be uniform and of a certain speed maintained throughout the whole separating process, that took perhaps five to ten minutes total. Once the correct speed had been reached, a release valve on the bowl was turned, releasing the milk to be separated onto a metal float that sat on top of a steel hub containing a dozen or more slotted metal discs. This rapidly turning hub, activated by the turning handle, acted as a centrifuge. As the milk filtered down through the discs, the cream that was heavier, separated off into a smaller spout, and was caught in a container sitting on one of two large, round metal plates at the front of the separator. The skimmed milk, that was lighter, separated into another larger spout into a pail, sitting on the other metal plate. Now, thinking back, this process, taken as a twice-daily routine, was quite something, and difficult to describe, although the principal of operation was quite simple really. Apparently there were also electrically driven separators, available after the advent of power to farmsteads, and Gordon's family had one. However, we always just maintained the hand-driven one.

This separator had to be washed on a daily basis, as the milk would sour if left longer, and ruin the whole process. The bowl, strainer and discs had to carefully washed and scalded with boiling water, and the discs hung to dry on a special hanging rack shaped like a giant safety pin. Washing the separator was one of the farm woman's thankless tasks, always waiting for her, that had to be done before the morning's milk could be processed each day. After the morning separating was done, the operator poured hot water through the bowl and disc system, turning the cream spout into the skim milk pail so as not to dilute the cream. This water would effectively rinse the bowl and discs so that, the separator only had to be taken apart and washed thoroughly once a day, to rid it of milk residue and build-up.

Sometimes, whole milk was saved out in a container, not separated, and chilled to the coolness of the basement only, so it was vulnerable to a short-life span before spoilage, especially in summer. Mom mostly used this whole milk for baking, as none of our family drank milk on a regular basis then—now I know why. The chilled, pasteurized milk of today has so much more appeal than did that whole milk back then, barely cooled. The skim milk was used to feed the non-nursing calves, soak chop for feeding chickens and pigs, and also for the pigs to drink. Milk that soured could be used for baking, or for making cottage cheese, although Mom never made this, Gordon says his mother used to.

Separated cream was very rich and wonderful to use in desserts, whipped cream, cereal, etc. There was nothing like it, and we all fondly remember "good old farm cream". Needless to say, it was loaded with calories, but no one knew much about such dietary restraint back then, or cared either. What we ate was one of the pleasures afforded by farm-life, and we enjoyed our food, mostly produced by the labor of the farmer, wife and sometimes children, right on the farm. The cream not required for family use was kept cool and saved for shipping for money.

The more milking cows, the more quickly enough could be saved to fill either a five or ten gallon cream can, that was a common container to all farm families back then (now a much sought-after collector's item). Of course sweet cream brought a higher market price, so it was a priority, when possible, to ship sweet cream and have it arrive at Broadview or Elkhorn Creamery in this same sweet state—needless to say a losing proposition in the summer months! I can still recall Mom's anger over dockages for sour cream, as she depended heavily on this cream cheque and the egg cheque from the candling station to buy her groceries from the stores each week. Later, when the Binst family opened a creamery in Wolseley, this problem of shipping to a creamery further east was much alleviated, although I can't say as I remember Mom and Dad bringing cream to sell locally; of course I was attending high school then and not always aware of all that went on as part of our farm operation during those years

With regard to cream cans, they were silver steel with handles on each side for carrying and a lid with another handle across the top that fitted snugly down into the neck of the can, to keep the creamy contents in place. Probably they were made at the local metal shop, as I seem to recall they were soldered together. Names, Post Office Box Number and Town were always painted in black letters on each can for easy identification. A delivery tag had to be attached to each cream can lid, designating creamery being shipped to, date, etc. I recall the thin wire that came with these tags was an excellent wire for Crafting, and I was often guilty of snipping a piece of it to help me with some project, much to Mom's chagrin, as then she wouldn't have enough wire on the card for tagging her cream! Oh, for craft, stores back then!

Since cream was shipped by train in those days, the local train station was usually the first stop we made when coming to town—to deliver a fresh can of cream for shipping and to pick up the empty can being returned; it was a common sight to see twenty to thirty empty cream cans out on the station platform waiting for their respective farm owners to pick them up. Cheques were sent separately to the post office boxes. Some shipping was done by truck in the later years when the train wasn't as reliable, with the train station still being the drop-off point.

Empty cans had to be washed and scalded thoroughly before they could be refilled with another week's allotment of cream. In winter, keeping the cream sweet was a much easier task than in summer, when we stored it in the basement in the earthen hole Dad dug for it, as mentioned previously. In the absence of large, clean containers to transport other liquids, cream cans were also used as receptacles for hauling drinking water to Field Days, Sport's Days, to the fields at harvest, or in our case to supplement the amount our water can would hold, when we acquired water from Raymond's well (to be discussed later under "water").

Some cream was kept aside by most farm families for the purpose of churning it into butter. We had two churns, as I recall —a small glass one that held perhaps 6 quarts of cream, and a very large metal one that would hold several gallons. The small glass one was more practical for our purposes, having a metal lid, handle and blades. Mom could achieve the desired buttery result in approximately ten to fifteen minutes of steady, quick turns on that little curved handle, and as time was always at a premium for her, she usually churned with this one. The larger amount of cream the metal churn would accommodate, resulted in a huge yield of butter. Dad usually took his turn with this procedure, and even us kids enjoyed hearing the large wooden paddles or blades "kerplotsch" in the creamy mixture, and would take a turn at the handle now and then! However, we quickly lost interest when the butter would not appear as quickly at we thought it should, and Mom or Dad had to finish the job.

When the churning procedure was over, the butter was removed from the churn with a spatula into a large wooden bowl. The buttermilk that remained was sometimes used to bake with or in some households even used as to drink, although never in ours. The mass of butter had to be "worked" with a large, flat, wooden paddle to remove the remaining buttermilk that was then poured off. Table salt was then added to taste, and worked into the butter with this same wooden paddle. The resulting butter was very pale yellow and very soft and creamy in texture. Sometimes a few drops of yellow coloring, bought especially for this purpose, could be added to the butter for extra color. I recall farm butter didn't ever taste very good to me, and I dearly loved what was then referred to as "town butter" or butter bought by the pound at the store, although we rarely bought any, as I seemed to be alone in this taste preference, and cream to churn into "farm butter" was always so readily available back then.

In addition to churning butter for our own family use, Mom sometimes sold butter to several ladies in town, who were interested in buying it, usually through previous arrangement, by word of mouth, etc. It was a real novelty to watch the procedure required to turn the mound of freshly churned butter into rectangular, pound shapes with a wooden press-type mold, and then to wrap it just so, and fold the two ends of the butter paper into perfect points to enclose the butter. I recall this butter paper was especially bought just for this purpose; it came in single sheets the size of standard letter paper, but like parchment, imprinted with a sunrise scene in pale blue. It seemed to have a non-stick quality to it, and was also cut into circular shapes to line round cake pans when making a layer cake. In the days before power on the farm and refrigeration, the pounds of wrapped butter were quickly dispatched to the basement on a tray to chill, and await transport to town, a day or two at most before spoilage. In view of this also, the small batches of butter Mom's smaller churn turned out, were more ideal for us, as could be used up more quickly, especially in summer, before spoilage or rancidness could occur.

About this time, margarine made its appearance on the scene, and could be bought as an alternative to butter. Some government directive prohibited its sale then in a yellow colored state, so it was sold in pounds or plastic bags in its natural white state, and color capsules or patches were enclosed for the consumer to color the margarine at home. I don't recall us ever using that much margarine as we were growing up, with cream always being so available for butter, and as mentioned previously, calories or cholesterol content of food was not an issue then.

Ice cream was a real treat back then, and could only be enjoyed when we went to town and bought it "by the dip" from the several restaurants there, our choice usually being the Chinamans under Wing Yuen and sons ownership. I recall one attempt Mom made to make ice cream from a kind of custard mixture that she whipped and chilled in the porch one winter, when we weren't able to get to town for a long time, due to the weather, and were craving a treat! It didn't quite measure up to our expectations, and I don't remember her trying again. Gordon recalls his family having a hand turned ice cream maker, and one time when a severe hail storm ruined their crop just prior to harvest, they made the most delicious ice cream from the hail stones. They also used it in winter when ice was available to make other ice cream treats, however, the hail made the best ice cream he reports!

The restaurants used to store their ice cream in huge thermal lined bags that kept the creamy contents chilled for a limited time during the summer months. I expect in winter the task of keeping ice cream was made easier, as cold storage would be more readily available. I can still recall the delicious taste these dips of rich ice cream had, especially if it was bought to take home—the dips would be placed in a white cardboard vertical specially designed box with a top closure, and always flavored the ice cream just a bit, as we always scooped out the last drops to enjoy, after the scoops were out and the remainder had melted! Of course a cone with this ice cream on it was equally welcome in the restaurant, or else a float with pop, that was one of Dad's favorite treats, especially orange. We usually always stopped at the "Chinks" as it was referred to back then, for a treat when in town, especially on a Saturday night of shopping. Dad would often even have a Denver sandwich and we would have fries or ice cream, etc. As mentioned previously, eating was one of the pleasures we always enjoyed as a family, and there often seemed to be a bit of money for a restaurant treat, even though we didn't have much else, and we always appreciated going for one, whenever we could. We rarely ate a full meal in a restaurant though back then, now such a common thing to do.

Dixie cups were a new concept at about the time we were growing up; they consisted of a small, round, lidded cardboard container filled with ice cream. A small dab of strawberry, raspberry or caramel flavoring topped the ice cream and was always directly under the lid when opened. A small wrapped wooden spoon accompanied each Dixie cup to eat the treat. Vanilla was the most common flavor ice cream came in back then, although chocolate, cherry custard and strawberry were available as we became older, and now finally any flavor imaginable is available for us to enjoy these days, and readily available to all at any time through modern refrigeration. It is hard now to imagine the rare and satisfying treat ice cream was to us back then in the days of our childhood.

Having discussed dairy products previously, just a few other recollections come to mind with regard to the farm animals and livestock. A block of salt was always kept in the farm yard around the barn somewhere for the livestock to lick, to supplement their diet. This salt came in a white, red or blue block about a foot square, with a depression in the bottom to secure it on a post; it could also just sit on the ground. The animals would gouge large depressions in these blocks with their tongues and turn it into unusual shapes, finally licking it all up, and a new block would have to bought in town at one of the several stores that carried it. It was always a great fascination to my cousin Audrey and I as girls, to share this salt with the animals, often breaking off a little piece to put in our pockets to lick on now and then! Our mothers were always aghast that we would want to lick something the animals had been licking; however, looking back, this must have been part of the fascination I think! Certainly, we weren't lacking salt in our diets, and could have had table salt with much less trouble, whenever we wanted it—it just seemed to be some "daring" thing we had to do!

In addition to the cattle kept in our own pasture, for milk products and food, Dad and his brother, Uncle Herb kept range cattle together for a few years, with the sole purpose of selling them at maturity for monetary gain. Calves born to these cattle just fed from their mothers and grew up as part of the herd. They pastured them in summer on some land south of the highway, and had to drive them there as a herd, riding horseback. It seems to me, they sold most of the yearlings off each fall, only keeping heifers to mother the additions to the herd for next spring, Uncle Herb keeping those in his much larger barn over winter. I think for the amount of work involved, together with the poor price of beef at the time was cause to abandon this project as non-viable; the South Pasture, co-owned with other siblings and relatives was later sold.

Keeping livestock over winter meant quite a lot of work for the farmer, with regard to supplying feed and water for them, as well as disposal of their manure. Oat sheaves and hay had to be put up each summer into the barn lofts or in stacks outside, for them to eat, or oats were harvested and stored to grind as chop for feed. Water had to be hauled from the dug out in barrels for them to drink in very cold weather, or else they would drink from a hole chopped in the ice, on nicer winter days. Manure and soiled straw had to be removed from the barn stalls each day in winter, as the cattle spent their nights in the barn. As mentioned previously, the stone boat was the vehicle of conveyance to do this job, being pulled by the horse or tractor. Many farmers dumped this rich waste on their surrounding summer fallow fields in winter that then acted as a good fertilizer as it decomposed. Some manure was piled in the pasture, where it decayed more slowly, and was often lighted to burn as a "smudge" of smoke to fend off insect pests that bothered the livestock in summer—they sure knew to stand in the smoke too! The chicken coop and pig pen had to be cleaned less regularly, but still had to be done quite often.

Of course, cleaning out all this manure was one of the many thankless but necessary jobs the farmer had to do—the manure often sticking to boots and the smell adhering to outer clothing worn to do the job. Lucky the farm home with a heated porch where such clothing could be taken off and hung up, or left to "air out" before being brought into the house. Our family was not so fortunate, and I can still recall the pungent smell of manure permeating our home, when Dad came in from cleaning the barn, especially in winter. It was one of those things that couldn't be helped, and we just learned to live with it. Dad would often refer to the Bible verse Hebrews 13:8, as he came in from doing his chores, that refers to things being the same yesterday, today and forever—nothing much changed for the farmer back then—always cows to milk, always chores to do, crops to plant and harvest and fields to work, with little thanks except a rather self-paced, independent life-style many would envy now! It wasn't the big-business farm concept of today, but a small operation, with each farmer eking out a small modest living, providing for his family as best he could.

A few more thoughts come to mind, with regard to food in general, and recollections of how things "used to be" that I have failed thus far to mention. In addition to farm butter, churned for daily use, as mentioned previously. Mom always baked her own bread, as did most farm women of the day. Although the heavenly aroma of fresh-baked bread and buns was something we enjoyed on a regular basis, I must confess I preferred "town bread" or baker's bread bought only occasionally at the store in town. Mom usually made white bread, from huge 100 pound bags of white flour bought in town as necessary. Flour sacking, the fabric used to make these huge bags for flour, was usually white, and after being washed several times, made into excellent tea towels and cloths for many household uses. For a time, as we were growing up, this sacking came in floral and prints that enterprising farm women and girls turned into fabric for dresses, blouses, curtains, etc. Matching flour sack fabric then became an issue when buying a new supply of flour, as some garments or projects took more than one large sack's worth of fabric! Aunt Ruby especially made use of this sacking for dresses, etc., I recall, as she sewed for herself a lot.

Homemade bread tasted O.K., but to make those thick slices into toast was another matter entirely and the thing I disliked most about homemade bread! There were no toasters back then, and the only way to make toast for breakfast, or any other time a piece was fancied, was to hold slices of bread enclosed in a wire rack, over the open flame of wood or coal burning kitchen stoves. A moment of inattention, and the lot could be charred in a second or two! The crusts were always "too crusty" and crumbly for my liking, and usually the "toasting" was over-done or under-done, depending on the time, skill and alertness of the person making it, usually Mom. Two pieces were all that could be made at a time, and then spread with that "farm butter" as opposed to "town butter", (as mentioned previously), wasn't a taste treat for me back then, although most farm people thought it was good, and probably now, I would think so too! Mom also made brown bread on occasion, but as she was the only one that liked it, didn't buy whole wheat flour often, and although we had the facilities, in the form of the barn chopper, to grind our own grain into whole wheat flour, we never did it back then, as a lot of farm women do today. Of course then, we didn't realize the nutritional value we were forfeiting using only white flour for baking either. A cute recollection comes to mind with regard to Mom's bread-baking and Connie; we often watched Mom punch down her dough and expertly pop it into seven or eight loaf (lard) pans she used to bake each batch in. After watching the preparation of this dough one day, Mom asked Connie, just a little girl at the time, if she thought she would bake her own bread someday when she grew up. Connie mulled this prospect over for a few moments in her little mind, probably considering all the steps and work involved, and wistfully replied "No, I'm going to buy my bread!" We sure thought this cute, and true to her word then, even though she has grown up to be an excellent cook, she most often "buys" her bread and rolls now!

Mom's homemade toffee was known far and wide as a delectable treat. She also made buns, wonderful Yorkshire puddings, delicious meringue pies and always had baking on hand for us and company to enjoy. She was an excellent cook, in the traditional English-style, patterned after Gran Teasdale, also a wonderful cook, and always prepared nutritious and delicious meals for us; we always ate meals together as a family, at the usual mealtime hours, and often a bed-time lunch besides. Dad had his favorite foods, and it seemed to be Mom's goal in life to please his gastric pleasures; she often said "The way to a man's heart was through his stomach", and her efforts seemed to bear out this dictum. It was nothing for her to be up running around throughout most of our meal, putting finishing touches on the dessert or bringing additional items to the table Dad or one of us children needed for our meal. I think she found she ate less this way, often having only a few minutes at the end of the meal to have her plateful, as being over-weight was a bit of a problem for her back in those years! However, it was not altogether restful for those of us eating; Connie and I sat behind the table, and couldn't easily jump up to help her, and of course Dad never got up, once seated. I think this is why I try so hard, now I manage my own kitchen and meals, to have everything ready and on the table, before calling family to come and eat. That way, we avoid, as much as possible, people jumping up from the table during a meal. Also Gordon is not opposed to helping me with forgotten items; probably an attitude change has taken place over the years, with this idea of "servitude" being exchanged for a "shared" commitment to household duties, now both parents work outside the home. Gordon's German heritage and his mother's fine flair for cooking has definitely enhanced my own cooking and meal preparation abilities over the years, for which and I am indebted and grateful.

With regard to certain dietary habits, I must mention how Dad always had the same breakfast without fail, all the years we were growing up—puffed wheat cereal, a fried egg, toast and coffee. He always ended this meal with a bit of Bee Hive syrup poured on his plate, to finish up with his last bit of toast. At the other end of the day, bed-time lunch, he always prepared himself this same snack—orangeade, from a fresh, squeezed orange, and soda crackers spread with a bit of peanut butter. Even if we had company over, and a lunch of something else was being served our guests, Dad would faithfully have his usual orangeade and cracker lunch. A creature of habit—that he was, but now looking back, it was kind of cute, and made him unique!

As mentioned previously, we seldom went out to a restaurant to eat a meal back then, limiting ourselves to a treat when in town. Visiting back and forth at each other's homes, for a meal seemed more popular, especially in the winter months, when there was more time. Gordon recalls it was always his little job as a boy, to dust the living room and parlor Sunday mornings before church, in the event Sunday visitors would come calling, and when this happened, it was more or less a given, they were invited to stay for supper, as there was usually a roast dinner being prepared, and would be enough food for all. The Mortons and Gran often came calling on us for a visit Sunday afternoons and always stayed for supper. We often stayed for lunch with Gran after church, having soup and sandwiches she had prepared before church, hoping we would share this meal with her. Since we had no phone in those early years, while we were growing up, ladies of the district would send invites for a supper and card evening back and forth with us school children, the replies going back in the same manner. Often several families would be invited, depending on the size of the home—we were always limited to one family because of our small home. These get-togethers were fun for adults and children alike, a change from home, and where there were children in that family, a chance to play together. Card games of whist, rummy, canasta, followed a delicious repast—the farm women exchanging news, recipes, bits of gossip, child-rearing tips, over the dishes, while the men visited in the living room or parlor, then all got together for the card games.

In earlier years, these trips between farms were often made by horses and sleigh, as in winter the roads were often impassible to vehicles. Teams of horses were kept in the host's barn, during the visit. In later years, when roads were kept open and cars more modern, Connie and I always secretly hoped to get stuck in the snow on the way home, to add adventure to the outing, and sometimes our wishes came true, with shoveling and pushing until eventually we arrived home. (Now I know why our own children used to wish for similar kinds of "adventure" on the way back from visiting out of town at our respective parent's homes—however, as parents, the prospect of becoming stalled or stuck on winter roads with young children frightened us, just as I'm sure it did our parents, who were more aware of the consequences than children—then and now!)

We sometimes had bachelors of the district come for a visit and meal, like Ed Thompson, Roy Debenham, salesmen like Ed Poels, etc., who because of their circumstances weren't able to reciprocate the meal, but their company was welcomed anyway. However, one bachelor, previously from the district, that came calling for a meal and visit, now and then, used to send my sister and I into a tail-spin, because he was usually filthy, rather crude and uncouth, and smoked a smelly old pipe, and we wanted to disappear, rather than spend an evening sharing our meal and time in his company. His only home was a primitive caboose, parked where ever he happened to be digging a well, or doing other odd work, that probably lacked any amenities, like water, sewer, or washing facilities. Mom always felt sorry for him, as had known this gentleman's family, none of whom lived in the area anymore, that could provide the old drifter a bit of hospitality now and then. Thus, he came calling on district people whenever he was in the area. Mom always felt he got "cleaned-up" from usual, when he came calling, but we could never tell! Looking back, it was probably a good lesson in The Golden Rule—doing unto others as we would have done unto us that our parents provided, by welcoming this fellow into our home, however, we weren't able to see the lesson in it at the time!

A "good neighbor policy of sharing" always prevailed when it came to food in farming communities back then, and our district was no exception. I suppose this edict resulted from the earliest pioneer days, when helping each other with tasks as well as available food, was often a means of survival. As mentioned previously, when butchering meat, neighbors came to help each other, and then all shared in the resulting bounty, in an effort to provide a bit of fresh meat for everyone, before spoilage could occur. Similarly, when gardens produced abundantly, whether it was vegetables or flowers, a lot of sharing the bounty went on between neighboring women. I recall Orval and Ivadell Brown always sharing their orchard fruit, especially crabapples, with many families in the district, and with us, before our own fruit trees reached maturity.

Before the days of plastic, and Tupperware, with sealed lids to keep food fresh and free of flies and other flying insects, homemakers used to use a covering of circular cloth or a thin plastic with elasticized edges to pull over bowls of left-over food. I can recall Gran Teasdale having a set of these food covers in graduated sizes and in different pastel colors. She would then place the food in her ice box to chill it. With regard to flies, that always seemed to be about in the kitchen, or wherever there was food, just like today, and in the absence of modern spray pesticides, homemakers had at their disposal and made common use of fly coils. These items consisted of a three inch-long cardboard canister, about an inch in diameter that enclosed a pull-out brown, spiral paper, sticky on both sides that could be suspended from the ceiling or other convenient place of suspension. The sticky material must have attracted the hapless flies, as they seemed to flock to these coils, and then become stuck fast, and died there rather quickly. Needless to say, these coils were awful looking, with hordes of flies stuck to them, but they served a useful purpose, and could always be replaced when full, or no longer as sticky. The other method of extermination, for flies in the house, was then as now, a good sturdy fly swat. Screens over the windows in summer were also a big deterrent, as long as they were in good repair, without holes, as certainly a fly would find the smallest hole and zoom in, if food was available. The thought of where else flies had been, in a cow dung or manure heap somewhere on the farm, always added to the need to exterminate them quickly. With regard to screens on windows, Gordon and I can recall as children, the sound of going to sleep with the evening breeze swishing through the screens on our bedroom windows—much as it does today, but somehow the memory of it seemed sweeter back then!

Probably next to the producing and procurement of food, obtaining water for drinking and family use was of high priority, and not too easy to come by on our small farm. Several attempts were made at well-digging over the years, and when water was finally struck, in a well close to the dug out, it was sent away for testing and found to be unfit for human consumption! Even the animals wouldn't drink it, as it had a strong chemical taste. It was a disappointment, to say the least, and forever after we had to obtain our water from a well at Raymond and Isobel's home about a mile from where we lived. "Going for water" was almost an outing, and one or both of us children would often go along in the car when Mom and/or Dad drove over to obtain this necessity each week. Those folks always seemed ready for a visit, while we filled the water cans from a hose hooked up in their basement. All the neighbors in the vicinity obtained drinking water from Raymond's well—the "good neighbor policy" prevailing—if we have lots, you are welcome to share it for free! It was a wonderful arrangement and looking back, except for the hard work involved for Dad in hauling it downstairs, and the constancy of need, got us away from our place for a little while, and a visit besides!

A large round metal water can (that held perhaps 15-20 gallons of water), with a snug-fitting handled lid and metal handles on each side was made for us at the metal works shop in town, and it was in this Dad hauled all our drinking water home and carried it downstairs each time, so it would stay a little cooler and fresher tasting. As mentioned previously, cream cans were sometimes employed also to carry extra water at canning time, etc. Needless to say, not a drop of drinking water was ever wasted in our home, and was carefully guarded and monitored, although we weren't reprimanded on a daily basis to conserve water, everyone just knew to do it.

To this day we keep water in the refrigerator for drinking, rather than "running the tap" just for the sake of obtaining extra cold drinking water. I still cringe when I hear water running straight down the drain from the tap.

Unfortunately, we have all become victims of the easy access to soft, hard, hot and cold water from one of several faucets and taps located in all our homes today, and it is easy to forget about conserving this still precious commodity, which of course does not come in unlimited supply.

A 5-gallon crock, filled with drinking water, always sat on the end of our cupboard, with a metal dipper hung above it, for all family members to share when we wanted a drink. It was never cold, and of course adding ice was not an option, so we learned to drink luke-warm water all the time. No wonder the tinkling ice in glasses of water in a restaurant caused so much excitement for us as children back then!

A large metal kettle was standard equipment on most coal and wood stoves back then and was the only means of obtaining hot water for hot beverages to drink, much as it is today, only now we have electric kettles to help with this task. The kettle always sat "at the ready" on one of the back burners and could easily be pulled towards the hotter, front end of the stove when needed.

Soft water for bathing, washing clothes and hand washing was a little easier to come by, with rainfall and snow being utilized for this purpose. A cement cistern was built into most concrete basements at the time, on an outside corner, ours being on the southeast corner of our basement at our farm. Gran had a huge metal cistern in the basement of her home that served this same water storage purpose. Her bedroom and bed were directly over this cistern and more than once, when the cistern was filled with water, she entertained horrible thoughts of drowning, should the floor of her old house cave in! (Fortunately for her, this never happened). The only access to our farm cistern was through a square hole of two by two and a half feet, cut into our living room floor, much to Mom's decorating distress! In winter, huge snow blocks were cut from snow banks, carried into the house and dumped into this reservoir, where it finally melted in the existing water, into beautiful soft water. This access hole would also be used to periodically clean the cistern manually, usually a spring job, before the spring and summer rains.

In summer, rainfall was diverted into the cistern from eaves troughs, along the house roof's edge, as we have today. A metal director, housed in a metal box on the outside of the house, could be channeled into the cistern, or if it was full enough, would be turned out, so the water would run away from the house into a pipe and drain box system, or into a rain barrel for outdoor garden watering as we do today. Many a rainy night, Mom or Dad had to scurry out to turn the director out if the cistern was full enough—always a good feeling—a cistern full of water!

I recall Gran Teasdale having a similar eaves trough system.

The soft water thus obtained, was pumped up for use at the kitchen sink, by means of a metal pump containing 2 valves in a cylinder, that allowed water up but not back and was attached to a metal pipe suspended along the wall of the basement cistern into the water. This pump with handle and spout was a smaller version of an outside well. The handle required several priming pumps or even a bit of water poured in the top, to start the process. The water that issued forth was cistern temperature of course, and had to be warmed on the stove in a pan or kettle, other than the one used for drinking water as it was not clean enough, and often being stagnant, had a smell. However, it was very soft, not requiring the usual softening processes of our soft water supply today, especially our naturally "hard" Regina water. Some cook stoves of that era, that burned wood and coal, had reservoirs with a hinged lid, at the furthest end from the front burners, that could be filled with soft water, and heated by the stove's heat. As long as the stove was stoked and fuel was burning, the water remained warm, but cooled as the embers died and the stove went out overnight. Gran Teasdale's cook stove had such a reservoir for warming soft water, with a metal lid that could be lifted up. It was always sedimenty in the bottom, and one had to "dip from the top" to avoid riling this sediment, with a dipper, when filling a basin for washing. Our cook stove had no reservoir, so all our soft water had to be warmed on top of the stove in a basin or kettle.

As might be expected, this soft water was precious, and often out of necessity, rationed. It was not unusual to re-heat dish water for a second or third use, in the large dish washing pan on the stove. Bath water was used by all family members, beginning with the children, who were supposedly least dirty, and parents following, Dad being the dirtiest, especially during summer months with land work, etc. The addition of a kettle full of hot water, after each person finished bathing, seemed to also "freshen" the water! It was standard practice to bathe only once a week, in an attempt to preserve this precious commodity of water, with sponge baths from a basin designated for this purpose, in the kitchen sink, having to suffice the rest of the week. Saturday night was usually bathing night, in preparation for Saturday Night shopping in town, in the summer months, and for church Sunday mornings, year 'round. B.O. was common, as deodorants weren't in common use at the time either!

I recall, while a teenager in high school, having an on-going battle with Mom and Gran for permission to shampoo my hair, which tended to be very oily at the time, oftener than the once a week recommended, which seemed to suffice for each of them, both tending to dry scalps, with the never-ending need to SAVE water, being the best deterrent quoted! I never did win those battles, having to put up with greasy, stringy hair during most of that time, until Dad intervened one day, telling Mom to let me wash my hair as it was so oily it smelled! Also, in winter, with only towel and air drying available back then, as opposed to dryers we have now, frequent shampooing and bathing was almost a health risk in drafty, cold homes, common at the time.

As mentioned previously, I am still appalled and amazed at our flippant and wasteful use of water today, the gallons flowing down the drain for daily showers, shampoos and baths that take place in most households, in the name of cleanliness, and in hot tubs and Jacuzzis for the pure "pleasure of it"! How our parents, especially our Dads, coming in hot, dusty and dirty from working on the land, would have loved and appreciated a nice bath or shower at the end of the day! It makes me sad to think of it and how far we have gone astray in our wanton ways because everything, including this once-precious commodity is so available and easy to obtain now.

Our bath tub consisted of a rectangular, galvanized steel tub, constructed for us, at the local sheet metal shop in town. It was stored, on end, in our basement, and carried upstairs each bath time, to one of the bedrooms, to afford a bit of privacy to bathe. The only sink in our house was the kitchen sink, made of white enameled metal with a drain. As previously mentioned, various, separate, enameled basins for washing dishes and daily sponge bathing of our bodies, or hand washing of clothing took place in this one and only sink. There were no taps or faucets on our sink as is known today, as there was no source of water to make them useful. Warm water to be used came either from a soft-water kettle on the stove or the stove reservoir, and cold water was pumped from the cistern as previously explained, finally obtaining a satisfying mix of each. A metal or rubber drain plug could be inserted in the drain to stop up water until the job at hand was completed, then when it was removed, dirtied water ran a short distance through a metal drain pipe into a large pail placed under it accessed through the lower cupboard door under the sink. Commonly called the "swill pail" in our household, it had to be watched carefully from overflowing, as would make a watery mess in the lower cupboard area if this happened. I can recall on many occasions this very thing happening, and how distressed Mom would be about it, as the water was often greasy and of course cold, and made for an arduous, time-consuming, messy clean-up that only she was allowed to attend to—usually a few choice swear words accompanied this!

This loath-some pail, usually a cleaned-out farm grease pail with a handle, was wide, cumbersome and needless to say quite heavy when filled with used water, and I recall as children we couldn't even lift it. However, Mom usually managed to remember to empty it before it became too full, and on occasion when it was full "to the brim" and really awkward to carry, Dad would carry it out and empty it for her. The far end of the clothes line, about mid-way between house and barn seemed to be the designated dumping spot for this swill water, the ground usually soaking it up after a time, in summer anyway. In winter, it became a greasy, frozen area on top of the snow, and we kids were strictly forbidden to slide or play on it, even though it made for a kind of mini-skating pond, good for sliding on, the greasy residue left on our overshoes and later tracked onto the step and ultimately, into the house hallway, was not worth the bit of sliding fun we might have derived, (or so Mom felt—Connie and I never quite agreed with our mother on this point!) It seems to me, on occasion, when we had pigs in the barnyard, this swill water was sometimes augmented with kitchen scraps, vegetable peels, etc, and carried down to them, but because of the distance involved to the pig pen was not a common practice on our farm anyway.

With the lack of running water and sewer, what would have been the bathroom in our small farmhouse, was converted into a bedroom for Connie, so other common items one might expect to find in a bathroom nowadays were then located in other parts of the house. The mirrored medicine chest to house common over-the-counter health care products etc., was located above the kitchen sink, with some stored in the cupboard above the sink or in the cupboard at the side of the sink. Hairbrushes, combs, nail file, etc. hung in a hand-sewn plastic divider bag on the side of the cupboard. "Pee pots" made of heavy china, often decoratively painted with a handle, and/or enamel buckets with lids and handles were employed as urinals under each bed for night-time use in case nature called. I recall Mom relating that at the Teasdale farm home when she was growing up, her siblings Harry and Alice determined how cold it was in winter in their bedrooms by checking if there urine was "frozen" or not in their pots under their beds! Thank goodness, we were more fortunate, having a central source of heat from the furnace (to be discussed later) in our home. These pots had to be dumped of their watery contents each morning, into a swill pail and were kept fresh-smelling with a tiny bit of water and a drop of Lysol or Dettol disinfectant, before being replaced under the beds again.

A canister toilet with a lid and vent into the chimney was located behind the furnace in our basement to afford some semblance of privacy. This canister housed a large pail that was used more for solid-waste toilet needs, and had to be emptied on a regular basis before it became too full—this aromatic, heavy, unpleasant task falling to Dad. He either carried it down to the barnyard and dumped it on the cattle's manure pile, or he carried it down to the lower garden area, dug a deep hole and buried it there—this area only being cultivated, but never planted into garden. (Lye sprinkled over the refuse before covering with dirt greatly hastened its breakdown and decomposition and was frequently used). Goodness knows what a modern health inspector would have thought of this practice, however, nature's necessities had to be accommodated somehow, and I expect this procedure was quite common back then on numerous farmsteads.

Although we weren't among them, quite a few farm people, as well as town-dwellers not on a sewer system, had outdoor toilets or "out-houses" as they were commonly called back then, that they employed as toilets, some even in winter. B-r-r-r-r! These consisted of a deep rectangular hole dug in a convenient, strategic place near the house, but not too near, with a small wooden enclosure over it and a handled door that could be closed with a hook on the inside for privacy. A wooden floor and a bench seat were built over the hole, with three or four round or oval holes to accommodate various derriere sizes, depending on the household. Again Lye was used to accelerate decomposition and keep down odor and flies, especially in summer. Some people used old newspapers, magazines, Christmas orange wrappers and/or catalogues for wiping, rather than toilet tissue, that was expensive and not always as readily available, which mustn't have been very pleasant! Thankfully, we always had tissue to use by our indoor toilet. I recall making early morning treks down through the garden with Gran Sexsmith and my cousin Audrey, if I would stay overnight for a visit, to make use of their outdoor toilet that their family always used in summer, even though they had a septic tank toilet system they used in winter. Likewise, when I lived with Gran Teasdale, during high school, her out door toilet was the one we always used in summer. Located at the end of her garden, off by itself as it was, her out-house was nearly always knocked over by Halloween pranksters every October (a common joke to play back then, as there were lots of these type of toilets in people's back yards). Finally, Dad moved Gran's out-house over by her shed and secured it there to the shed, using the dirt from the newly dug hole to fill up the old one.

The septic tank system was employed in some farm homes, where household wastes went into outdoor septic tanks, where bacteria and chemicals broke down most of the solid matter into simpler substances. It then drained into the ground through a system of underground clay pipes called a tile-field. Gordon reports this type of sewage system was utilized after the 1960's at his parents farm home, and this must have been the system used at the Herb and Raymond Sexsmith homes also.

Water for livestock and farm animals to drink was obtained from natural rain and snow run-off into sloughs or dams and most of all in dugouts. Almost every farm had one or sometimes two dugouts—deep, rectangular bull-dozed depressions twelve to fourteen feet deep dug in pastures or a slough area, to provide water for animals in winter and especially in summer. The long parallel sides were vertical, while the shorter parallel ends were sloped up to allow animals and/or the farmer/owner easier access to the water's edge. These dugout water storage reservoirs usually remained 3/4 to full all year 'round, in dryer years but in winter, the depth depleted somewhat, sometimes even going dry. Gordon recalls when this happened, they melted snow in metal troughs by building wood fires underneath the troughs, however I don't recall Dad ever having to do this.

In summer the animals helped themselves to drink at water's edge, however in winter a round hole had to be chopped in the ice, near the sloped edge, allowing animals access to the water under the ice—a daily chore for the farmer, as the hole would freeze over each night. Also water was hauled from this hole into two wooden barrels and transported on the stone boat back to the barn for the animals to drink from pails in their troughs in really cold winter weather. Care had to be taken at the icy edge of this hole by the farmers and animals.

Lizards made the dugout home, and in summer could be seen scurrying along in murky clouds near the sloped edge, if frightened by passersby. Also in summer, water from the dugout was hauled in the same wooden barrels to water the garden if it was dry, without rain. We were regularly warned to stay away from the dugout as children, as these monstrous ponds claimed their share of casualties, especially farm children, ie. Clippies sister, Vera and son, while we were growing up. Imagine our surprise when a hired lad from Sintaluta, Glen Vickers, went swimming in it to cool off one harvest day, while working for Uncle Herb and Dad—wonders never ceased! I can still see him coming back around the blough, all refreshed—made us wish we could swim too, until we thought of those lizards!

Several other bloughs in our pasture and farm yard usually filled with water for the animals to drink, in spring and over the summer, and I recall liking to sit to the west side of the one nearest the farm yard on hot, summer days, as long as the dreaded cows weren't about, to sun myself, and day dream a little. In winter, Dad would clear the snow on the surface and Connie and I skated there. Once in a long while, wild strawberries could be found beside the next blough to the west, if the spring had been wet and just the right conditions existed, as mentioned previously.

Before the advent of electricity in rural Saskatchewan in the mid-1950's, some homes were heated and lighted by a system of power derived from a wind-driven windmill that charged a generator and batteries kept in the basement, although we weren't this fortunate. Power from this source depended on the wind, always fairly prevalent in this province, but because it could not be depended on entirely, this source of power was sometimes unreliable, and had to be carefully monitored. With the advent of hydro-power all these homes had to be re-wired for the stronger-voltage.

It is perhaps noteworthy to record that homes with the generator/battery sources of power outlined in the preceding paragraph were also able to have running water from their taps in their kitchens and bathrooms (provided a water source was readily available like a well or dam of water), because it could be pumped up by this internal electricity system to upper levels of these homes and also soft water could be heated by this electricity. The other system sometimes utilized to have soft water run from taps was to have a large receptacle on the roof or in the attic of three story homes to catch rain water and then have it run down to the taps by gravity. To heat this same soft water it had to pass through a high-standing water heater usually located on the ground floor kitchen, heated by the kitchen wood or coal burning stove. This heated water could then be utilized in kitchen or pantry taps by gravity from the high-standing water heater, but had to be pumped upstairs again for bathroom use.

Most rural homes utilized natural daylight as much as possible, as when darkness fell, artificial lighting consisted of candles, wick lamps that burned coal oil and/or gas lamps that burned kerosene. Close work of any kind was difficult to say the least, and often caused a great deal of eye strain! Candles, now considered ornamental, decorative or romantic, were essential for night lighting and some households even made their own with string wicks and tallow, although we never did. As I recall, we always had wick lamps with glass chimneys, but most of our light was derived from a gas lamp that burned fuel under pressure, that had to be added before each lighting, and even during the evening hours with a little hand pump. I can still picture this little apparatus as being a brass cylinder about 8 inches long, with a nozzle on one end and a black round-handled plunger on the other, that sucked up air when the plunger was pulled back and deposited it into a valve on the lamp base from the nozzle end. It seems to me only Mom or Dad were allowed to perform this pumping procedure, especially if the lamp was burning, as I suppose the danger of too much air being inserted could result in a combustible explosion. (Likewise, gas irons of that era and Mom's little gas stove that will be mentioned later under heating, all operated on this same air/gas combination, made the same hissing noise and frightened me half to death, I recall). As just explained, these lamps were noisier sounding, because they burned a fuel and air mixture or vapor, but their light was much brighter than wick lamps, emanating from a fragile mantle, covered by a glass chimney.

These lamps were available in a number of shapes, sizes and colors depending on need, purpose and affluence, I suppose. Some had bases of shiny metal, or decorative pot painted with floral or oriental designs that could stand on a table or be hung from a ceiling hook. Our main lamp stood approximately two feet in height, was green metal with rounded base and tall slender stand with a mantle and glass; it also had a two foot long rod at the top and a ceiling hook. Dad had a more stout and sturdy handled green lamp, with a heavy-duty glass he hung in the barn for chores illumination after dark and to light his way back to the house. Needless to say great care had to be exercised at all times with these burning lamps, none greater than in the barn where straw and hay could ignite into an inferno in seconds. As children, we were always acutely aware of the need to be careful around fire, because of a neighbor boy's tragedy, whose face and upper body were badly burned by a lamp fire at their home, as we were growing up. A glass globe fire extinguisher (bought from a traveling salesman) filled with red liquid fire retardant always hung on the archway of our farm home. We were never to touch the spout end that dispensed it—thankfully we never needed to—it still hangs there today.

Mantles, light-giving median of gas lamps, were always precious, fragile and guarded with great care, as if shattered, had to be replaced. New mantles were like a little knitted silky white bag with pale green writing that tied onto the lamp. Some kind of radical reaction took place in a mantle once it burned and it was always a source of wonder and awe to us back then—it became about half its original size looking like a sheer filament, a form it remained in until broken—perhaps a period of several weeks, depending on care. A fluttering summer miller moth was the mantle's worst enemy, as even though the mantle was protected by the glass globe, by its very nature, a moth was always drawn to the light—the closer, the better, always resulting in a quick demise of both mantle and moth! Flashlights being battery operated, were in common use back then, much as they are today, although I don't recall us using one very much as we were growing up (probably due to the battery's expense).

Wick lamps were turned up to shed more light by means of a little round metal disc handle, that threaded more of the coal-oil soaked woven-string wick up out of the lamp's bowl. Turning the wick up too high resulted in smoking and dirtying the glass chimney with a fine film of soot. Lamp globes had to be cleaned frequently, old newspapers seeming to work very well for this cleaning and polishing. Wicks had to be trimmed regularly for even burning and replaced as needed. Kerosene (coal-oil) was purchased at hardware stores in town, and brought home in gallon spouted cans. Eddy brand wooden matches with red Cardinal decal, were used for all lighting purposes back then, and in our house hung in a little metal holder located beside the basement door cupboard. This holder accommodated a small sliding lidded match box and had a little tray in front to keep a match supply readily available, but out of the hands of young children. (When empty, these boxes could be stacked and glued together to make the neatest set of doll dresser drawers with a bit of foil for a mirror). I have already related my on-going fear of matches as girl, and always heeded Dad's warning "fire made a good servant but a poor master"—good advice for all ages to heed for all time.

Probably no other electrical commodity was more appreciated and regarded as almost "magical" than electric lighting was to farm homes when hydro-power was finally made available to rural Saskatchewan in the mid 1950's from the coal mines at Estevan. The advent of indoor and outdoor yard lighting extended everyone's capabilities for work or pleasure into the evening and night-time hours. How well I remember the thrill it gave each of us to flick a switch and a room would literally "flood" with light. I guess electricity must be the hardest modern convenience to imagine being without, as looking back, it is even difficult for us to believe we ever could have survived without it and the wonderful ease and comfort it has wrought in everyone's life since it's inception way back then.

Power crews worked on lines and poles coming right up Dad's field from Raymond's farm to ours. Later Dad used this inconvenience as a demarcation to divide his half section of land into quarters for summer fallow and planting. The line going at an angle across his southwest field to the school was a bit more disconcerting and always a trial to work around with heavy implements and tractor. The connecting poles between these two fields ran down our pasture at a south-west angle; the power pole housing the barrel-type transformer, also became our "yard light" (lard-light as little sister Connie called it as first I recall) and was the source of a flood-lit yard of light that could be seen for miles at night. (Also a great attraction for moths and other summer night-flying creatures I can still picture in my minds-eye—even huge black locusts one particular summer).

The actual electrical "wiring" of the house, prior to the advent of rural power being turned on, was provided by a couple of electricians Johnny and Otto. We were to recall many times later, the good-natured comradery shared by these two technicians as they secured the wire, plug-ins and fixtures. They were obviously skilled in their work; however Jack was quite foreign and was always calling to Johnny from the attic, as they passed cable and wiring in the walls down to make corresponding connections at the outlets. Jack would call out "You got it Johnny?" (meaning the electrical wire) from his attic sanctum, and Johnny would call out he did or he didn't have the wire to make the connection, etc. They were a couple of nice fellows and best of all had a hand in bringing to us a most memorable gift, the power that would eventually transform our world and quality of life on the farm forever.

Furnaces were converted over to gas/electricity combinations and all manner of electrical appliances including kettles, toasters, irons, stoves, refrigerators, washers, tools for garage, yard and barn became available and in time, many more. Probably the refrigerator was Mom's most cherished electrical appliance—she even found a spot for it in the living room of our small home! Her electric stove had to run a close second—no more messy ashes or stovepipes to clean (that will be discussed in home up-keep). Television, bright new home-based entertainment centre of the future, was just beginning to make its appearance on the horizon, but would not be part of our family home for some years to come, even though readily available, mostly for economic reasons, thinking back.

In addition to the procurement of food and water, shelter and heating, additional necessities of life had to be provided for farm people, as well as their animals, pets and implements, etc.

With regard to shelter, of course, the quality of building materials was not what it is today, most homes being constructed of wood on concrete basements or some just with earth basements like Gran Teasdale's home when it was first built. Shingles were common on roofs, but various coverings of brick and stone were much more common than today. A material called Insul-brick was often used as an outer covering back in the war years, consisting of a tar-backed covering pressed with colored chips of various shades, and looked quite attractive as on Gran's home in Wolseley. We also covered our hen house with a similar material, but all other farm buildings were white siding with black roofs and dark green painted trim. The house was covered with a white tiled covering, also popular in the late '40's with the same trim as the rest of the farm buildings. This tiled material proved quite durable, as it is still intact today on the same house Mom now lives in at Wolseley. As far as insulation went, bats of a wooly-fiber type of material, or pressed bats of grey felt shreds encased in paper, were placed in attics and walls during construction, but needless of say, would not meet today's high standards, mostly because of the types of materials like fiberglass, etc. available now. In farm homes older than ours, layers of newspaper often was used to chink up structural gaps and Gordon thinks even horse hair sometimes sufficed. Prior to this stage of building construction, one thinks of wooden log and sod cabins of the pioneers, "way before our realm of remembrance".

As mentioned previously, the other buildings on our farm besides the house were made of wood and siding, the barn providing warmth for the cattle, horses, the cats and an occasional mouse! In very extreme winter conditions, the dog would reluctantly agree to over-night in the barn, but usually preferred to remain "under-the-step", the one and only home he seemed to choose for himself, located under our back door porch. It was to this location he brought all his "dog treasures" over the years; old bones, scraps of leather, etc., and would defend it valiantly if we even came near "his domain" growling and baring his teeth. Now I think back, he was a good, gentle and tame dog otherwise, except in this one regard.

It was imperative to Dad that his car and tractor were properly housed in a nice double garage with a cement floor, windows, etc., and he prided himself on keeping a neat garage, with tools and a work-bench between the windows at the front and lots of space on the walls to hang other essentials. The lawn mower and yard equipment were also stored in the garage. Old license plates from years gone by were tacked up along the west wall as they expired, and still remain to this day at Mom's home in Wolseley, as the garage was moved there, along with the house, when she moved from the farm. It was common, in those days, to build a machine-shed for land implements, combines, etc., but I suppose lack of funding was Dad's biggest draw-back in this regard, and probably the reason we never did build one, plus Uncle Herb had such a shed and housed the swather, combine, etc. he and Dad co-owned and shared. The implements Dad owned and kept at home (drill, one-way or disker, cultivator and harrows) he always lined up neatly in the field just east of the buildings, following harvest, to act as kind of an easterly windbreak I suppose. I seem to recall he placed the harrows on end in tent-like shapes over winter, several sections together.

The chicken house was a small wooden enclosure with a wooden floor, located to the left of the barn, that housed the chicks, mature laying hens, several roosters and the pig barn and pen off to the back of the barn yard. As mentioned previously, barn swallows always built a nest, in our henhouse rafters for as many summers as I can remember, and their graceful, swooping aerial antics, as well as the flashes of metallic navy blue plumage and orange-russet breasts, and their chatter, are a fond remembrance to me. Of course, a number of new and older bins located close to the farm yard and in several field locations housed the grain after each harvest, until it was sold. Sometime after I left home, Dad built another wooden shed to the east of the established buildings, for his truck housing on one side, and two granaries on the other.

Heating, an essential commodity required in all homes, especially for warmth during prairie winters, and also of course for cooking, was procured with much more difficultly prior to the advent of electricity. Discussion of this era will follow.

Provision of heat was made much more difficult than it is today because of the inferior types of building materials available to be used in any and all types of homes and shelters built back in those days. The coal/wood-burning kitchen stove played a major part in the household, providing heat for warmth, heat for cooking and warm water for washing/bathing, as well as a burning garbage disposal for smaller kitchen refuse. Some models came equipped with a reservoir (already discussed with water), other models had a back and warming cupboard above the burner-area with a kind of roll down top for storage, etc. There were usually six lids on the top of this type of stove that were removable by inserting a lifter into a corresponding slot, but fitted into round depressions when in place, making a smooth flat cooking surface. The two front burners, as well as a hinged portion of the stove top (on some models) could be raised as a unit, by a coiled metal handle, to accommodate large chunks of coal and/or wood for burning. The back burners had a space under that went over the oven that heated the back part of the stove, further away from the actual fire-box—hence, the expression to put something on the "back burner" where it could still simmer, li k e a soup or stew, but wouldn't be exposed to the direct, high heat. Vents along the side of the firebox could be opened or partially closed, by means of a sliding, knobbed metal closure, to feed air to the fire; also a vent in the stovepipes just above the stove could be adjusted to allow chimney air to the fire—a tricky undertaking to get just right, given the blasts of wind coming down the chimney in Saskatchewan! (Sometimes a really strong wind-blast would blow soot down the chimney and even out into the kitchen, especially nearer spring, when the chimney tended to need cleaning and was lined with more soot—needless to say, a very messy clean-up, if this happened!) Because of the heat given off by these stoves they sat on legs up off the floor (a favorite place for house cats to sleep for example Gran's Tigger).

Of course, a large oven with a heat gauge on front, was located just right of the firebox, for baking, roasting, warming and the like. Often the oven door was opened to let heat into the kitchen, to warm cold feet and hands, to keep little baby chicks warm or even human babies! Gordon related how he was placed in blankets on the warm oven door, after being born at his farm home in March 1943, as a kind of incubator effect for a newborn. In those days people had to use what was available—"necessity was the mother of invention", I recall Gran Sexsmith often saying!

A steel furnace was constructed and installed by the local plumbing and heating shop, to suit the needs of our small home. Fuel was huge chunks of coal and some wood. Furnaces and stoves had to be stoked regularly, and in winter were never allowed to go out. This stoking process was accomplished with a long metal rod that reached into the burning embers, adjusted them (spraying up millions of sparks!) and then more wood and coal was added as needed. This job and removal of furnace ashes usually fell to Dad, while stoking of the kitchen stove could be done by either parent, usually Mom. (I don't recall Connie or I having much to do with the wood/coal burning stove, mainly because she would have been too little, prior to electricity, and I wasn't very domesticated by age 10-12, when we still used this type of stove.)

Heat from the furnace reached each room in the upper level by a duct and huge stovepipe system and brown, metal wall registers of some 14 x 14 inches located in each room that could be opened or partially closed to adjust heat in any room, by a curved lever handle located on top of the register. Neither Connie nor I would budge from our beds on winter mornings, to dress for school until Dad had stoked the furnace (that would have died down to embers overnight) and heat could be felt coming from the registers. Our favorite haunt was in front of the living room register I recall, but not sure why the one in our room wouldn't have sufficed. It would have been more private, although Dad was always out doing chores at that time and only we girls were in the house.

Fuel of wood and/or coal had to be kept in plentiful supply in a wood pile in the back yard, then be brought into a wood box in the kitchen, if space was available, as in Gran's kitchen, or in the porch as was the case at our home. Coal was kept in a coal bin in our basement or in an outside shed. Everyone had a wood pile back then (ours was behind the barn). Dad sometimes cut his own wood pile from the blough's deadwood or else the Indians from near-by reserves often called with loads of wood to sell, depending on these deliveries as part of their livelihood and they liked to have regular customers. Several of them could unload a truck of wood as quick as a wink; the wood was good and cheap $5 to $7 for a one-half ton truck load. Logs were usually poplar wood, about 12 to 14 inches long and 3-4 inches thick and could be readily split by an axe into kindling for fire starters or left in log form for maintaining established fires to supplement coal.

Coal had to be ordered by the load, usually each Fall, in anticipation of the coming winter, and delivered from town—it seems to me Ted Lewthwaite sometimes did these deliveries, as had a big truck, or perhaps Dalt Folbar, as he also had a big two-toned green truck I recall, that seemed to be his pride and joy. The massive flaking chunks of shiny coal always fascinated me, especially after hearing tales of how it was obtained from the bowels of the earth's coal mines at great risk to life and limb (Spring Hill Disaster—Anne Murray's home, happened about this time). It could easily be broken into smaller chunks with a bit of bashing, and was obtained with a little coal shovel and scuttle or bucket from the coal bin in the basement as needed for heating. In fall, when the coal was first delivered through an outside foundation chute and the bin was full, the coal was contained by a wall of 1 x 8 boards in sliding encasements along each side of the opening. These boards were removed one by one as the coal was used up, until in spring only one board remained in place, to contain slushy, small pieces of coal in the bin.

Another form of pressed coal called briquettes could also be used for fuel at the time (a larger version of our barbeque briquettes of today). Gran Teasdale always burned these, claiming them equally as efficient and easier for her to handle by herself, living on her own as a widow, than the ungainly large lumps of coal, even though briquettes were a bit more expensive. She kept them in her side shed, carrying enough for her needs each day in her coal bucket for her kitchen stove, and the oil for her front room space-heater, she kept in a spouted can and filled the fuel reservoir at the back of the heater, as needed, from this can. These space-heaters were employed in homes where there was little or no basement for a furnace, and would basically heat a room by radiant heat, however the floors were always still cold, and of course the further away from the heater, the cooler the room.

Of course, this burning of wood and coal as fuel for heating and cooking, presented another disposal problem—ashes and soot! Ashes fell through the firebox grate into a long rectangular metal ash can with a handle, on the kitchen stove and a larger flat ash box for the furnace, that could be removed and the ash contents thrown away, outside on the "ash heap", also located at the end of the clothesline, in our yard. A shuddery, grating sound resulted when this ash can was removed from the stove, and I can remember often awakening to this horrible sound as a girl, as it was one of the first tasks Mom did each day before she could stoke up the stove for breakfast, and her cursing all the time at the mess and falling ashes on her clean green and black tiled kitchen floor! Emptying of the furnace ashes seemed to fall to Dad, and I seem to recall he emptied them into a large pail he kept for this purpose by the furnace, and then carried them upstairs and outside to the ash heap. (With all the carrying from upstairs to downstairs and back up again with water, milk, disposal needs and ashes, no wonder poor Dad played out and had an early demise—all that hard work, and Mom often doing her share too, never complaining, just doing it out of necessity as part of our life-style—makes me sad now to think of it!)

Stovepipes arched upwards from the back of the kitchen stove and vented into the chimney, the length of stovepipe being governed by the distance from stove to chimney. In our house, the chimney was just beside the stove, but in Gran Teasdale's house the stovepipes had to go across her kitchen (above the kitchen table), to the chimney on the opposite wall, and were suspended from the ceiling with sturdy stovepipe wire. These necessary pipes were always shiny black metal on the outside, but were messy and dirty inside, because of the heat and residue from burning they carried to the chimney. Therefore, they had to be taken down periodically and batted and brushed clean, a hellish job and a dirty one, usually done each spring, when the stove could be put off, and the stovepipes taken outside in the yard, usually being placed on old newspapers first, to catch the soot as it was knocked and brushed out. A decorative metal ring usually fitted over the stovepipe as it entered the chimney, serving to snug the stovepipe into the chimney hole more effectively, as well as for aesthetical purposes. Likewise, the back lids on these stoves had to be removed periodically, and the soot that collected under them raked out with a long metal handled scraper, another messy job.

The inside of furnaces and their stovepipes had to be cleaned likewise, but usually by a professional chimney sweep, that had proper long brushes and equipment to do the job, and as before, in spring, when furnaces were no longer required for warmth. In homes with an upstairs, greater lengths of stovepipe had to be employed, if heat was to be carried up there. Gordon reports requiring lots of feather comforters or feather ticks as they were sometimes called, as well as extra blankets, to try to maintain enough warmth in their upstairs over cold wintry nights, after the furnace fire died down. Bedrooms off the kitchen were of course the warmest ones to have back then, acquiring most of their heat from the kitchen stove. Our small home, all on one level was quite satisfactorily heated with the basement furnace in all areas, in winter, augmented of course, by the kitchen stove.

However, I recall when I stayed with Gran Teasdale during my high school years, that the front bedroom I used in her home had no source of heat, except for the space heater in the living room. Many-a-winter's night we had to close off that room altogether, especially in extremely cold weather, and I slept on the living room couch, to conserve as much heat as possible in the rest of the house. Also, to keep frosty air from seeping in under outer doors, stuffed fabric rolls, especially made for this by enterprising homemakers, were often laid along the floor in front of these doorways to keep heat in and cold out! Likewise, often heavy blankets were hung at windows for the same reason. Thinking back now, one can really appreciate central heating as we know it, with warm floors, no chilly sleeps, ashes, stovepipes, etc.!

Fireplaces, so common and fashionable in modern homes today, weren't used in any homes known to me during this era—even in the grand homes of Dave and John Sexsmith, or other larger homes in the district where we lived. I am not sure why this would be, as one would think the heat given off by a fireplace would greatly augment furnace and kitchen stove heat just as it can today.

Needless to say, hot water bottles were frequently filled with hot water and taken to bed to warm chilly feet and bodies at night, or frequently, more than one hot water bottle was placed in beds prior to bedtime to ward off the chill and dampness in minimally heated bedrooms, especially upstairs in two-story homes etc. Gran Teasdale was a faithful hot water bottle fan, using one frequently in winter; I recall she felt it important to cover these bottles with a knitted cover, with a drawstring top and pom pom tassels, and since she loved to knit and was quick and talented at this craft, she always made sure all family members had these knitted covers for the hot water bottles in their homes also. To this day, the cover used on our hot water bottle, is one Gran knitted.

It would be remiss not to mention the love affair Mom maintained for years, during this era, with "her little gas stove" as she called it. Since she always felt the heat so much, especially in summer, and used to perspire profusely, she employed this little stove to save lighting the kitchen cook stove for preparing meals. This little sucker could cook up a meal in no time under her very capable direction and many a fine one we have enjoyed from its heat! Mom sat it on top of her unlit cook stove for a counter; it was powered by an air/kerosene mixture from a copper-colored gas cylinder that was held onto the base of this little stove with hooked, metal brackets on each side, and as I recall a long, metal, fuel-rod hookup that fitted in under the burners, when in place. Once filled with kerosene, air had to pumped into this cylinder into a nozzle at the right side, with the same little pump (previously mentioned in the gas lamp write-up). Sufficient air had been pumped into this cylinder, when the pump could no longer be depressed easily (a pressure-sense known only to Mom), so that when the burners were turned on, and a match held to them, a beautiful blue flame instantly glowed under one or both, whatever was required, burning this air/kerosene mixture—very intense and quick. The quickness suited Mom just fine, as she always seemed to be in a hurry back then!

Mom even used this little gas powered stove to bake her bread, as she did each week, and also to do other baking in summer. It seems to me an oven was acquired from the Simpson's Catalogue or perhaps Eaton's (as both major retailers had a mail order catalogue back then). It was a grey, metal, rectangular box that just fitted over the gas stove perfectly. It had a door and a heat gauge and understandably became hot very quickly, but by the same token, cooled off immediately after the twin burners of the stove were turned off, and could even be carried outside, once emptied, to cool off, as it had handles on each side. Whereas the cook stove once stoked and lighted, burned for hours, heating the house when it was not needed or wanted! I recall this little stove was beige with grates over the burners, sitting on four little legs; when not in use it lived under Mom and Dad's bed for want of a better place, and was easily accessed from the kitchen from this spot!

Some women overcame the heat from the kitchen stove in summer by having a "summer kitchen" or stove located in a porch or in another building in the farmyard, close to the house for easy access, but removed from the main kitchen. Gordon reports his mother used to cook in their porch, attached to the house. Either arrangement provided the family, (at harvest time, or other busy times), other hired hands and neighbors with hot meals, without "roasting the cook" so to speak!

With the advent of electricity of course wood, coal and briquettes were mostly abandoned for heating, as furnaces were converted to electric with a pilot light and a thermostat to regulate heat. A large silver tank that stood on a trestle outside held fuel oil, that ran into the house basement by gravity to fuel the furnace as required. This fuel oil was delivered faithfully to our farm, and surrounding district farms by brothers. Vic and Albert Sexsmith, cousins to Dad, who ran a gas station in Sintaluta at the time. An order had to be put in for their delivery, usually several times/winter, depending on the severity; I recall it always being a chance for a little visit with these two congenial relatives, as the tank filled with fuel.

Eventually the cook stove was converted over to an electric one, as the house was much more easily heated in a uniform manner with the electric/fuel oil arrangement. Kitchen stove-pipes were no longer needed to vent kitchen stoves, and chimney holes were now covered with decorative plate-like chimney flue covers. An era had ended, and not many were sorry to see an end to the dirty stovepipes, ashes, etc., as well as the ever-present danger of a fire, always a risk where people, their belongings and flame were in such close proximity!

Isn't it ironic, now that we have easy access to modern cooking modes of all types, such as electric, natural gas, convection, conduction and microwave ovens, for use indoors, we humans get such a kick out of taking all manner of food outdoors and cooking it on a gas-powered, electric or briquette barbeque? Or better still, over on open campfire flame? And we exclaim and drool over the smell and taste of this type of cooking, and can't seem to satiate our appetite for such gastronomical repasts!

Barbequing, as we now know it, was just coming into common vogue in the mid-60's, about the time Gordon and I were married. I can recall my Dad commenting that during his life-time he had seen unusual changes—we had gone eating inside to outside (a practice he failed to find enjoyable, competing with the bugs and nature in order to eat), and moved our bathrooms from outside (referring to outhouses mentioned previously), to inside. He felt he had pretty well summed-up how far modern society had strayed from what was sensible and straight forward by then—wouldn't he have been surprised by still more "backward" socio/economic changes we have experienced since his passing—most mothers in the labor force, while their young children are cared for in Day Care centers, the trend away from religion and respect for authority, the number of common-law marriages, high divorce rates, the high cost of every commodity, the taxation rates, both provincial and federal, wanton use of our natural resources, land owners farming huge tracts of land with gargantuan tractors and implements, but most living in towns or cities and not on their farms, wars and still more wars (Dad always felt since all wars are ended around a peace table, why not have the "powers-that-be" sit up around that same table before forcing the ordinary people to fight each other on the battleground, thus saving a lot of bloodshed and heartache, which always sounded very reasonable, but still has not happened that way). Loud, modern music, dance modes and clothing fashions would have surprised him, as well as space travel, etc.

However, life is full of changes—the longer we live, the more we realize it. We don't necessarily have to like them or agree with them, but we have to accept them in order to keep going on, clinging to our faith in God, who never changes, and our hope of everlasting life in eternity available to all believers. What a glorious reunion that will be for all family members and dear friends now departed!

On a more mundane note—with "cleanliness being next to Godliness" as Gran Teasdale always used to say, the business of keeping clothing and home clean and cared for will follow, personal hygiene having already been discussed under health care and water.

Clothes washing was usually done only once a week on Monday mornings, with hand washing of frequently used and needed items being washed in the kitchen sink basin throughout the week. I recall, only vaguely Mom using a ribbed glass and wooden hand washboard in a tub, as was the usual mode of washing clothes in our grandmother's day. Quite soon after we moved to the farm, Mom invested in a gas driven washing machine that made a very annoying pup-pup-pup sound, and had to be primed with a foot starter. Thus, there was no sleeping in on Monday mornings, even during holidays, as that incessant gas motor sound permeated our whole sma1l house!

There were bonuses to wash day however. Because Mom's washer was downstairs, and once she began the washing, she more or less stayed down there until it was completed, she used to put an "oven meal" in to cook before starting, usually a stew with dumplings or suet crust and yummy baked rice pudding for dessert. Of course, these kind of meals could cook away in the oven without attention, and be ready to serve for the noon meal. I recall Gran Teasdale used her kitchen for washing clothes, rolling out her washing machine from her bed room, where it stayed when not in use, for want of a better location. Also hers was always electric, with her living in town, whereas until rural electrical hook-up, we always used the gas. (See "traumatic incidents" on previous pages for Gran's unfortunate episode with the wringer on her washer).

This gas washer had to be vented by a small, ribbed silver metal hose into the chimney, since it ran with a motor and had an exhaust for harmful fumes. A large round tub on four legs contained a silver metal agitator for washing, much like our electrical machines today, that could be activated by a handled knob on the side of the tub, for starting and stopping washing. Two rubber rollers fitted into an upright housing that attached at the back of the washer. A knob on top of this housing could be turned to activate these rollers backwards, front wards, or to stop them, depending on the need. The forward/reverse function was especially useful when clothing was being wrung from the wash water for rinsing, the operator would want the rollers moving from front to back, as a tub or sink of rinse water was always set up to collect washed, wrung out clothing in order to rinse out the soap from the wash cycle.

The whole roller housing could also be released to swivel around, away from the wash tub, to accommodate this above mentioned rinsing cycle, if rinse sinks were available to use. I recall Mom used a small, pale green, enameled bathtub (I think she used it to bathe us as children, when we were smaller) that she stood on an upright wooden crate behind her washer to create a make-shift rinse sink. Sometimes a substance called "bluing" was added to the first rinse water, because white clothes were understandably the first clothes to be washed. The idea of this bluing was to provide a slight, blue tinge to the white clothes, much like the fabric softeners of today, that are always blue tinted. I recall bluing was bought in boxed, cubes about an inch square, made of a pressed, bright, vibrant blue powder. It crumbled off easily in your hands and had to be contained in a little cloth bag of some sort, the bag just dipped quickly and squeezed ever so lightly into the rinse water, to release a scant amount of color. I recall I knitted the little bag Mom used for this procedure, out of a bright yellow string yarn, with a little drawstring top. It was stored with the rest of the wash-day paraphernalia, allowed to dry out and be re-used again the following Monday, until the cube was all used up and had to be replaced. Understandably a box lasted a long time.

Clothes in the rinse tub were agitated by hand to remove soap from them, and allowed to remain in this cool water for a time, to help release more soap, or else sometimes even rinsed in a second rinse water. In order to wring the rinse water from them, clothing was then passed back through the wringer rollers, this time with the rollers reversed, and the operator standing behind the washer, or to the side, catching the wrung clothing by hand, and placing it in a wash basket, to be hung later for drying.

A silver release bar, located on top of the wringer housing, could be given a sharp rap with the heel of the hand in event of an emergency, for example, fingers accidentally being pulled into the rotating rollers, (which could happen quite easily, unless care and attention was taken when the rollers were in motion; it was not unheard of for long hair to also be caught thus), that would cause the housing to jump up out of place and release the top roller—if Gran would have done this her wash-day catastrophe back then could have been averted, but she was afraid of ruining her washer! Imagine! On occasion, instead of passing through the rollers and on to the rinse tub, a piece of clothing would stick to the rollers and wrap around one—this was especially likely to happen with a small, thin item like a handkerchief, etc. Then the operator could use this release bar, to separate the rollers, stop the rollers and/or adjust the tension as described below.

The rollers could be adjusted for tension, depending on the type of clothing being wrung, by a tension knob on top of the roller housing that could raise the upper roller slightly. Soft, light fabrics would require more pressure, while heavier work clothing was bulky, so the pressure would need to be adjusted accordingly.

As always, the need to conserve as much soft water as possible, held true for the washing/rinsing procedure also, thus the same water was used for all the washing each wash day. Kettles and pots of water were kept hot on the kitchen stove to augment the wash water as it cooled and became dirtier with each subsequent load added, going from whites, to colors, then dark work clothing, that was often the most soiled of the lot. When all the dirty clothes had been put through this wash/rinse cycle, the pup-pup washer was finally turned off (much to the relief of everyone within hearing distance) and the washer drained from a side spout into a pail. Sometimes, Mom used this water to mop up her cement, basement floor that was always neatly painted in a tiled pattern. Then finally, the task of carrying this water upstairs and out to the swill dump at the end of the clothesline post. Likewise the rinse water had to be poured into a pail from the little green tub and disposed of in a similar manner. It seems to me, if this rinse water wasn't too soapy, and it was summer and the garden was especially dry, this water was gently poured out over the garden rows.

Nowadays if we want to starch an article prior to ironing, we use spray starch. Back then, boxes of starch (navy with white writing and decals) could be bought for this purpose. The starch came in white irregularly shaped chunks (that I recall I sometimes liked to nibble on as a girl), that dissolved in cold water, placed in a basin. Dress shirt collars, and cuffs were always dipped in this starch/water mixture, after washing and rinsing, and prior to drying. Likewise linens, doilies, lace collars, cuffs, etc., could also be stiffened this way. Laundry soaps were usually purchased in some of the same brands still in use today like Tide, Oxydol and Ivory soap flakes for fine washables. Gordon reports that his mother and grandmother used to make bar washing soap from a lye/lard mixture they boiled up with water, allowed to cool and harden, cut into bars and used for washing clothes, although I don't recall Mom or Gran ever using this type of soap. A golden yellow bar of Sunlight soap was always on hand though, to hand scrub extra soiled areas on articles of clothing, much as I use it today—what a fine enduring product! Bleach, as I recall was always bought, at the store and added to the washer as needed for extra cleaning, just as we would add it today, sparingly and with caution!

Gordon reports that when electricity was available on their farm, they converted their gas washing machine over to electric, but I don't recall if this was the case with ours. It was this same type of wringer-washer that I first did my washing with at Andris after nurse's training and at the John's residence after we were first married, so I can write about this washing procedure from first-hand experience! The exception was electric automatic washers and dryers in nurse's residence that I rarely used, preferring to take my washing home to be done there when I went, or else hand washing in bathroom sinks. (The hospital did our uniforms, bedding, towels, etc., so we were only responsible for personal laundry).

Drying the freshly washed clothes proved to be a frustrating task, especially in the winter months. A wooden clothes horse was standard wash equipment in all homes back then and really served a useful and much needed purpose. They were composed of wooden spindles on a compact, fold-up frame, that when extended and set up full-out on wooden legs, could eventually dry a whole wash, just from the heat of the house, although also created a lot of dampness in the whole house that day! Clothes horses could also be set up outside for the sun and wind to do this same drying, but usually a pulley-type of clothesline suspended between two posts located close to the house sufficed for outside drying. I recall Gran had a metal pole type of outdoor clothesline with heavy string lines in a square shape, in a similar design to the ones we use today.

Gordon's Grandma had the neatest clothesline arrangement set up in her home in Neudorf, that every woman would have loved come wash day! She could hang her clothes on her clothesline in her closed in porch, safe from the wind and elements and the reel them out of a narrow door space in the porch wall! Wooden or plastic clothes pegs were used to secure items minus the tension gauge, common in today's clothes pegs.

Mom often preferred to hang her clothes on the outside line, even in winter, if the weather was at all clement, as she hated the "soggy house scene" of inside drying and loved the smell of clothes dried out in the fresh air, even though the clothes usually froze on the line. I can still recall the different shapes the frozen clothes took on, especially Dad's long underwear, with legs and arms inflated by the wind and then frozen in that position—it was always so cute to see! Usually the frozen clothes were difficult to remove from the line and still had to be hung up inside to finish the drying process. Numerous lines were hung from the basement rafters for this purpose. Mom and Gran always had a clothesline of thin, white rope suspended at ceiling level, corner to corner in their kitchens, to hang tea towels, and other small hand-washed articles to dry.

Of course, with the advent of electricity, electric spin dryers came into common use, usually along with a matching electric washer. Separate small spin dryers, in the form of an upright canister, with a basket inside to hold wet clothing and a little flat rubber lid to keep them in place, could be plugged into a wall outlet, at the end of each wash cycle, and used to spin dry clothing. This type of dryer worked on a rapidly rotating housing principle that sucked water out of the clothes, and pumped it out of a hose at its base, that had to be drained into a sewer or wash tub drain. Grandma Issel and Gordon's Mom both had this type of spin dryer, but Grandma's was a separate unit, whereas his Mom's was a part of her washer unit—the same type as my Mom still uses today, since moving to town.

I recall having the use of Grandma's little spin dryer when we still lived at John's home, as newlyweds, as Grandma had moved into a Senior's Home, It helped "dry" the clothes a lot faster, but they came out of this dryer completely compressed, and dried "full of wrinkles". I wasn't sorry to have use of an automatic washer and a dryer that fluffed wet clothing as it dried, when we moved to our own home in 197O, after Heather was born.

As just discussed, indoor drying caused all clothing to dry hard and wrinkled, and ironing was a necessity for almost all articles. This proved no problem for Mom, as by her own admission, she loved to iron, and drew great satisfaction from her ironing expertise, and the great, "fresh" look she could achieve after ironing a piece of clothing, (a feeling not shared by many homemakers I have known, including myself)! Needless to say, she had lots of practice in this area, with several kinds of irons during her lifetime from girlhood on.

I vaguely recall Mom using sad irons; I am not sure how they became known by this name, probably because they were such a sad excuse for an iron! This type of iron consisted of a solid piece of steel, shaped into a point at both ends, about the size of today's irons. They had polished surfaces for ironing and slots in the top where a curved, wooden handle could be clamped onto them. They were heated on top of the burning wood/coal stove until hot, the hotter the stove, the hotter the iron! At least two sad irons were necessary, so one could be heating, while the other was being used, and cooling down. There was another type of handle and clamp available that was shaped the same as the metal base, only a little bigger, so it would fit over it. A release clamp could be depressed one way to release the iron, and back to secure it. (I have a small replica of this type, handed down to treasure, patented May 22, 1900, according to the inscription under the handle, from my Aunt Martha, Dad's sister. Apparently, she used it for small ironing jobs, sewing, etc.) This type of handle was much safer than the slotted-type described earlier, as there was no possibility of the metal base falling out, once secured, however this could and did happen occasionally with the slotted type. Imagine that heavy, hot sad iron falling to the floor, or worse yet on the operator's foot or leg— makes a person cringe to think of it!

The type of iron I recall Mom using most as we were growing up was the gas iron. Operating on the same principle as other gas appliances at that time, burning a kerosene/air mixture, the air being pumped into the little round gas canister through a valve, with the same gold-colored cylinder gas pump, as mentioned previously, that was used for the gas stove and lamps. When lighted, they burned with a little hiss, and blue flame, that always frightened me to death, and I wanted no part of learning how to iron with it! I recall Mom's iron was a pretty green, her favorite color, while Aunt Elsie's was blue. Thinking back to how these irons looked, the little fuel canister was located just behind the handle at the back of the iron, making it rather cumbersome to operate, however, the heat it gave to the iron was intense, and to homemakers of that era, a big improvement on sad irons. Because of the location of the little gas tank behind the handle, these irons couldn't be sat on end when not in use, as we set our irons today, so a footed metal base was employed, that sat on the end of the ironing board, and housed the iron, while the operator was adjusting her piece of clothing for another sweep. There was no heat gauge, as I recall, so accidental scorching of items being ironed was a constant threat! Heavy fabric pressing cloths were a must for delicate ironing.

If it was possible to begin ironing clothes when they were at a dampened stage of drying, it saved the necessity of "damping down" clothes. This process literally lightly wetted pieces of clothing prior to the ironing procedure, so they would iron up nicer, without wrinkles, much the same principle as our steam irons achieve for us today. This damping down process was usually achieved by hand-shaking droplets of water, from a container, over the clothing, then snugly rolling the piece of clothing up, and placing it in a wash basket or other receptacle, and covering it with a towel. The idea was to achieve a uniform dampened state prior to beginning the ironing process that took several hours or even overnight. Thus the little rhyme, "Monday being washing day, and Tuesday being ironing day." I recall Gran Teasdale having a zippered plastic bag, made especially for keeping rolled-up dampened clothing damp, until such time as she could iron it. I can still recall seeing the rolled up shirts, blouses, skirts, linens, etc., wrapped up in Mom's large laundry towel, she used for this purpose, sitting on the kitchen table, awaiting her ironing process. Of course, towels, facecloths, work clothing, etc. were exempt from this damping-down procedure, and were usually ironed in a semi-dry state from the line if possible, and then hung on the clothes horse or kitchen line to finish drying. Some homemakers employed a bottle with a shaker cork lid that held water to sprinkle on clothing for this dampening process, Aunt Ruby being the one I recall. I always felt this was a neat way to dampen down those unruly, wrinkled clothes off the line, however, I don't remember Mom ever having such a bottle, only using droplets of water from her hands.

Ironing boards were usually made of wood back then in the same shape as we are familiar with today, except standing on a wooden frame, that folded up when not in use, for easier storage. The board was covered with layers of felt, or other such fabric to give firmness and insulation and then covered with a heavy cotton fabric that would periodically have to be changed due to scorching and water spots, etc. Mom and Gran always used ironing boards, made from heavy, flat board or plank, cut into an ironing board shape that they laid on their kitchen tables, when they needed to iron, without stands of their own. Still others kitchens had them built right into a kitchen cabinet, that could be opened, and the board pulled out on a wooden extension while in use, my favorite idea, and put back when not needed, and the door closed. I recall being the proud owner of a collapsible, wooden, toy ironing board that always seemed to be a favorite toy, along with a little red metal iron, that would heat up slightly if left on the hot stove top, like the sad irons, that could be used to "iron" doll clothes. I guess little girls have always liked to imitate their mothers, even though the grown-up version isn't nearly as much fun!

Hair ribbons, in common use back then, for securing braids and other common hair styles, etc. could be "ironed" without the use of an actual iron, by wrapping wet ribbons tightly around tall, smooth-sided drinking glasses, and left to dry. The end result was equally as good, or better, given the uncontrolled heat irons gave off, and the silky, delicate nature of most ribbons, that would probably have been ruined under the high heat.

As can be determined from the previous descriptions, washing and ironing of clothes was a time-consuming, difficult procedure, repeated week after week, year in and year out, through all the seasons, with winter making the process more difficult, but summer making it hotter, especially the ironing. It has made me tired just thinking about it all, and explaining it! As with all electrical appliances that followed the advent of electricity to rural areas, electric irons were welcomed for their lightness, heat control, steam and general over-all efficiency. The only thing left to get used to was that blankety-blank electrical cord dangling around the back of the handle, a necessary evil, to keep the iron working!

Articles that couldn't be laundered by the above procedures, and there were many, made with wool, silk etc., before the days of wonderful polyester, had to be dry-cleaned, either at the local dry cleaners in town, or at home using purchased cleaning fluid. Great care had to be taken with this home-cleaning, as the fumes were toxic, and it could only be used outside. It was great for "spot" cleaning small areas, and Mom often employed this type of cleaning, rather than pay rather exorbitant cleaning fees, much like today. There was always a very strong smell left on clothing by cleaning fluids used back then, even by the dry cleaners, and upon bringing it home, clothing had to be hung outside on the line for several days at least, to rid it of the smell, before wearing or storing it.

Storage of clothing between seasons back then was made more difficult by the type of fabric available at the time. Moth balls, little round balls of crystallized moth repellant were often employed by homemakers in an effort to save heavy, woolen clothing, linens, comforters, and other stored items from the ravages of house moth infestations that seemed to be common at the time. Probably because so many fabrics couldn't be laundered back then, or in the absence of proper dry cleaning facilities, items were sometimes, unavoidably stored in a soiled condition, in trunks, closets or boxes in attics or basements for long periods, where clothes moths seemed to thrive. (This brings to mind our one and only encounter with the little devils, as we were growing up in the episode with the second-hand piano—see previous pages—yes they even lived and thrived in piano felts, apparently!)

As children, we hated the sickening, aromatic smell given off by mothballs, and happily, living in a newly built house, we weren't ever subjected to our clothing smelling of mothballs, except for this interval when we first inherited the piano. Even then, it seems to me Mom used sprays etc., with a more agreeable scent than those dreaded mothballs! Gordon's Mom, on the other hand had an on-going battle with moths in their older farm home, and I recall being almost paranoid about acquiring them from stored items Gordon wanted to bring to our new home, and her using mothballs in everything she stored, in an effort to dispel them. Clothes moths were an ongoing scourge it seems back then, for many households.

Mom had a lot of trouble with mildew on stored items, as she had two large blue wooden trunks for storage in our small home that sat in our basement, for lack of an accessible attic or better place. In summer, when the furnace wasn't required the basement became very cool and damp. Consequently, during these times, articles stored in these trunks became subject to that coolness and dampness that fostered the growth of mildew. What a shame to have clothing, books and other stored items covered with this greenish/grey powder that couldn't be removed easily, and a musty smell that lingered, even after exposure to dry conditions and sunshine.

Many larger homes had accessible attics back then, their dry, upper level location making them ideal for storage. As a child, I recall often playing with my cousin Audrey in the attic of her home—it was a magical place filled with seasonal clothing, old trunks, boxes, newspapers, pictures, old letters, magazines, a dress form for sewing, and the like. Memory upon memory lingered there, and we would spend hours looking at these old things, playing dress-up and make believe. Entry was made through a closed door and a wooden flight of steps, from the-upstairs hallway, just a ways from Audrey's room. I remember a faint mothball kind of musty smell up there, probably because the windows weren't opened often, but looking out from them, we felt the world belonged to us, and we were fairy princesses—for that day anyway! It was a heavenly place to play, and living in the small bungalow that was our home, the only time we got to play in an attic was when we visited Audrey, and as previously mentioned Aunt Elsie's attic at Sunny Hill farm, full of all her girlhood treasures.

Other remembrances come to mind with regard to caring for our home, and assisting Gran Teasdale in caring for hers, as being a widow, the bigger jobs of home maintenance were beyond her capabilities, requiring help from Mom and/or Dad, from time to time.

Wall to wall carpeting for floors was not in wide use, probably because of lack of availability and difficulty of maintenance. Homemade and purchased rugs, mats and runners were popular, probably because they could be lifted up and carried outside for shaking, or hung on the clothesline and beaten clean with a carpet brush/beater that would literally envelop the homemaker in clouds of dust! Some homemakers had Bissel-type cleaners, they used for this purpose, although not usually. It was common to braid rags into circular or oval mats to be placed at entryways and doorways to entrap dust and dirt being brought in from outside. These could be shaken out, as part of daily home maintenance and readily washed in home washers when heavily soiled—drying them proving more of a problem, especially in winter.

Mom always had a spongy kind of rubber/foam purchased mat to stand on by her kitchen sink cupboard, as she spent many hours standing there, performing many daily tasks, and liked the little lift and softness it gave her feet, as opposed to the rest of the kitchen floor covered with dark green and black asphalt tile, a new, popular floor covering at the time our house was built. Mom always loved clean, shiny floors, and always kept this kitchen floor gleaming with wax and lots of "elbow grease", as she called it, polishing after the wax application with soft cloths by hand. On occasion, Connie and I would do this same polishing job with soft dusters under our shoes, sliding around, making a game of our polishing job, and usually ending up in trouble, when we got too exuberant or one of us fell. Of course, an electric vacuum and polisher years later, made this maintenance much easier.

I also remember an incident involving this kitchen floor covering, that I will relate, because it seemed so important at the time, as the tile was just new! An acquaintance was visiting us one evening with her husband, and was wearing, red, high-heeled shoes with clickers on the heels, very popular at the time. This woman somehow sat with her legs crossed and her one high heel resting at an angle on the tile, at various locations, around her chair over the course of the evening, resulting in half-moon, clicker-shaped gouged areas at each spot! Of course, no one was aware of the damage until later, but it was a constant source of irritation to Mom, and difficult to clean. It seems to me, she and Dad finally replaced the individual tiles most affected, but that tile flooring remained in place for all the years spent on the farm, and even after Mom moved the house to town, always shiny and neat looking.

Cocoa matting, a course, braided type or runner mat, that could be bought by the yard at hardware stores and the ends hemmed with strips of cloth, was popular back then to place in back door entry ways, its rough surface being especially good for wiping shoes of outdoor dust and dirt. I remember Mom and Gran both having this type of matting at their back door entries.

Linoleum, a floor covering made of a hardened mixture of ground cork and linseed oil on a backing of burlap or canvas, was also popular, and could be purchased by the roll from local stores, the catalogues or sometimes from traveling salesmen. It came in a myriad of colors, designs and patterns to blend with any decor, from kitchen, bedroom, bathroom, living/dining room and hallways. Its shiny surface was easily maintained by washing with soap and water; when dry, it was then spread with a thin covering of paste wax, a solid, pale orange/gold clean smelling wax, bought in lidded tins. This wax covering had to be buffed to a shine. Linoleum was the type of floor covering we had in our living room, being floral green. In heavy traffic areas, the shiny top finish would eventually wear off linoleum, and would show through brown, the flooring finally having to be replaced, but this would not happen for many years.

The bedrooms were varnished hardwood, and required very little maintenance, except the occasional mopping for dust. Bedside mats were always in place for warmth, either purchased, made from rags at a mill in Manitoba, (homemakers could send rags and have rugs or heavy, knitted blankets made I recall), or homemade. I recall Gran had two beautiful Persian rug runners in her living room that always made the room so cozy and neat.

The most common floor cleaning modalities available back then were corn brooms, soft bristle push brooms, and later soft plastic bristle push brooms, used together with a faithful metal dustpan, could clean up most dust and household grubbies that accumulated from normal living. Mom had a favorite little soft bristle broom she used for sweeping up her kitchen several times/day and I believe still has today. Mops were used more in bedrooms and hallways where linoleum flooring only required light dustings. They consisted of a wooden handle attached to a base of multiple, twisted cotton threads, usually of a gold color, that made up the mop's functional head. It was always suspected that mops pushed around more dirt than they ever picked up, however it was all that was available back then! This fluffy head could be detached from the handle and thrown in the washer for cleaning. Gordon reports that his mother had a white thread mop, of a similar style and function.

Rag mops on a handle, with a matching scrub pail and built in canister for wringing out the wet mop between applications to clean the floor, were commonly used for washing floors, (hospital cleaning when we first worked at Grey Nuns'), and later sponge mops on a handle, with a push lever for wringing were more popular than the rag mops, as were neater, with less splashing to baseboards and furniture. Mom seemed to prefer getting down on her hands and knees for floor scrubbing, with a basin and cloth, or scrub brush, with a wash cycle, then a dryer rinse rubbing. Dad even had a course, bristled push broom he used in the barn, for cleaning the cement floor of the final dregs of manure and urine, left by the cows and horse in winter. He used another similar broom to sweep his garage as dirt and dust accumulated there.

Dustbane, an oily, wood shavings material could be bought commercially, for floor cleaning in large businesses or as mentioned previously, sweeping school floors, as at Allindale. The idea behind this material was that the oil in the dustbane caused dust and dirt to cling to it, thus cleaning the floor, however it left a rather oily residue on the floor surface, and as far as I know, was not in common use for home floor cleaning.

Long-handled, brightly colored, feather dusters aided the homemaker in dusting her home, much like today, although soft cloths also sufficed. Occasionally the children in the family would be called upon to perform this simple task; I can recall doing this little job to help Mom, and Gordon reports doing the same. Of course, there wasn't the myriad of commercial cleaning products available on the market then as there is today, to assist the homemaker, but often common household products on hand, sufficed. Vinegar and lemon juice were commonly employed, as well as baking soda, salt and old newspapers, to clean lamp glasses and polish stove tops, etc. I recall a purchased product, Bon Ami was used to cleanse sinks and basins back then—enamel, rather than stainless steel, was the common sink and basin finish, and this product, seemed to work well to clean enamel. Gordon reports his mother even used Bon Ami to clean chicken eggs prior to sale in town, whereas we always just used a dampened cloth dipped in vinegar.

Varnish was a very popular finish at the time, and since Dad built most of the cabinets and cupboards in our small home, after we moved in, most of them were plywood finished with varnish, with the exception of the kitchen cabinets that were painted white. Paint was all oil-based, as latex hadn't come on the scene yet, so most painting was done in spring and summer, when houses could be well ventilated, because of fumes and strong odor from this paint. High baseboards were popular in all rooms when our house was built, all sanded and varnished, that remain thus in Mom's home at Wolseley today.

Walls were painted in various colors or wall papered at regular intervals to give a fresh, new look. Wall papering was usually done in spring, after furnaces and space heaters could be shut off, and smoke and soot were at a minimum. For as long as I can recall, Mom and Dad did all of our wall-papering at home, and also at Gran Teasdale's home. Mom prided herself on being a master of sorts at it, learning her skills from Grandad Teasdale, who was apparently quite good at it, and inheriting his tools of the trade, so to speak. Trestles, a long, flat wall papering board, just wide enough for the strips of rolled wall paper, an apron for tools, and a long, black bristled brush for smoothing the pasted sheets on the walls.

Weeks before, rolls of wall paper, white or lightly patterned light beige ceiling paper, and more patterned/colored wall coverings and matching borders, had been chosen and purchased either locally or from the catalogues, and were ready and waiting. A huge pot of wall paper paste had to be prepared, consisting of a special mixture of water and flour/cornstarch, that was cooked on the stove and stirred carefully to get out the lumps—lumps did not look very good under newly applied wall covering! This mixture was allowed to cool in readiness, being made the morning of wall papering day or just the day before, as it would readily sour and spoil.

The room to be papered had to cleared of furniture as much as possible, and walls prepared by dusting and sometimes removal of old wall paper, if there were layers underneath, that had bubbled or peeled. The ceiling was usually papered first, followed by the walls and finally the border was put on last. Two trestles and the wall papering board were set up, usually in an adjoining room or even outside, if the weather was clement. The ends of the rolls of wall paper were knocked off with a sharp rap to a hard surface—these ends being the "kids share" of the wall papering venture; unrolled, they made glorious pretend ringlets, earrings or other "jewelry" for us to play with, but mostly, in the end only created extra mess that had to be cleaned up at the end of a tiring, exhausting day for the adults!

Strips of wall paper a little longer than required, were cut from the rolls, and laid face down on the awaiting table top. A huge wide paint brush, dipped into the pot of prepared paste was employed to carefully spread paste onto paper. Any visible lumps had to be removed, and the thickness had to be just right. This pasting job usually fell to Dad, as Mom would be up on the step ladder by this time, awaiting arrival of the pasted, dripping strip. The paste table top had to be carefully wiped along its edges, with a damp cloth, after each strip was removed, so that subsequent strips weren't subjected to the paste, on their facing edges. This job usually fell to Gran, if we were at her house, or sometimes to me, when I was older, or we were working at home.

In Gran's older home, the walls weren't always too straight, putting more challenge into the job, and in her kitchen, the stove pipes had to be taken down first, cleaned outside, as previously outlined, and then put back up. For us children, wall papering at Gran's house was always kind of fun, a day away from home, spent with our dear grandma, having meals at her house, and also having the good feeling of "helping" her out. Of course Mom and Dad much preferred wall papering at home, where the walls were straight, and old, peeling previous wall paper wasn't a bother to them!

With the exception of pre-pasted wall coverings that now just have to be wetted in warm water troughs, the rest of the wall papering procedure went much as it does today, and the fresh new lift it gave a room was well worth the time and effort involved. Naturally, wall paper and paint on walls was much more subject to smoke, soot and soiling, with wood and coal burning stoves and lamps, as opposed to the clean burning gas of today, so it was necessary to paint and wall paper often.

Windows had to be maintained each spring and fall, much like today, with storm windows being put on for winter, and screens for summer. Storm windows consisted of a regular sized four-paned window with three or four little round holes bored in the wooden base, with a flip up piece of board over them that could be raised or lowered to let a bit of fresh air into the house in winter. The double panes of glass surrounded by a wooden frame served to act as an insulation unit, together with the same sized inside four-paned window, to aid in keeping out cold winter blasts. The panes of glass were held in grooves in the window frame, and then a material called putty helped put a protective seal over glass and wood. Putty was a pliable clay-like color and texture when purchased in packages from the hardware in town. Since this material hardened, cracked and fell out of the window crevices after several years, it had to be replaced in spring, and painted over before the storm windows were stored, usually in the garage or a shed. As usual, all glass required regular cleaning.

Screens for windows only covered the lower half of the inside four-paned window, as in summer, there was no need for insulation from the cold, and a great need to get a breeze through the house, to help keep it cool. Both front and back doors also had windows with screens that could be replaced with glass in winter also. Mom always loved to have lots of fresh air in our home, I recall, usually always having several windows open at all times, and in summer both screened doors. It was amazing how much fresh air those little holes in the storm windows actually let in. Small 2x6 inch boards, made especially by Dad, lived on each window sill year 'round, for the purpose of holding up the inside house windows to whatever height might be desired for ventilation. Now, thinking back, this was a great, inexpensive way to raise or lower a window and keep it in place. Windows could also be outfitted with a hardware grooved metal adjustment, that would serve to lock the window in whatever position was desired, however, they weren't part of the window scenario at our house. Screen windows as well as storm windows were secured on the outside of the window frame by small metal butterfly clasps with a screw in the centre, that allowed the clasp to be turned; inside, screens and storm windows were sometimes also held with hook and eye closures for added security.

Blinds were always utilized on all windows, partly for privacy, but mostly to keep out light and a certain amount of heat. I recall Mom had green blinds on the two kitchen windows that faced east, that were always drawn on sunny mornings. It seems to me Mom and Dad's bedroom also had a green blind, even though their room faced north—I think Dad liked it best, as he hated mornings to come, and loved to sleep in as long as possible, even after Mom got up, as she loved getting up early in the mornings. The green blind would have facilitated prolonging darkness a little longer for Dad, I think. The rest of the bedrooms and front room had yellow/beige blinds. Some homes utilized outdoor shutters and awnings that could be drawn to keep out hot summer sun, but this wasn't something we had on our farm home.

Venetian blinds made an appearance about this time, although we never had them. They were a much heavier version of today's Venetians, with wide metal horizontal slats held together by canvas strips, but pulled open and closed with a string-pulley system similar to the ones known today. Curtains for living rooms were often sheer, with heavier patterned side drapes, often quite colorful and attractive, as I recall the ones in Gran Teasdale's home, being maroon colored with floral/ beige pattern. I remember Mom had plain, silky patterned maroon side drapes over sheers in our front room. Kitchen curtains were often patterned cotton, made from flour sacking or similar purchased material, and later when plastic became available, patterned plastic with plastic tie-backs. Metal rods were employed at the top of window frames, much as today for curtains and drapes.

While on the farm, we never actively used our front door that faced south, to come and go through, even though there was a little step leading up to it. In winter it was closed and sealed up, and only opened in summer to let in a breeze through the screen for ventilation. I think the reason we may never have used this door, was because our very small front room opened directly through this door, with no hallway, and usually there was a piece or two of furniture located in front of this entry, for lack of wall space.

The back door, facing north, was the one actively used by our family while on the farm. At first a small deck with railing and stairs was built for access, and later Dad built a small porch inside the railing, partly as protection for the back door in winter, and partly for some added storage, and a place to hang outdoor, manure-laden clothing and boots. It was unheated, but better than nothing, as Mom used to say! A raised board walk about 3 ft x 8 ft that Dad built, served as a sidewalk of sorts leading up to the back steps. Prior to this, old planks boarded together on the back, served this same purpose.

Doors were never locked back then on farm homes—now a necessity, to protect house and contents from would-be robbers and ransackers. No one would have thought of violating this kind of unwritten trust everyone had for other's property back then. Schools, churches, garages, sheds and barns likewise were never locked, as there didn't seem to be a need. It still saddens me to think of God's houses having to be locked up; a church should be available to everyone, at any time, without threat of being vandalized! So much has changed with regard to respect for what belongs to others—a sad state for our society today.

Keys to both front and back doors always hung on a nail on the doorframe of both front and back doors, but I don't ever remember anyone ever feeling the need to use them. Likewise all doors in the house had door knobs with locking devices and keys, but I don't ever recall any of them ever being used.

Before the advent of arborite or granite for counter tops, cupboards were covered with pieces of linoleum, much like floor covering, secured around the edges with metal strapping and screws. I recall this was used for our farm cupboards and also our wooden table top. Later, oilcloth, a patterned, plastic covering, melded onto a woven cloth back, could be purchased from the dry goods department of stores in town, from rolls, by the yard for table coverings. I can still recall the rather unusual smell newly purchased oilcloth had, I suppose because of its manufacturing, but it was not unpleasant, rather fresh smelling, to match "the new lift" it always gave the kitchen table! Later still, the woven backing was no longer needed, as heavier gauge, patterned plastic became available by the yard for this same purpose, that could also be made into matching kitchen curtains, etc.

White, painted wooden chairs accompanied our white painted wooden table that Mom, Connie and I sat on, at table, while Dad had a different chair made with aluminum tubing shaped into a chair, with a plastic, maroon covered, seat and back screwed in place. This became "Dad's chair" and hardly ever any one else sat on it, as it seemed to tip forward easily, unless a person seated well to the back of the seat, and as kids we were never able to manage this very well. Many an hour he would sit there after coming in from his chores, talking to Mom, and drowsing off now and then, often still dressed in his outdoor clothing and boots—just "warming up" before going out again to tackle the rest of his chores. The tube base sort of grated and slithered on the hard tile floor, and after a while actually marked the tile—needless to say a small stone or grit under the runners had to be dispelled quickly, for a smoother, quieter, sit.

I recall Mom bought red and white plastic covered cushion covers (that went "whoosh" each time we sat on them when they were first new, and always gave us a little laugh) for our chairs, as they were just flat and hard wood, without a seat groove or anything, and awfully hard! Later, as those coverings wore out, she covered our cushions and Dad's tube chair with a floral patterned green plastic material (in other words she and Dad re-upholstered them, as we would call it now).

A Duncan-Fyfe drop-leafed pedestal wooden dining room table with matching chairs was purchased through the catalogue, and was Mom's pride and joy. It would extend with two leaves and was often put to good use on Sundays, as we were growing up, as the Mortons, Gran and sometimes the Wilsons were frequent visitors. It is still the table Mom uses today in her home at Wolseley, having had it re-finished to its original beautiful luster. It seems to me, an upright china cabinet, on legs, was also purchased through the catalogue, to house Mom's good set of green/white and gold china, glasses/pitcher set, knick-knacks, etc. However, it was later replaced for whatever reason, with a lower, more compact unit that sat directly on the floor and seemed more in keeping with the limited space in our living room. It was this same cabinet's glass front door, that sister Connie accidentally fell through from the little low round living room chair, sustaining a nasty laceration to her forehead, when she was a young child. Luckily, the location of the wound, close to her hairline, caused no disfigurement, as I don't think she was taken to town for sutures, as we would have done today.

A wooden, lidded silverware chest, with a mirror in the lid always sat on the china cabinet, housing Mom's good silverware of 1847 Rogers design, called Everlasting Love. It seems everyone had sets of china, silverware, crystal and the like back then, as well as everyday dishes and cutlery that stayed in the kitchen cupboards. Silverware had to be polished with polish, much like today, as would become tarnished if allowed to stand, not in use. Silver tea sets on a tray, as well as silver spoons, or sets of silver were a treasure to own, often being handed down from generation to generation as family heirlooms but again, also had to be polished regularly.

For a time the piano was part of the living room furniture, later moving to my bedroom, due to lack of space, and to allow more privacy while practicing lessons, however, mostly, because of direct opposition with the newly acquired television set, that also occupied that room! A floor model cabinet radio and later one that stood on a table were always part of the living room furnishings, as well as a davenport couch and another arm chair with wooden legs, in a blue, velvety, patterned fabric covering. I recall Mom had an unusual table lamp given to her as gift, after we acquired electricity that was circular, on a base, with a picture of Niagara Falls on it. When plugged in and lighted a little disc inside turned, appearing to cause the Falls design on the outside to be actually "falling". It was most attractive and quite a curiosity at the time, I recall.

Bedroom closets housed inside clothing and good clothes, while the back doorway wall housed outer, everyday clothing with a series of hooks located on the wall by the window, and underneath, winter boots, etc. An open cupboard Dad built, above the clothing hooks always housed the mail order catalogues and sometimes mitts, scarves and hats in the off seasons, although because of its height, was not really very accessible to anyone but Dad. As mentioned previously, all the cabinets and cupboards in our home were hand-built by Dad, with the exception of the lower kitchen cabinets that were purchased as a unit, with the enameled kitchen sink included. Knick-knack shelves were built into each corner above this sink, and later Gordon installed a fluorescent light above Mom's sink, hiding the bulb with a fancy valence. The kitchen cupboards were always painted white, and all other cupboards and closets were varnished.

Dad was quite a "handy man" and seemed to be able to fix almost anything and get it working again, much like Gordon can today. I recall Dad liked to do fret-saw carpentry, and even taught me to do some as a girl! An intricately designed corner shelf he made from a pattern he had, of plywood, and then varnished, always hung in the living room at home; Gordon's Dad then took the pattern years later, and made similar corner shelves for all our children's bedrooms to house their small collectables.

Everyone used doilies back then, under lamps, pictures, and knick-knack ornaments, either crocheted, tatted or embroidered runners being most often seen. In crochet, the pineapple design had just become popular, and a lot of ladies used it in their crafting. Arm and head rest doilies were common for use on chairs and couches. Mom was not "a crafter", perhaps because of lack of time, or more of inclination; however she did sew quite a lot for us girls as we were growing up on her trusty portable Singer sewing machine. Any problems she encountered could easily be solved by Gran Sexsmith, as she was an accomplished seamstress, and later when Mom was on her own, Dad would often help her work through a pattern, after she had flung it in the corner, with a few choice words of frustration! I recall as a girl loving to visit Isobel's home where she would have several crafts always on the go, and was always more than willing to show me them, and how she did them. She sewed, as well as knit and crocheted, did beadwork, worked with leather and did plastic thread weaving. She also molded plaster-of-paris figurines to paint, with sets of red rubber molds, popular at that time. I can recall one of my favorite birthday presents ever received as a girl was a box of these same figurines to paint, from my cousin Wayne, which his mother Isobel had made for me, and on another occasion, two rose paint-by-number pictures, that were becoming popular crafts at that time. How I did enjoy working on these pictures and figurines.

Another time after I had woven a drawstring bag on my little hand-loom, Isobel offered and proceeded to line this little purse for me with white satin lining that had been a hem cut off Eileen's wedding dress, if you can imagine. Other crafters that I recall during these formative years were Aunt Ruby, who often had a delicate petit-point picture on the go, or else tatted doilies, and she had a special skill in both. A beautiful hand-crafted, ecru, crocheted tablecloth she had made always graced her dining room table, centered with a mirror, with parakeet ornaments on top. I had always admired this elegant table whenever I visited and played with cousin Audrey. Imagine my dismay when, one day while Audrey and I were running by this same table and cloth, we accidentally pulled cloth, mirror and figurines to the floor, with a sickening crash! We both deserved severe punishment for having caused such a mishap, however, after a little cry, and inspection of her beautiful cloth, that miraculously had not been damaged, we were only sternly reprimanded. I have never forgotten this incident, and feel sorry to this day about it, as I think it was a little knot on my moccasin-type shoe that had caught the cloth in the first place, although, no blame was ever laid.

A neighbor man and friend, Ed Thompson, a bachelor, came quite frequently for a visit and meal—and he was a "crafter" in all sorts of areas, especially leather and plastic thread weaving, popular at the time. When he learned I was interested in this latter craft, he gladly showed me how to weave a two-toned pull for zippered jackets, and also a pretty patterned bracelet and scarf clasp from grey and pink plastic thread. Whenever he went to the craft shops in Regina, he would get new colors of thread for me and lent me his patterns, etc. I still have these items today, and some of the plastic thread saved in a toffee tin box. Also during these years, I learned to knit, from Gran Sexsmith, embroider and sew by hand and on the machine from Mom and Gran Teasdale, and to crochet at school from Miss Railton, grade IV and V teacher at Allindale, nourishing life-long, treasured abilities I still greatly enjoy today.

Mom was always a "plant" person, and indeed seemed to have a real green thumb both indoors with houseplants and outdoors in her garden. She and Aunt Ruby always grew beautiful Gloxinia plants back then, Mom's being velvety purple trumpeted flowers, and Aunt Ruby's wine colored flowers. Mom also had beautiful Fushia plants in the kitchen windows, and in the front window a Hoya plant wound around, bearing pink clusters, that fairly dripped nectar when in fresh bloom. I can still see the pink buds waiting in their clusters to bloom, perhaps 20 little flowers to a bloom, wrapped like little waxen, hexagon-shaped hats, that later opened to expose their velvety side. They would last for weeks, and the smell, especially in the evening, was just divine.

In the garden, yellow roses were Aunt Ruby's forte, while Mom grew gladioli, sweet peas and often, bright orange and yellow nasturtiums in the south flower bed and later a yellow rose and peonies. A huge vegetable garden with a wonderful strawberry patch at the south end provided Mom with endless hours of work and pleasure, and us, her family with wonderful meal accompaniments, fresh in summer, and frozen or canned in winter. A large raspberry patch at the north end of the garden provided all family members with delicious fruit and lots of picking hours!

Just a few more notes on care of house and home, and remembrances of these, having got off on kind of a tangent in the last few paragraphs with crafting, hobbies and how they related to recollections of home-life back then as we were growing up.

A kitchen light fixture placed in the centre of the kitchen ceiling when we got electricity on the farm in the 50's, remains in place in Mom's kitchen to this day, as well as her favorite lighting fixture in the living room ceiling and a pole type tri-light she also had back then. Bedrooms lacked ceiling fixtures, and lamps sufficed, with the exception of the bathroom, that had a ceiling bulb, now covered with an imitation chandelier that is kind of attractive. The garage, henhouse and barn all had bulb lights and of course as mentioned before the yard light lighted a good part of the yard with its height and high-powered bulb, shielded by a metal shade. Nowadays, farm yards have modern halogen lighting that brightly lights up the yards and surrounding area for miles!

Our basement was regularly painted with white-wash over the cement walls, for a cleaner, brighter look, and as mentioned previously, Mom always painted the cement floor with drawn tile squares, spending hours down there with a paint brush! Of course, plotting all the tiles was the hardest and it seems to me Dad helped with this part, then repainting them was much easier. As I recall, that floor was always bumpy, with a lot of rough surface, whereas, her cement floor in her house at Wolseley was much smoother and easier to do.

The two homes of Herb and Raymond Sexsmith were always so grand, in size and appointments, that I still recall them fondly, from my girlhood days, because they were so utterly different from our home, especially in size! A small bungalow compared to a two-story home is quite different, even today, although ours was always filled with love and contentment for the most part, and we never grew up feeling deprived per se.

It seems to me, those two homes would have been built at about the same time, early in this century, by the former fathers, Dave and John Sexsmith, Dave's of brick exterior and John's of stone exterior. Both had huge kitchens, pantries with dumb waiters to the basement, long rectangular dining rooms and parlors with front doors and huge staircases and hallways, as well as back doors with another set of stairs leading up to the main level and even side doors with outdoor steps. The Dave Sexsmith home even had another staircase down the south side of the house off the upstairs level, as access to an upstairs apartment, occupied first by Herb and Ruby when they were first married, and later by Gran Sexsmith, in the later years.

There were bedrooms on both levels of both these homes, but I always felt the upstairs layout in the John Sexsmith home was so nice, with all the bedrooms and bathroom going off a circular centre hallway, with a winding staircase up to that level, whereas in the Dave Sexsmith home, the staircase swept straight up from the front door, resulting in a huge hallway in the middle of the house, and only four bedrooms on that level, that could be accessed also by a stairwell off the kitchen.

The dining rooms in both homes were definitely built for huge gatherings, and could easily seat 25 to 30 people or more at large, oval expandable tables, that came with 6 or more wooden leaves. Plate rails ran around the entire perimeters of both rooms at about a seven foot height, and were usually filled with decorative, treasured plates, placed at frequent intervals. Between the plate rails and the high wooden baseboards at floor level, the walls in the dining rooms were covered with a golden brown colored wall relief featuring various figurines, the quality appearing heavier than a wall paper, and more like a decorative wall board of some kind, that must have been in style at the time. (Lincrusta wallpaper).

Beautiful bay windows were a special feature, as well as an alcove with southern facing window seats and glassed cabinets, in the Dave Sexsmith home, that I am more familiar with, because of visiting there more often to play with cousin Audrey. It seems to me the wood in this alcove had a beautiful high gloss dark reddish brown quality, and at its entry, large carved pillars on each side led up to the ceiling. I recall this being a delightful place to play, seemingly "away" from the rest of the dining room area, in our own little world! Boston ferns stood stately and tall on unique plant stands in the bay windows facing west. Apparently one of the finishing carpenters made these plant stands in his spare time. They were approximately six inch square pillars with square bases and tops covered with a putty-like material and then imbedded with small pieces of broken colored glass, pottery, china, beads, buttons, etc. I can remember as a child being fascinated with the many different designs on these stands, and now looking back can really appreciate the hours of careful work and attention that went into making them, the craftsman having to work quickly, while the clay/putty was soft enough to have the ornamentation imbedded into it, with no sharp edges protruding for safely sake. I wonder what ever happened to this pair of stands, after Gran Sexsmith's time?

The upright piano, beautiful large leather-covered arm chairs, several couches and a small, built in, maroon-colored velvety sofa behind the dining room swinging door are other furnishings I recall. A rounded, cylinder shaped velvet cushion with a jester's face on it and large black velvet buttons on the ends always sat on this little sofa, and was always kind of a curiosity to play with when visiting.

Huge, ornate gold-framed black and white portraits of Gran Sexsmith's mother and father, the Donalds, hung in her bedroom, the only bedroom on the main level of the house, just off the front hallway and back stairway. It seems it was popular back then to have family pictures made "larger than life" for posterity's sake, but I can recall, as a child, the size of these pictures being quite overwhelming, especially when staying over at night, and sleeping with Gran in her bed! However, after a guessing game of writing/drawing on backs, bedtime prayers and goodnight hugs, the ominous-sized portraits seemed less threatening, and were soon forgotten, once the lights were out.

Grandfather clocks that sat on the floor were popular at that time in some homes; however, I cannot say that I recall either of these grand homes having one. It seems to me there were mantle chime clocks that tolled out the hours, and I remember Gran Teasdale always having one of these in her home, tilting it forward to stop its noisy tolling and ticking at night so as not to disturb her sleep! Of course wind-up alarm clocks were common in all households, and this is the kind we always had at home. Silent-operating battery clocks had not yet made their appearance, probably because small-cell batteries had not come on the scene either.

Several other remembrances come to mind with regard to these homes that I wish to mention. Both homes were wonderful places in which to play, especially hide and seek, as the possibilities for hiding were "endless" because of their sheer size! Likewise the barn, hayloft and several straw-filled corridors leading out several doors at Audrey's home were a joy to play in. One time, I recall Audrey befriended a mouse family in their basement, picking up the little pink babies, and cradling them in the waistband of her sweater, so they chased each other around her waist! It seems to me, after several days her new-found friends were discovered by a horrified Aunt Ruby, and quickly put to rest, much to Audrey's dismay! I recall playing at Harold and Eileen Sexsmith's home (formerly the Chew home, where the Teasdale family grew up) with cousin Dwight, having delightful times outside playing hide and seek in double rows of hedges that ran all around the yard, and also visiting at the Reid's stately home and playing with friend Grant, who was also ages with all of us cousins at that time.

Looking back, as a matter of observation, for all their size and grandeur, the many amenities we would include in such a home today, were sadly lacking back then in those homes, probably because no one had thought of bedrooms with half baths, and also because there wasn't the emphasis on cleanliness there is today, both for personal hygiene or for our clothing, etc. There was only one toilet and tub on the upper level, although sinks were more plentiful, with one at the back door entryway, one in the pantry, one in the upstairs bathroom, of course, as well as wash and rinse tubs in the basement. Showers hadn't become common, and bathing in a bathtub, perhaps once a week, seemed often enough, as has been mentioned previously. Kitchens separate from pantries made many additional steps back and forth for the homemaker, with kitchen cabinets located in the pantry along with the sink, while the stove, kitchen table and another small counter and set of cupboards were located in the kitchen. The dining room was inconveniently off down a hallway, past the pantry, in the Dave Sexsmith home anyway. The John Sexsmith home seemed to have a little better design in this regard, I always thought. Spring cleaning must have been a massive undertaking, due to the sheer size of these homes!

With this thought in mind, this is probably as good a place as any to mention, hired hands. As we were growing up, it wasn't very common-place for the "average" farm family to have an employed or hired man to assist the land owner with his work, or the homemaker with hers. I can recall only several instances during my youth knowing hired hands, and several names come to mind. Raymond and Isobel had a hired couple, Wilf and Sylvia, for a time, Wilf helping with the barn and field work, while Sylvia helped Isobel, who was sometimes in poor health back then. Another hired hand named Bill also worked for Raymond, for the longest time of all. One of his accomplishments during his employ was digging a new, deep tunnel, perhaps 10 feet deep, all by hand, from the well up to the house, for new concrete pipes to be laid, etc. It was quite a thing back then, to watch the progress Bill had made on this tunnel, each week when we went for drinking water—the straight, precise job he did, and all the hard work. As Gordon says, several hours now with a back-hoe—and this same grueling work would be done quick as a wink.

Several summers at Harvest time, Uncle Herb and Dad hired a young lad from Sintaluta, to assist them, since neither family was blessed with sons. He boarded at Uncle Herbs, only coming to our place if harvesting was scheduled there. I recall he was an excellent worker, and used to cool off at noon by swimming in our dug out. I remember being so envious of him being able to swim, since it was something neither Connie or I grew up learning, not because Mom didn't offer to drive us to Wolseley where swimming lessons were taught at the local dam every summer holidays, but we were just too wimpy to make the commitment back then, a decision I am sorry about to this day. Who knows if we ever would have actually swam in the dug out, thinking back to the lizards that lived along the edge each summer, and the dangers lurking in the soft mud at each sloped end, but in the unbearable summer heat, it was often a dream we had, and then to witness this young lad actually going to swim there, really was something, as mentioned previously.

I can remember Dad telling us his mother, our Gran Sexsmith, often had a "hired girl" to assist her with her chores, household duties and child rearing, as her children were all young and very close together. Daughters grew up and eventually assisted in the homemaking, while sons helped with outdoor chores and land work, preparing them for taking over their own homes and farming operations someday. Few farm children left the farming community in those days, but grew up and married young people from similar backgrounds, usually from the area. Husbands rarely performed household tasks, meal preparation or assisted much with child care, as it wasn't common to job-share tasks back then. Thankfully, there has been a turn-around in this thinking, beginning as we grew up, and becoming quite common now, with so many wives and mothers being employed outside the home.

It was common in the era when our parents grew up, to hire whole gangs of workers, especially at harvest time to assist the farmer with threshing, to accomplish the work now done by combines. Lots of young Eastern lads would "come West" just for this employment to earn a bit of money and for the experience. They would "ride the rails" (free-load on top of railways boxcars on trains headed west) to get out here, sometimes remaining to eventually settle and acquire their own land. Others would return to the east at the end of harvest season, and return the following year, often to the same farms in successive summers. One such fellow, whose home was in the Maritimes, a lad by the name of Yates, had come to work on the Sexsmith farms back then. When as a girl, I submitted my name to a pen pal club in a farm paper, whose circulation was Canada-wide, his daughter wrote to me, wondering if we were of the same family, for whom her dad had worked so many years before. As I was not keen to write to the girl for some reason that now escapes me, my Mom wrote to them, and she and Bertie Yates (the wife) corresponded for many years, through this one small link with the past. It seems to me they were potato farmers then in the Maritimes, but have since passed away.

Needless to say, while these gangs of men could accomplish a lot of work each day, they also had huge appetites, and had to be fed and given a place to bunk, etc., often sleeping in barns or even outside. I can recall Gran Teasdale telling us of the mounds of extra food that had to be prepared from early morning to dusk during this threshing season, often in very hot August heat, with limited facilities and no modern amenities or refrigeration. The abundance of home grown garden produce, at that time of year, must have been a blessing, but the cooking and baking over hot stoves must have been difficult. If the weather held and was clement, the threshing at each farm could be accomplished in several days to a week, however, inclement weather resulted in a lot of stranded workers who still had to be fed, but who were only paid while working, which of course sometimes happened.

Having briefly touched on harvest, through the discussion of hired hands, the following paragraphs will portray the many fond recollections I have of the harvest season, the culmination of each farmer's annual effort and struggle with the land, the elements, insects and all other variables not in his control!

Probably no other recollection from my girlhood days brings back such fond memories for me as that of the harvest season. Usually by my birthday on August 26, a good start had been made on the golden fields of grain that surrounded our buildings, bindering and swathing was often completed by late August, and sometimes even some combining was done. It seems to me harvest season has definitely fallen later over the years, with September and October being more the norm now to harvest, especially the specialty crops of today like canola, lentils, sunflowers, field peas, etc., that were unheard of in our area in those days. Crops were mainly wheat, oats, barley and occasionally flax. Weeks of preparation had usually gone into servicing of the harvest machinery, the swather, combine, binder, auger, grain wagon and of course the bins to hold the grain. Bins were all made of wood back then, square in shape, not like the rounded metal ones most common today. Aging ones had to be fortified, often with paper, lathes, etc.,—a little job I sometimes helped Dad with, and our farm seemed to have its share of this type! Then there was the glorious summer when Dad built the new bin in our yard, and Connie and I used it for a play house prior to the harvest, as discussed previously.

Golden swaths, pyramid-shaped stooks of oats and scratchy stubble covered the landscape as in the last weeks of August, the district children excitedly gathered together new notebooks, pens, pencils, crayons, erasers, rulers, and lunch kits etc. in anticipation of the first day back to school at Allindale. Most years a new lady teacher had to be "oriented" and "broken-in" so to speak, (with the exception for me of Grades IV and V and VII and VIII), but this kept school-life lively and fresh, and as discussed previously, I always loved school and all associated with it. So the beginning of school, my birthday and the harvest always made the late summer an especially happy time for me.

Cousin Audrey and I loved it when the harvest was in progress at our farm, because of its close proximity to Allindale, and we would rush home after school so we could get in on a little part of the "action". One harvest when I was about seven or eight years old, I developed epistaxis (common for me back then), every day after school, and had to rest, in the house until it subsided, a very frustrating scenario, when Audrey and I had this important harvest business to take part in! Looking back, this malady was probably due to the excitement of the moment.

Uncle Herb and Dad always harvested together, as they shared all the harvest machinery, stored when not in use in a gigantic machine shed in Uncle Herb's farm yard. I always felt sorry that Dad ended up doing the brunt of the combining and a great deal of the swathing, because Uncle Herb had a visual handicap and was older. Looking back, I think the harvest put a tremendous strain on Dad, especially in the later years, when unknown to us, his health was beginning to deteriorate. He always seemed grumpy and tense, and not his usual kind and smiley self during harvest, but he was usually off on the machinery, except during meals, while Uncle Herb took grain away and tended to auger and bins, and it was with him, that Audrey and I spent most of our harvest experience. We would ride on the tractor, back and forth, taking grain from the combine back to the bin for unloading, etc., and then play around the bin until the next field trip.

Occasionally, as the grain neared the peak of the bin, someone would have to go inside and shovel it back into the corners. Of course we were always more than anxious to do this important task, however, were never allowed, as because of our small size, the grain could have "swallowed" us up, or we could have been overcome by the grain dust, floating in thick, clouds from the end of the auger. Mom sometimes came and helped with this, or as mentioned previously, the hired hand would help with it. Several older fellows known to Uncle Herb, a Mr.Weibe and another gentleman known as Uncle Bill came several years to help at harvest. I always remember this man saying to Audrey when she asked what she and I could do or how we could help him in some way, that all he wanted was "Peace and quiet"! I suppose in our exuberance to "help" we were a little overwhelming to the old fellow, (and no doubt a bit of a nuisance), as whenever children are around moving machinery, the adult in charge has to have "eyes in the back of their head" as the saying goes.

Our other favorite development during harvest, were meals served out in the field, to save the men the time and effort involved to return to the house for eating. Looking back, it probably would have been a welcome and much-needed respite from the long, grueling hours Dad spent running the combine, however, everyone did it back then, as time was of the essence, the weather could turn bad, or a machinery break could mean precious hours lost, so if everything was running smoothly, it was kept running at all human cost!

Mom would pack up the trunk of the car with the most delicious meals, keeping the food piping hot in pots and pans covered with lids and then a blanket. The card table was employed for serving, and nail kegs, logs and an occasional kitchen chair came along from the house to sit on. Full course meals with meat, potatoes, vegetables, and desserts of pie or pudding and lots of cold water or hot coffee were Mom's specialty, and she prided herself on these culinary feats under the extremely difficult conditions of wind, heat, cold, and staggered meal times. Of course, to us children, these unusual field-type meals that occurred only once a year, at harvest, were better than any picnic in the park, and we loved to be part of them.

Hay crops for feed were often cut in mid-summer from road allowances and dry slough grasses prior to the grain harvest with hay mowers, allowed to cure and was stacked or stored in barn lofts. There wasn't the emphasis on planting of land to actual hay and forage crops as there is today. However, most farmers with cattle planted a small field of oats.

The early harvest back then involved cutting these beautiful lacey looking oat fields of grain for winter feed. This crop, one of the prettiest looking crops I recall, was first diamondy-flecked shades of green, and later turned golden, and was then ready for the binder. The machine that Dad and Uncle Herb used was indeed a relic, literally held together with binder twine—the same used to tie up the sheaves it was used to cut and make! In earlier days, it was pulled by horses; however, the tractor was employed to pull the binder in my days of recollection. Another person had to ride on the binder and operate it, rising and lowering the table, making sure the machine tied the sheaf of cut grain, and then to trip the release dropping 6 to 8 sheaves in one spot.

Later these same sheaves had to be "stooked" for curing. This involved heavy, back-breaking work for one or several men with pitch forks, picking the sheaves up, placing them against each other in a peaked position, then two more facing across from the first two, until a stook was made using the 6 to 8 sheaves dropped at each spot by the binder. A stooked field of sheaves was a beautiful sight to behold, and is still in memory held dear. Apparently Dad was an excellent stooker, and did a great deal of it as a young man, when the south half of section 17, (where he would eventually have his farm) was all sown to oats, and he helped his father by stooking this whole field, spending whole days there until the job was done.

Stooks in a field, in their typical pyramid shape, were curing, and could be left there until late fall, safe from the elements until all the other harvest was completed, before being picked up in racks, pulled to the stacking yard and formed into stacks. Several district men usually got together for this task every fall. Making a good, sturdy stack was another skill Dad prided himself in, directing the placement of sheaves in a circular fashion on the ground, often on a snow base, heads facing in and cut ends facing out, filling in the centre, and each additional level, building on top, becoming smaller after the middle of the stack was formed, until a peaked top was achieved. This shape repelled moisture and the elements, until the sheaves would be needed as winter feed, and would be taken to the barn and broken apart to feed the cattle.

Some oats were also combined, stored in bins and later fed to horses in their natural state or chopped in a grain chopper located in the barn to feed cows, pigs and chickens. The bin Dad chose to keep oats in was one of his oldest wooden ones and sat near the road about 1/2 way between our lane and the church road (called this because in olden days the only church in the district, Alexander United, was located a mile or so south of the grid road crossing). I suppose he located the oat bin there for easy access across the field whenever oats were needed to feed the animals in winter.

Later in August/September the wheat harvest took place with swathing often preceding the combining process. Dad and Uncle Herb always owned a pull-type combine as mentioned previously, and as a girl this large orange Case machine seemed like a monster with belts, pulleys and levers everywhere, as well as a pick-up in front, a hopper for holding threshed grain, a spout for emptying the grain into a wagon or truck, and finally a long chute for dispersing of the straw and chaff. It was always a thrill to watch the golden heads of grain being taken up into the combine, either from swaths directly onto the pick-up, or if the grain was still standing, seeing the reel push the grain towards the cutting blades. From this point the monstrous machine did its work, and soon golden grain poured forth from the spout into the hopper and clouds of straw and chaff spewed out the back, to be "spread" by a rotating spreader blade onto the stubble and later worked back into the land, or else left, in rows to be baled or burned. Similarly, crops of barley and flax were combined, often after the wheat. (I have not mentioned threshing machines, except in passing, in the hired hands section, since we were never familiar with their operation as were from our parents and grand-parents era).

Gordon recalls their farm operation having a baler to pack up this combine straw into neat 40 lb. rectangular bales to be fed to livestock in winter, but Dad and Uncle Herb never owned one, preferring to use the oat sheaves as mentioned previously, and working in or burning straw.

I recall the stubble after cutting was usually left about six inches high, and was very hard on legs and ankles, unless covered. Mom and us girls often came back from the field meals with bleeding ankles where this sharp stubble had scratched us—Mom would dab bits of Kleenex on hers to stop the bleeding, I remember.

Wheat swaths most years were so wide (at least two and a half to three feet) that a small person could barely even jump across them, let alone walk over them, and as children we were always cautioned not to come across swaths if possible, as there was always inadvertent trampling. Likewise, straying animals in grain fields at harvest or herds of wild deer could make quite a mess of swaths. Flocks of ducks and geese landing in fields to feed weren't too welcome either and made some mess of swaths. That's why Dad always liked his crows in the fields, with their leader Jack that flew about discouraging fowl-type birds from landing in his fields he always thought.

Stubble burning took place after the harvest was completed in late fall. It was quite a common practice back then and was done to alleviate the fields of excess straw, especially in years when it was abundant, long and heavy, before fall or spring cultivation. It was quite a job, especially in a dry fall, to control the burning, so it wouldn't get out of hand. The wind had to be minimal, (quite a feat to obtain in windy Saskatchewan), and often burning was done in the evening after the wind went down for the day. The object was to have "controlled" burning in the rows of straw swaths only, however, usually some of the stubble burned also. Ideally two people worked together, burning row after row, so Mom often helped Dad with this task. I recall always being afraid for them, in case they were burned, or the fires got out of control, especially as it became dark, and flames and smoke billowed skyward. Still to this day, if we see fields being burned in fall, I have this uneasy feeling—as always fire being a good servant and a poor master, as Dad used to say! It was dirty, tedious work, smoke and pieces of charred straw floating all about and underfoot. In wet falls, or if harvest was late, this burning step was often left out, and the straw allowed to dissipate on the fields over winter. What remained was then worked into the land in spring.

Nowadays, with the emphasis on land conservation, and the desire to minimize soil erosion by wind and water, etc., stubble burning is minimal, with zero tillage being utilized by some farmers for weed control over fall and winter, or else the harvest straw is just worked into the land. Strip farming was never common practice in our area, as it is in areas west of us around Swift Current etc., however crop rotation was common.

Dad always divided his land in half, as mentioned previously, using the power line poles to the north east to divide summer-fallow from crop that rotated every year. I recall many more bloughs on the land as we were growing up, than are in place now, as over the years there was a tendency to remove these pesky nuisances, usually filled with water, taking up land that could be planted and productive, as well as having to work around them with implements. Several bloughs were located in the farm yard and pasture, that remain there today, the one behind the barn extending way out into the west field, as it still does today, and often used to harvest hay from. Another, with a huge stand of quivering poplar trees, was located to the right of the lane, going south, as it met the grid road. I recall always being frightened to death as a young child on my way to school, that some wild beast, namely a wolf, would be lurking in that blough, waiting to attack me! (mentioned previously). There was another brook-type little pond near the school on the right of the grid road that we often played in come spring, and on the other side of the lane, a large round blough about half way down the field to the east, that was too far away to be a threat re: the wild beasts, etc.! Although shelter-belt trees were available to help prevent wind erosion from as near as the Forestry Farm in Indian Head at that time, at minimal cost to the farmer, or even free, it never seemed to be a priority to Dad, and we never planted any.

Crop spraying for weeds or insects was accomplished in one of two ways, and was only utilized in years of bad infestations of either pest. For a number of years district farmer, Albert Luther ran a spraying operation and could be hired for this job; he went all over the area with his equipment, probably because he needed the funding it could provide, with his family of five children, but must have been very hard on him physically, breathing in all those toxic fumes with little or no protection except a handkerchief tied over his nose and mouth. (He has lived well into retirement age, with no apparent ill effects, so he must have been extra spunky or cautious or both!) A certain amount of "trampling" resulted, but usually recovered eventually. The other option was to hire a plane through an agency that did this type of work, (mentioned previously) and several years Dad did just that, even though the cost was prohibitive, he felt the end result would be worth it and then trampling was not a problem.

The size and magnitude of today's tractors and implements would have awed Dad, as with his little operation, a medium-sized tractor, (John Deere, as mentioned previously), and other 12 -foot implements were all that his land required. It seems to me he owned all the implements for seeding and land maintenance, and only shared the harvest implements with Uncle Herb. Dad had a disker for seeding and ploughing, and an old drill he sometimes used and liked for seeding, that did a fantastic job with the rows, so even and straight, especially as the crop was just coming up. A small cultivator, and a set of harrows to smooth the land after cultivation, were the extent of his implements, that he kept neatly stored in the field nearest the yard, by the buildings. When not in use, over winter, harrows were placed upright out of the dirt, in pyramid shapes against each other, to help preserve them, as could be uncoupled from each other. Dad had a saying he often used as we were growing up, that typically suited a farmer-father. He used to say, when we had harrowed all he had ploughed, we would be older and wiser (in the ways of living he meant!) Cute! And now we are older and wiser, we can relate to this little saying exactly!

Because we couldn't take part in the seedtime or other land operations as we felt we did in the harvest, apart from an occasional ride on the tractor, the other seasons of the crop year never seemed to figure very highly in our thoughts as we were growing up, although I'm sure held equal magnitude for our parents, especially Dad, as it was his reponsibility, through his choice of wheat/oats/barley to plant, excellent maintenance of the land, and ultimately the harvest each year, that meted out our living and subsequently our life-style, which out of necessity was often frugal.

Grain prices never seemed to be very high, and with a small farm, (less than one quarter section planted to a cash crop any given year), an abundance of grain wasn't usually obtained, although the land produced good quality wheat, and it certainly wasn't from lack of goad farming practice on Dad's part. Quotas were sporadic, and few and far between, and as mentioned previously, egg and cream sales often had to augment or were the only source of farm income some months back then. Thank goodness so much of our day to day food was produced and stored for use right on the farm, as just discussed with food.

With regard to hauling harvested grain to the elevator, for sale, Gordon and I have different recollections. Sometimes, there was a quota and grain could be hauled at harvest, but usually the grain had to be stored and then hauled as quotas came available. Since neither of our Dads owned trucks, with the exception of Dad having a smaller one in later years, after I left home, Gordon says his Dad hauled grain to the elevator in Neudorf in a wagon or trailer behind the tractor, or even teams of horses. (Apparently horses hated going into the elevators, because of the floor grating, noise, etc). In the days before augers, the grain had to be shoveled from the bins by hand with a special scoop shovel, into the wagons at home, and at the elevator the wagon was tipped and dumped. Probably this shoveling and trailer arrangement took place at our farm also, although I only recall the years when augers were available, and Dad hired a fellow from Wolseley with a large box truck to haul his grain to town for him, further reducing his take-home grain cheque, by having to pay for this hauling.

No wonder farmers overall seem to be a patient, hopeful lot, relying so heavily on the good Lord to provide "seed-time and harvest" as the Bible says, as so many variables figure into their day to day operation. There was always "next year" to rely on when everything would turn out right and things would go better! A good motto we could all follow and live by, as so many things in this life are out of our control; we have to take the good with the bad and "keep on a-truckin"!

Clothing, another necessity of life has yet to be discussed, and since what we wear, then as now, plays such an integral part in our everyday lives, and we invest so much interest and funding into providing this commodity, especially now, this next section will deal with clothing, how obtained, styles recalled of our growing up era etc.

Whenever possible, as a cost saving as well as lack of clothing stores back then, clothing was made at home. Gran Sexsmith was the seamstress extraordinaire of my childhood. S h e could sew anything from scratch! Just show her a picture of what was required or wanted, and she would whip up her own pattern and make the garment, quick as a wink!

I remember once showing her a picture of a little girl in a coloring book, wearing a ruffled pinafore type of jumper, and a day later I had an identical one made of pretty pink cotton with pink flower-shaped buttons dancing down the front, just like the little girl in my coloring book! And, all accomplished on her foot driven treadle sewing machine—I don't think she ever had an electric one. My sailor quilt mentioned previously was also a favorite gift made by this marvelous grandmother seamstress.

As I look back, I realize what a wonderful gift and skills she possessed, and I am in awe of all she did and was able to do even as an older woman, when I knew her as my Gran. She was always making Audrey and I clothes for our dolls, as well as for us, and was never limited to simple pieces of clothing, but made coats, jackets, dresses as well as knitted mitts, socks, scarves and toques all winter for all of us children and adults. She was such a quick knitter, and could knit up a storm and carry on a conversation, etc., without ever missing a stitch! She could darn a hole in a sock with such perfection, it looked like new. Apparently, she always sewed for herself as well as her daughters and others, as I recall Dad often mentioning all the fashionable clothes she sewed for Aunt Martha, trying with all her skills to get a new creation "just right" for Martha's rather fussy standards and tastes, then at the last minute before going out on her date, Martha would wear her "old blue", a favorite blue dress she could always count on!

Mom sewed after a fashion, but by her own admission, she hadn't the skills, time or patience to persevere and become good at sewing, although she did make Connie, herself and I quite a few items of clothing over the years, and mended a lot for Dad, etc. Aunt Ruby sewed a lot of her own dresses, often out of the cotton floral flour sacking that could be bought with 100 lb. bags of flour in those days. Gran Teasdale sewed a little on her treadle machine, mostly mending for herself.

Simpsons (Sears-Roebuck) and Eatons mail order catalogues provided farm families with many clothing options, as well as all manner of items necessary to maintain a household back then. With limited access to city stores because of distance and means of mobility, and stores in the small prairie towns having small selections, rather carrying more essential commodities, the catalogues provided a means of browsing, much as we would "window shop" today, and to dream a little! Current fashion trends were often first noted on the glamorous catalogue models, and as soon as a glossy new book would arrive by mail in Spring and Fall, favorite selections would be made from it, especially by the female members of the family, and then pennies were put aside in the hope of "sending for" the desired items before the catalogue out-dated or the season ended!

The arrival of the thinner Christmas Wish Book was a particular favorite time, especially to the children in the family, as all conceivable manner of toys, dolls, etc. were listed there in page after page of living color to long and wish for. Toy pedal cars were always my favorite, and I recall spending hours dreaming of how it would be to have one to pedal and ride in. Of course dolls with changeable wardrobes ran a close second, and all manner of crafting toys were wished for too, as well as clothing.

I recall being on the "brink" of my teenage years, finding myself caught in the dilemma of choosing between keeping a fashion doll and wardrobe I had received as a catalogue gift that Christmas, or returning it in favor of a favorite dress I had my heart set on. With limited resources, it had to be one or the other, and finally my grown-up self won out, and we ordered the dress, a lovely pale blue/grey flannel dress with pleated bodice, white collar and an ornamentation of two silver buttons joined by a silver chain on the left shoulder. It was an absolute favorite dress, and was worn time and again, often generating compliments, especially when worn with my new black strap-over wedge shoes, also ordered from the catalogue. If I had to give up my fashion doll, at least the sacrifice had been worth it!

In Wolseley, there were only two stores that carried clothing, and as mentioned previously, variety and selection were limited, due to space and necessity of carrying only what would be needed and useful to the farming community served. Coles, owned and operated by Mr. Stan Cole for many years, and later Robinsons was the clothing and grocery store we always went to for our needs as we were growing up. There was a small ladies shop, Rene's Style Shop down the street from Coles that seemed pretty exclusive and rather expensive. The only thing Mom ever bought there was a peach shorty coat on sale.

It seems to me the operator/owner's name was indeed Rene; she always appeared to me to have just stepped out of a fashion magazine, or was perhaps from another planet as she and the clothing she carried in her little shop seemed so far removed from the reality of the farming community she served, and her prices somewhat exorbitant. There always seemed to be enough clientele among "town" ladies and the French-speaking community to keep the shop viable. In fact one of these ladies took the shop over when Rene left and ran it for a number of years, even in a different, newer location across the street—an asset for a small prairie town to have.

I recall, in about Grade XI during my high school years when a type of leather jacket became popular for ladies, available in an array of pale pastel colors, that was a definite "must-have". Of course they were available in Rene's shop and I remember nearly dying of envy when a class-mate showed up one fine spring day flaunting her new pale blue jacket, bought for her by her working mother from this exclusive shop! It came as a hard blow to my budding female vanity to be told by my parents there was no possible way they would or could pay for such a jacket, and since my baby-sitting jobs were few and far between (always going home to the farm at weekends when most young families needed a baby-sitter), I was only able to save enough for a less expensive version in the same pale blue color from the catalogue! However, it served the purpose and I got many years of faithful service and wear from that jacket, being warm, waterproof and reasonably stylish.

Looking back, it seems the weather played an integral part in how we had to dress, especially in winter to keep warm. Were the winters more severe back then or are we just better equipped today? It seems to me a little of both—there was definitely more snow most winters as I recall, and our centrally-heated homes now make a big difference in how we have to dress even for inside, as opposed to the wood and coal burning stoves and furnaces that heated our farm homes in childhood as mentioned previously.

This was of course before the days of ski-doo suits, nylon outer-shells, fiber-fill or thinsulate! Down and feathers were available from raising poultry on the farms etc., but use of these seemed limited to pillows, eiderdown quilts and other bedding. No one thought to make use of feathers in clothing as inter-linings for light-weight, warmth back then. Synthetics had not yet made an appearance, and natural fabrics like heavy wool, heavy cotton like denim and furs were used for clothing and blankets to keep warm while outdoors working, playing or getting from place to place in cutters and sleighs.

Fur coats and stoles were very popular winter outer-wear for ladies as we were growing up, and I recall both grandmothers owning furs. Gran Sexsmith had the most, luxurious full-length muskrat winter coat with a satiny lining and ties inside. Then large ornate buttons for closure and even a muskrat hat to match. Gran Teasdale always owned a Hudson Seal full-length coat, beautiful black, shiny shorter-cropped fur with similar ornate buttons. It seems to me one Gran or other matronly ladies we knew owned fur or sable stoles around this time, some even having the little furry animal's head, complete with beady, staring eyes attached at each end! These must have undergone some kind of preservative process prior to being part of the garment, and I recall never being too keen on being around or touching these stoles, however, the Grandma's coats were quite something else and we loved to run our hands over their silky, furry surface, or better still to "try them on", whenever allowed, flouncing around like princesses, the length dragging on the floor and the weight, especially of the Hudson Seal nearly immobilizing us! Whenever we saw Gran Sexsmith in her muskrat coat, in town or wherever, the pockets always seemed to have a magical, never-ending supply of quarters in them, or sometimes candy or other treats little ones love, and needless to say, endeared this lovely lady to our hearts even more, as if her love and kind ways weren't enough for any grandchild's needs.

Buffalo furs were made into coats and hats for men and for warm blankets and rugs at that time, the matted, heavy fur lending its warmth, especially for wear during long drives with teams of horses or early cars with limited or no heat. I don't recall knowing any men who owned muskrat or other fur coats at the time, but perhaps there were some.

For outdoor work on the farm in winter farmers wore "layers" of clothing for warmth, rendering tiresome, awkward movement. Long fleece-lined underwear was a "must" next to the skin, then one or two pairs of wool work socks (Dad always held up his socks with garters, elasticized, adjustable straps with a closure and garter attached that were worn on the leg just under the knee), were pulled up over the tucked in underwear. How unusual for these wool work socks, grey with a white and red top band, to be popular foot wear for male and female teenagers now! Rough, scratchy things—I have never been able to figure this out! (Must be a "generation gap"affair).

Mid-calf felt boots were a very common form of footwear worn by men and boys on the farm for winter warmth when we were growing up. They consisted of a 1/2 inch layer of pressed dark grey felt molded into a boot shape in different sizes. A little hole pressed into the sides near the top assisted the wearer in pulling the boot over foot and ankle. They were warm, soft, comfortable, very popular and could be left on all day while inside. For outdoors, a low, slip-on rubber overshoe would be worn, making the unit weather-proof, or else a higher, buckled rubber boot could be worn over this felt boot for negotiating higher snow banks, and for more warmth and dryness. I recall Uncle Herb loved his "felch boots" as he mistakenly always called them, and in winter was never seen in any other kind of footwear, except when dressed up to go out.

Although Dad had several pairs of these felt boots over the years, he also liked his "boots" ankle high, lace-up cork soled leather boots he always wore on his feet for work often in winter and always in summer. They were light yet durable and protective, and I think he found them more comfortable than the felt boots, as his feet tended to sweat quite a lot, like mine. Buckled rubber overshoes were again worn over these boots to protect against, snow and elements. In summer, men and boys wore ankle high laced-up leather work boots in dry weather and pull on high-topped rubber boots over socked feet in wet and rainy weather. Toe rubbers were common foot wear over lace-up black or brown dress oxfords, for men anyway, and for winter boys tended to wear fleece lined rubbers over boots with a pull strap closure around the top, like a belt and buckle or else buckled up the front opening. (Whenever I think of boys wearing rubber boots it brings to mind Allindale school days, recesses in Spring, playing in the culvert run-off in the near-by ditches and Meredith Lister purposely wading in over the tops of his rubbers, after his Dad, Bill had expressly forbidden it, and I, being one of the "older girls" at school, supposed to monitor Meredith's water activities—how exasperating! Having a little brother wouldn't have been much fun after all I decided then, but I always wished we'd had an older brother).

It was also common for school boys of that era to wear high-topped laced running shoes of black canvas with white trim, soles and laces for school in summer, and during holidays going barefoot some of the time. Gordon recalls getting a new pair of such runners every spring, wearing them all summer, until they were outgrown and worn out to be replaced again the following spring. There was nothing quite like these runners worn every day to produce bad cases of "smelly feet" Gordon recalls!

Hand-knit socks of finer wool in argyle/diamond patterns were commonly worn for dress-up by men find boys at that time. I recall Gran Teasdale knitted lots of pairs of socks with this design for her son-in-laws, etc., with Clippie having her knit him pale yellow ones. Romeo slippers made of leather that covered the entire foot like a shoe with a colored elastic vent on each side were also common relaxation footwear for men and boys, and I recall Dad always having a pair to wear around the house.

Denim overalls (BWG brand) were the common choice of pants for farmers in winter. Dad wore his overalls over a kind of drill, dark green cotton pants and matching shirt for extra warmth—the overalls and other outer clothing being shed at the back door after work in the barnyard, as was often wet and smelled strongly of manure from the animals, cleaning the barn etc. A lot of farmers wore denim overalls as their only leg and body covering (after underwear) on a regular basis all year round, perpetuating the common image we have in our minds of farmers in overalls! Farm boys also wore overalls or jeans on a regular basis for chores and school in winter and summer, as they were tough, durable and warm, especially worn over long underwear. Denim domed or zippered coveralls were also worn.

Flannelette shirts in multiple plaid colors were worn on the upper body for warmth and coziness by men and boys in winter, while cotton shirts were a common choice for summer. Pullover sweatshirts we know today had not yet made an appearance, but hand-knit vests and cardigan sweaters were worn. Cowichan siwash sweaters were available in limited supply in larger centers, or were hand knit and worn. I recall Dad had several purchased heavy knitted colored sweaters with white trim called "curling sweaters" he wore for warmth under his outerwear jackets and parkas.

Cotton knit t-shirts, vests and shorts were worn as summer underwear by most men and boys, although Dad always preferred to stay with his light-weight summer long underwear—said he felt "half-dressed" in shorts, and of course his sock garters felt funny against his bare legs! Gordon recalls having summer t-shirts and golf-type collared cotton knit shirts to wear as a boy in stripes and patterns, but most often long or short-sleeved shirts were the norm. Since polyester was not yet available to combine with cotton for a perma-press finish, even work and school/play cotton shirts had to be ironed like dress shirts, as they would come off the outside drying line or indoor clothes horse wrinkled and stiff—bah! Poor homemakers back then! (Good job Mom always liked to iron—by her own admission).

Denim smocks or loose fitting collared, short coats with snap closures and pockets were often worn as a jacket over overalls when needed for warmth winter and summer. Hooded parkas were then worn over these smocks for winter warmth. I recall Dad buying a gold-colored shiny fabric parka with a pretty fur-trimmed hood for "better wear" and also a bright jacket of orange/rust/yellow shades in square patterns at Coles store over the years while we were growing up. He always hated the gold parka, stating it had no warmth what-so-ever, while the brightly shaded jacket he wore and wore, first for better and then later for the yard. He always felt the cold so much in winter.

Of course hands had to be covered in winter for warmth and protection. Usually one or two pairs of hand-knitted mitts were worn under leather ones by all family members, for work and school. Consequently, the "knitters" in the family, were always kept busy providing these woolen mitts, especially as the children grew, or adults wore them out. Gloves with fingers were made of leather, suede, cotton or knitted of wool, but were mostly used for dress-wear, as they looked nicer, but weren't as warm as mitts. Dad often wore leather gloves for certain jobs even in summer, gauntlet-types that protected the wrists and forearms when stooking or stacking, or shorter wrist-length ones for fencing, stone-picking, etc.

Men and boy's headgear for work on the farm always consisted of a cap of some kind as head protection from the sun and other elements. Dad had a favorite wine colored corduroy cap lined with a quilted material that had a flap that covered ears and neck, for use on cold winter days. I recall him wearing this same cap for many winters. In summer vented, peaked caps were commonly worn. Some farmers wore "railway caps" made of striped black/white denim; still others wore brimmed straw hats in summer for work. As mentioned previously, hooded parkas were a must in winter, often worn over caps when needed for extra warmth. For better wear, black and white tweed caps with a domed peak were very common headgear for the male population as we were growing up. Gordon recalls as a boy, having a cap of this kind that was his absolute favorite hat for all occasions. He loved it with a passion, and was most distraught when his brother Helmuth purposely threw it into a stump-burning fire causing its untimely demise; he still recalls the incident with sadness, and no other cap could ever replace this special lost one. Dad had several natty looking brimmed straw hats for better wear over the years, often sporting a decorative band plus a little feather.

Boys and girls wore knitted woolen toques on their heads and often several scarves tied around head and neck for winter warmth—again keeping the knitters in the family busy! Ski pants, lined or quilted heavy cotton outer pants with reinforced knees and cuffed at the ankles were often worn by both boys and girls in public school as play wear or for chores. I recall as girls, Connie and I having several angora wool bonnets with ties under the chin, fondly knitted for us by Gran Teasdale. It seems to me we had mittens to match in this fluffy, warm angora, made from rabbit fur—soft, grey with pink trim. I recall angora was popular for knitted articles at that time, and some even had sweaters and vests knitted from it. Kind of fluffy to work with, getting up your nose and in your eyes, but lovely to wear and so warm, and we were grateful to Gran for making these items for us. I remember I even knitted my Annie doll a bonnet, with left over blue angora wool Gran had used to knit Aunt Alice a pair of gloves.

For church and better wear, men and boys usually had at least one suit or pants and sports jacket, long or bow neck tie and a white long or short-sleeved shirt. Pastel colored shirts for the male population had not yet made their appearance, and being made entirely of cotton, had to be washed, starched and ironed after each wearing, as previously discussed in care of clothing. I recall Dad owning two suits only during all of our growing up years, a dark green/turquoise striped one and a pale brown striped (the color of this suit always reminded me of chocolate cake batter, as it was the exact same color) one he wore alternately whenever a "good" occasion arose. (Dad, not much for buying new clothing for himself back then, finally relented and bought a new suit for Gordon's and my wedding—little did any of us realize at the time that, sadly, two short years later this would also be his burial suit).

Dad was especially proud of an outfit he bought, again at Coles/Robinsons store, of a fitted sports jacket in a mint green and white tiny check pattern, grey pants and hat. He liked to look nice, and was especially dapper in this particular outfit! He had a passion for nice ties, and always liked to receive one as a gift. He used monogrammed cotton handkerchiefs to wipe his nose always, and was never without one. White for dress-up and colored and patterned for everyday. He had no use for disposable tissues and continued to prefer "his hankies" all his life.

Long top coats were worn over suits or other dress-wear when the weather warranted more warmth. Dad always wore a long brown cloth coat with a yellow scarf and brown felt brimmed hat, again with a little fancy feather trim. Of course in severe winter weather parkas were the only sensible choice for warmth.

Sleepwear for men and boys then as now was pajamas of flannelette for winter with long sleeves and legs, and cotton for summer with short sleeves and legs. Some other accessories I recall Dad and other men wearing back then were braces to help hold up their pants, in addition to a belt. Being rather slim in build, I think Dad felt his braces gave him added assurance his pants would never fall down! He had several pairs, heavier for work and thinner and finer for dress, in different colors. It is curious to see them return to style and fashion now and then. Braces also made an excellent "swing" for a house-mouse when hung upside down on pants in a closet—this actually happened at home!

Stretchy fine wire arm bands worn over long-sleeved shirts just below the elbow, helped men adjust sleeve length to suit their particular arm length, as shirts weren't sold in individual arm lengths then as they are available today, and the arm band would take up the slack of a sleeve that was too long. Ornate or monogrammed tie clips were commonly worn to attach long ties to shirts, either with a spring clip or a little chain and piece to insert into a shirt buttonhole. Some men wore pocket watches with a fob chain attached, but Dad always owned a nice gold wrist watch he wore for dress wear, a gift from Mom. I recall him also using a collar stay with his dress shirts. This item consisted of a thin wire support that fitted under the tie at the neck, while the pin points extended down to be stuck in under each collar point to keep it down and flat against the shirt, much as buttoned-down collars do today.

Wallets and billfolds were used then as now for carrying money. Some younger men of that era carried upright leather wallets in their back pockets, the top of the wallet having a chain looped through a metal eyelet that attached to their belt loop for added security. It seems to me long handled rat-tailed combs were carried by young men in their back pockets, to frequently maintain their Brylcream-slicked back hair styles, popular at the time! Men who smoked carried their "pouches" containing loose tobacco in order to make a "roll-your-own" cigarette whenever the need arose. These pouches consisted of a leather 4x6 inch zippered pouch, lined with a kind of thin rubber lining that kept the tobacco carried and stored therein moist and fresh. This pouch was filled each day or every few days from a can of tobacco that always sat at our house on the kitchen window ledge. Dad always smoked Vogue tobacco and I can still recall the attractive tin of pale gold with the face and upper body of a stylish woman (in vogue) outlined in a pale orange pencil thin design. A silver lid embossed with the Vogue insignia and an official seal that we sometimes removed and used for play-money (as it grey and white and looked a bit like paper money), guaranteed fresh product, and heavy foil surrounded the tobacco.

Vogue cigarette papers in a little booklet of the same design as the tin were always carried in the pouch or shirt pocket, along with loose stick matches or lighter. These papers were thin like the perm papers of today with a glued edge that had to be licked and folded over the tobacco "just so" to complete the finished cigarette. There was a real knack to rolling a good cigarette, and Dad's seemed to turn out just right, as opposed to the ones Uncle Herb used to roll for instance, all squiggly and thin, not neat! Occasionally, we would take a notion to roll Dad some cigarettes, but they never turned out quite right. I recall the Mortons had a special metal instrument designed to fill empty rolled/sealed papers that could be purchased in boxes back then—the idea being to save a little on buying the bulk, tinned tobacco, but not having to roll and lick them. I always thought this was kind of neat—no one thought of cigarettes or their second-hand smoke as being a bad thing back in those days, and it was considered socially acceptable, even suave and stylish to smoke. Perhaps this is why teenagers were so tempted to start this awful habit at an early age and addict themselves before realizing they were ruining their health.

Dad got a nasty cut on his lower lip one winter from a flying chip while cutting wood, and because it wouldn't heal, and more and more was beginning to be written about smoking being bad for us, he decided to start using cigarette holders with his cigarettes and continued to do so for a number of years. Pipe and cigar smokers were quite common also at the time. Stylish women of that era often used long, elegant cigarette holders, and were pictured puffing away, wafting these holders around in the air, and we all thought it so avante garde! (They still had to be cleaned of their messy, tarry, smelly contents that built up inside from time to time—one could have assumed then inhaling such could not be good for a person). Cigarettes could also be purchased in soft packages already rolled and filled. Later still the packages were made of harder cardboard with two slip out carriers and wrapped in foil, just like today. The only difference being filters are on the ends now, for perhaps 3 decades, as opposed to just the tobacco ends back then.

There probably were other items of dress for men and boys of this era, that I may have failed to present, however the things I have recorded are the memories I have from the men and boys known to me at the time, namely Dad, uncles, neighbors, cousins and boys at school. It seems to me with regard to footwear there is one kind I have failed to mention, as I don't recall my own Dad owning a pair, however, I remember seeing them on other men at the time. I refer to high-topped leather boots with reinforced steel toes, laced with leather laces that were worn by some men for their farm work, and those involved in construction or working with heavy equipment. I remember Irvin Arndt having a pair when he helped Mr. Scheibler build our house on the farm—he was my idol back then, even though I was just a little girl, and I remember those high leather boots he wore all those years ago. Also a hermit-type man mentioned previously always wore this type of boot. Some Western types also wore leather cowboy boots in grey, brown or black with tooled designs and a high slanted heel, designed much the same as they are today.

The previous account has purposely recorded current fashions worn by men and boys in our farming community as we were growing up, with occasional cross-references that applied to both male and female clothing. What follows will be an account of what I recall about women's and girl's fashions at that time.

As with male clothing, female apparel was frequently dictated by the weather, and often style and fashion had to be forsaken for warmth out of necessity, especially in winter! Cotton, fleece-lined vests (shirties) with sleeves and panties of similar fabric were worn by girls for warmth in the winter months. Since it was not common for women and girls to wear slacks and pants, as they do today, (and wonderful leotards and panty hose had not yet come along), stockings had to be worn over legs and under skirts and dresses. Girls were limited to brown ribbed cotton knit stockings that wrinkled and bagged and simply were ugly! We could hardly wait to graduate up to the lovely silk stockings ladies wore back then, with a seam down the back that had to kept straight in the middle of the calf to look nice!

I can still remember getting my first pair to wear for the grade VIII Christmas concert at Allindale, and what a thrill it was to feel their silky softness next to bare legs after those horrible cotton ribbed ones. (On thinking back, were stockings still made from silk or nylon or perhaps a blend of both—with nylon [the new synthetic] taking over the scene in a few years, I can't be sure). I recall Mom telling me that during WW II when all available silk was used by the forces for parachutes, silk stockings were in very short supply, and women used to go bare legged, even for dress-up, penciling a make-believe line down the centre of their calves and ankles to give the illusion of legs covered with stockings! So, as late as "the War Years" (1939-1945) it would seem silk was still being utilized for ladies stockings, with a gradual change-over to nylon, then nylon with lycra and revolutionary pantyhose in the '60's—and whoopee—no more garters were required! I recall Mom hated this transition to pantyhose and continued to wear nylons that required garters until they were all but impossible to buy. She also had a passion for fancy "clocked" nylons—ones that had swirls and designs at the heel and ankle—they must have been "stamped" on in a kind of velvet material of some kind. These designs were always black and quite attractive for dress wear back then.

Lisle stockings, an "in-between" light-weight seamed cotton stocking were sometimes worn by girls and women as we grew up, and I believe are still available today, as brother-in-law Barry presented me with a pair as a joke at my 50th Birthday Party! They were better than those ugly ribbed ones smaller girls were forced to wear, and tended not to run as easily as the nylon ones. I recall wearing lisle stockings in the last year or so at Allindale, and feeling quite grown up!

It was common practice for women to wear a garment or girdle with control front, to keep tummy tucked in and as an attachment for garters that held up their stockings, that were worn for homemaking as well as dress-up. Girls wore a garter-belt (or "stays") around their waist or smaller girls a harness type over their shoulders with garters attached, that went over the shirt, but under the panties.

While girls then wore ski-pants over their dresses and skirts to keep their legs and lower bodies warm under their parka tops, women wore warm wooly over pants and protective woolen overstocking over their silk ones. The foot part consisted of only an elasticized heel strap, and elasticized top that simply "stayed up" on upper thigh when pulled on, as they fit snugly. For as long as I knew her, Gran Teasdale had to wear a heavy support stocking on her one leg for severe varicosities, and I always felt sorry for her because of that, especially in the hot summer weather. Nowadays, a simple surgical procedure or laser treatment could easily have relieved her of those diseased veins. How good we have things now, compared to back then.

Both grandmothers and I suspect all ladies of their era grew up wearing corsets to support their figures. So it was, that when I knew them, both Grans continued to wear their corsets to support their bosoms, tummies and backs, as well as to provide garters for their stockings. Corsets were always made from a pinky-beige or white colored brocade worn over silk or cotton vests. A series of laces on the right side could be tightened or loosened to fit the individual ladies figure. On the left side a row of tiny hooks and eyes enabled the wearer to secure the garment for daytime wear, and to take it off at bedtime. Long legged pantaloons of silky jersey or cotton were then worn over the bottom.

Corsets always seemed to me like some kind of torture chamber, with their confining metal "stays" sewn right into the garment, not to mention the uncomfortable heat they must have generated in summer, but ladies of this vintage were used to them and wouldn't be persuaded to graduate to a girdle, or worse yet just bra and panties—it seemed to come down to what they were used to and felt proper and appropriate wearing. A full or half slip of cotton, satin or rayon was worn under dresses and skirts. Camisole tops were sometimes worn under sheer blouses, especially as it became more fashionable to wear slacks, and a full-length slip was not required as it had been with dresses and skirts. Slip and bra straps were fitted with metal glides for adjustment, much as they are today, but without the comfort and give of synthetic blends as we are accustomed to now. Crinoline slips consisting of a top and skirt part with several layers of scratchy white net to pouf out full, gathered skirts were popular especially while we attended high school.

Younger women wore brassieres to support their bosoms of similar design to the ones worn today, being made of white or black cotton fabric, as opposed to the myriad of colors and synthetic fabrics available now. I can still recall the bitter-sweet reality of puberty, when it seemed appropriate to begin wearing a white lacey training bra (a hand-me-down in some box of clothes from Aunts or cousins), but it meant giving up my cozy cotton shirties that I'd became so accustomed to wearing over my girlhood years. It was a great feeling to be growing up, but sad leaving behind what had felt good and was comfortable for something that felt anything but comfortable, just for the sake of becoming a young woman, and having to wear the customary articles of clothing dictated by fashion. Nice to see a return of vests and camisole tops for women again lately.

In summer, girls wore sleeveless cotton knit vests with a little shoulder strap and silk or cotton panties. Ankle or knee high socks in colors to match outfits were available and worn on feet and legs as opposed to the ribbed stockings of winter. It was common to go barefoot in summer holidays, or just to wear sandals on bare feet. Mom often went bare-legged as well in summer, but always wore nylon "sockies" she had made from cut-off nylon stockings in her favorite tan-colored canvas lace-up shoes she always wore for working at home for as long as I can remember. Purchased footlets were similar to the lisle stockings mentioned previously, in weight and color, and consisted of a foot covering with elasticized top that were worn in shoes for a barefoot appearance but the feeling of a sock or stocking. (Nylon knee-highs were a '70's creation).

Although I don't remember much about them, Mom always wore ankle high white laced up leather shoes on me as a little girl, as I recall from pictures, the thinking back then being to give little feet as much support as possible in their formative years. Little ankle socks were worn on feet, the tops pulled out over the shoe tops and folded down all around. I remember having low brown laced up oxfords with three little lines designed over each toe to begin school at age six, and subsequent pairs of these same leather oxfords in black or brown through the younger years.

When I was a little older and could have more say in choosing my own footwear, I liked penny loafers, popular at the time, (a new shiny copper penny in the front slot made these loafers even more attractive), or else low moccasin-type loafers, inspired by the little girl featured in my favorite book at the time "On Cherry Street". I recall Gran Teasdale not thinking much of my choice of loafer shoes, and supplying me with a proper pair of low brown leather oxfords with lovely swirled designs on the toes, she had bought herself in Indian Head, because of her strong conviction to "proper shoes". I think I gave them "token" wear when I knew Gran would be seeing me, and then continued to wear my loafers as well, as they were my choice!

I also remember these same loafers getting me in trouble one day while playing with Audrey, as one of the knots along the heel got caught in Aunt Ruby's beautiful crocheted lace dining room table cloth, as Audrey and I ran by it in play. The cloth sustained a tear from a mirror and parakeet ornament on top that came crashing to the floor with the cloth. (If only I'd worn my oxfords on that day—it would have saved a lot of grief!) I still feel bad about this incident to this day, although neither of us got a spanking, just a verbal reprimand, the embarrassment and guilt were enough penance. (I may have mentioned this before, but it is an indelible memory, I have always felt sorry about, and bears repeating).

Girls also wore saddle oxfords as we were growing up and I can recall having two pair during this time. They were white low leather laced up oxfords with a "saddle" of navy blue leather along each side extending to the laced part. They were considered very stylish back then during the bobby-sox era of rock-n-roll, and were probably a very sensible type of footwear, considering the fast-paced type of jive dancing we all did at the time! Also, about this time white bucks were also worn by young people, girls and boys, patterned after Pat Boone, a popular pop singer of the day, who always wore these shoes. They were a low laced up oxford made of soft white suede (buck) that were lovely to look at when new, but the pits to maintain for active teenagers in high school—not very practical but of course to be in style with one's peer group was everything! They could be "brushed" clean at first when new, then finally white polished that cleaned them but ultimately ruined their suede leather finish. Both Grans always wore laced black oxfords with a 2-inch heel for every day wear and dress-up.

Sock pins were popular as ornamentation on girl's socks, and I recall owning several pair. They were small broaches with safety clasps in silver or gold metal patterned in small designs like butterflies, flowers, little birds, etc. These pins were worn on the outside folded over edge of ankle socks, and if possible, matched to the girl's outfit of the day. Cotton socks with folded looped terry edges were all the rage at the time I recall wearing sock pins.

Sandals in white, brown, black or some pastel colors were commonly worn by girls in summer and strap over shoes for winter as well as oxfords. Low laced-up canvas runners were also common footwear in summer, with white being the most popular. High heels were at least three inch at this time, often clickered, and considered the only appropriate dress wear for women, enhancing the foot and leg in fashionable elegance, but the devil to wear for any length of time. Mom always loved her high-heeled shoes and danced many a mile in them with Dad. She often said she would have liked to wear them to work in for every day, but wouldn't have been practical, or very good for her back, legs or feet in the long run I'm sure. Thank goodness by the time we were of an age to wear them, the height of the heels was a more tolerable one or two inches, but the toes were more pointed, impinging on the toes and subsequent comfort. Sandals were also common footwear for women in summer, with a flat, wedged or high heel, and were available in white or colors.

For outdoors, rubber boots in white and some colors were worn by girls in summer, while for ladies an ankle height type of rubber was available with a flat sole while a button and elastic closed a flapped-over piece on the outer side. I recall these rubbers were made of a kind of clear blue/grey rubber and could be worn with a flat or high-heeled shoe to keep dry in rainy summer weather. For winter, girls wore cute little laced up ankle boots of white rubber, trimmed with white fur, often with a fur muff that was worn around the neck, and had a slot at each end to put tiny hands in for warmth. I recall having such a matched outfit of rubbers and muff, my muff having a little doll's head and face perched on top as a fancy touch! Ladies wore overshoes with or without a heel, made of a kind of velvety covered rubber, and lined with a soft brushed material for warmth. They often sported fur tops and closed with a zipper on the inside of the foot or else buckles on the front. When I was in high school, I recall it became fashionable to wear winter boots directly over the socked or stockinged foot and to carry your shoes in a shoe bag. I remember having a pair of zippered, low-heeled boots with a little bit of faux-fur around the upper edge that I felt were very stylish and quite warm with their nylon pile lining. High leather boots became fashionable in the 1960's to wear with "hot pants" and "mini-skirts", lined or unlined depending on the season. Buckled-up rubbers were replaced almost entirely by zippered ones for ease and convenience. Thank goodness we were never subjected to the high buttoned shoes and boots popular when our mothers grew up, that had to be closed with a special hook, but are now popular again for some in the late 1990's as I record this.

As with male clothing, female clothes were limited to the fabrics available at the time like silk, rayon, crepe, jersey, cotton and wool. Some nylon must have been available, as I recall Mom having a pretty lime green nylon blouse with a pleated front and pearl buttons she seemed to wear a lot and when I took part in the Wilson and Stark weddings, my dresses were made of pink nylon, as well as my white Confirmation dress.

Hemlines have varied over the years, dictated by fashion. While we were growing up fashions for ladies were mid-calf and longer. Girls didn't seem as affected for dress/skirt length, and I recall most of my outfits were knee length or just below it. Mom would never allow Connie or I to wear jeans, subsequently we didn't even own any until years later when we were grown up, or perhaps Connie had some for high school. Mom always considered them as boy's apparel and not appropriate dress for girls, even for rough-housing or play. I always remember kind of resenting this, and being continually envious of my cousin Audrey who almost grew up in her blue jeans. Mom had a pair of pale green slacks she had sewn for herself to wear outside for warmth or gardening at times, and these were the only pair of pants I can ever recall her owning, as we grew up. We had slacks made of corduroy or cotton or overalls for play.

Mentioning overalls, I recall an unfortunate incident that happened to me at about age 8 or 9 while playing with my cousin Dwight during summer holidays one year. I was wearing my wine-colored cotton overalls to play in that day, and while using their canister-type toilet upstairs for bathroom duty, the one strap of my overalls accidentally fell into the toilet coming in contact with the messy contents. I remember being horrified to have let such a thing happen, especially away from home, and there not being any girls in their family to allow a change of clothing. I wiped the offending strap off with paper as best as I could, and washed it a bit in the basin of cold water and soap, however I remember spending the remainder of the day in a rather odiferous state, too embarrassed to consult his Mom, Eileen and too shy to tell Dwight. Fortunately, a good washing once I got home that evening of overalls and self helped everything seem right again.

Coats as mentioned previously were often fur or cloth with fur trim on collars and cuffs. Station wagon coats were popular for men and women as we grew up, and I remember envying Audrey again, as she had one as a girl. They were a fawn color of brown in a woven kind of fabric with a fine diagonal line, double breasted with two rows of large buttons in front and belted with a matching belt and buckle. Faux fur collar and lapels, heavily padded shoulders, side self-finished pockets and back kick pleat completed the look of this coat. It seems to me women of all ages wore these popular coats, as well as boys and men.

Mom had a brown, nubby fabric coat for winter with a lovely red fox full collar and lapels I recall she wore for a long time as we grew up. For summer, she had a full cerise-colored cloth coat with huge self finished buttons. The body of the coat fell in heavy gathers from a yoke at the shoulders and was unbelted. I recall she wore this coat whenever she went out in spring and fall and the particular fall she was pregnant with Connie, no one even knew of her expanding state with her wearing this very full cerise coat! She also had the rose colored shorty coat mentioned previously, as they were fashionable back then. Mom never had a fur coat—said she didn't need one and wouldn't be happy in one, however it was probably more lack of the means to buy such a warm coat at that time, than anything else.

I recall some of the coats I owned back then was a little full-length princess line coat of pale turquoise colored wool, with tiny flap pockets that had embroidery trim on them and the collar. It was always kind of itchy on my chin when done up, but I recall it was warm for spring and fall wear, and I remember wearing it to start school at Allindale. Gran Sexsmith fashioned several coats for me and I wore them a lot. One was a little green short coat with silky lining, gold buttons and pockets in kind of a boxy style. The other was a winter parka made from an Air-force great coat that had been stored "in the trunk" of clothes in our basement previously, and smelled of mildew, because of the dampness. Mom and Gran always assured me the mildew smell would wear off it in time, however it never did, and as warm as that jacket was with hood, lining and ski pants Gran also made to go with it, I never liked it because of that smell!

Gran Teasdale knitted me a royal blue sweater with grey-trim and cuffs and grey buttons that was lovely, but I couldn't wear it until she lined the sleeves with full-length white silk.

I must have been wool-sensitive even back then as I am today. I recall Connie and I having matching grey jackets with pink pile lining and toggle closures as girls, and later I had a black jacket with little white slubs and luxurious grey pile lining throughout that was very warm and cozy for high school. It seems to me Mom inherited it and wore it for years later as a yard and chore coat. Another favorite was a long blue princess line coat with faux-leopard trim on the collar and pockets I wore for good during public school years. A long wooly wine colored coat and later a blue/grey checked long coat with huge blue buttons and a beige/white checked with even larger buttons and a foamy lining also come to mind. I can't help but mention the joy I felt being able to purchase a shorty muskrat fur jacket shortly after getting out of nurse's training. Rose and I thought we had died and gone to heaven every time we put on these stylish coats. We had bought them together at Western Furs from a former patient of hers that happened to be the manager and who kindly gave us a very good deal on them.

Rain coats mostly consisted of clear plastic topper coats we wore over our regular coats with snap closures and hoods. All-weather coats had not made an appearance as yet that I recall. Umbrellas were sometimes used by ladies in town for rainy weather, however I don't recall Mom ever owning one. We used Orval Brown's tractor umbrella he kindly brought over to shield me from the rain on my wedding day, as I went from house to car on the farm on the way to the church. Silk parasols were a common play item for little girls, and I recall Connie and I each getting little silk ones made in turquoise and orange sections with a curved bamboo handle at the Exhibition one year when we were girls. We thought we were quite stylish and grown up, keeping the sun off us as we played in the farm yard etc. Parasols always seemed to be an item wealthy ladies carried in magazine pictures or in the movies, not in real life!

Hats were a very common item of dress as we grew up, and outfits for dress-up often came with matching or coordinated hats. Since it was necessary to wear them to cover heads in the Anglican Church back then, I have discussed hats previously with attendance at St. George's Church. It was common to wear head scarves and colorful kerchiefs knotted under the chin, to keep hair in place and sometimes for warmth. They came in light-weight patterned silks and later synthetics or heavier fabrics like wool etc. It seemed to be a joke back then that wearing a scarf tied over the head and under the chin was being "like an old German lady" especially when it was referred to as a babushka, as it seemed older women of this heritage especially, wore head scarves in this manner. As girls, we often received good quality, pretty scarves as gifts from Aunts in England, and still to this day I have some of them that I treasure, wearing them now as neck scarves with coats, etc., rather than on the head. Long knitted scarves were wound around the head over hooded coats to protect faces from harsh winter winds and snow as we grew up.

Occasionally women protected their hair from the sun or while house cleaning by tying similar scarves backwards, with the flat fold at the nape of the neck and the ends in a tucked in knot at the centre of the forehead. I recall turbans being worn by women-folk as we grew up, although the fashion seemed to have waned before we ever got to wear them. Gran Teasdale seemed to own several of these colorful head coverings that were made of a soft jersey-type of fabric. The crown was sewn in front into a kind of top-knot and then long ends wound around the head and tucked in at the back, completely covering the hair (these were especially good on "bad hair days")! Girls wore knitted bonnets, or toques as mentioned previously, and tams were popular. Cousin Audrey had a favorite red tam she always wore, and I recall having a white one. They were always made of a kind of pressed wool, with a little top knot in the centre, and often were worn at a stylish angle, the tight inner band keeping it in place.

Purses were often part of an outfit, being matched to shoes in a corresponding or complimentary color. However, a basic leather purse in white for summer and black or brown for winter, sufficed for most needs, especially for the farm women I knew. I recall Mom had two purses made of ornate squares of plastic all joined together with woven cotton thread that we called her "Chiclet" purses, as they resembled the little boxed, coated gums that could be bought in packages that became popular back then called by that same name. It seems to me she had a brown one and also a white one. Ladies usually carried purses with short handles, while girls tended to have the shoulder kind. Ladies purses came equipped with little clasped change purses attached to the inside of the purse with a little elastic string for easy access, and to keep money separate from the rest of the purse. Wallets were not carried in purses, as they are today.

I had a "passion" for purses as a girl and owned many of them over the years. Audrey always had an enviable collection, and I can still recall one particular purse she had made of soft brown leather, that had short handles, a clear clasp closure and had a delicate pink lining. I used to beg her to let me play with it whenever I was visiting, and she quite often would let me—I would feel like a little lady that day, playing with that particular purse! I had a little red purse with shoulder strap, zipper closure and a little pouch in front lined with white plastic ornamented with men and ladies dressed in old-fashioned clothing. A tooled leather purse that I laced together as a craft was another favorite as I grew up, as well as a white boxy one with "see-through" plastic sides, handles, clasp and little white flower ornamentation on the front side. I always longed for an actual authentic Mexican tooled leather purse, and finally received one from the Andris who had visited Mexico when I was renting a suite in their home as a young nurse—needless to say I was thrilled and enjoyed carrying it many years after that.

Change purses for girls consisted of fold-over decorated smaller plastic cases with zipper or clasp closure and inside a row of pronged divisions just the right size for each denomination of change, that could be slid into each divide at an angle and held securely. I recall being at a Sport's Day in Wolseley held at the local fair grounds each summer, going around with cousin Audrey. She had a friend visiting her from the States, who had one of these change purses simply "loaded" with change, each division full of quarters, dimes, nickels and pennies. I had never seen a child carrying around so much money, for indeed one or two quarters seemed to be the extent of my wealth most of the time back then! Several wallets I recall owning as a girl were made of plastic—the fold up type with a clasp, with places for change, bills and pictures of family and all my pen pals back then etc., much as wallets of today. One was pale blue, quite decorative, with a simulated woven and scrolled covering, while the other was smooth pearly white with gold ornamentation. A patient once made me a tooled leather wallet of similar design as just cited, with my initials tooled on the front. Later leather clasped Lady Buxton wallets, designed more like a small purse were popular, and I recall owning several over the years. My romance of shoes and purses continues to this day, and I am still very fond of each, owning many coordinated sets and separates over the years.

I recall both Grans owned fabric shopping bags with two wooden handles at the top, so they must have been popular with their age group as we grew up. The handles were smooth varnished wood finished with an oval opening for the hands and a spindle below this to attach the casing of the fabric body. Gran Teasdale made hers out of the same fabric as her front room drapes, kind of a maroon with panels of ivory and gold swirls covered with large flowers in subdued colors. She carried the best things in it, often taking it uptown to bring home her purchases, etc. When I was hospitalized with my earache as a girl, she visited me every night, bringing warm celery soup and crackers in this fabric shopping bag, and I remember it was just the right temperature to have right away, being in that warm toasty bag! Gran Sexsmith's shopping bag was made of beige woven fabric, patterned in an up and down stripe. She embroidered a pair of parrots on the front of hers, stamped first with a stencil and then the design was worked in brightly colored wool. She also carried many goodies in her bag when she came to visit, but my favorite time was when it contained her nightgown, as that meant she was going to stay overnight for a visit. It usually also contained her knitting, as she was always working on a pair of mitts or socks for someone, or some other craft or sewing.

As far as indoor clothing went, as mentioned previously, most was bought from the local stores, catalogues or hand-made. Dresses and skirts and blouses were the most common style of apparel for girls and women, and it was an exception to see pants on anyone of the female gender. Although I recall having a pair of slacks towards the end of Allindale school years that were referred to as "drapes" of a black rayon blended fabric with a little slub pattern, very full and pleated at the front waist. A matching fabric belt attached with loops at the back and buttoned down flaps at each side of the front. A school friend and I both had a pair and felt we were quite stylish in our "pants"! Hemlines were mid-calf for the most part or longer, fashion having just gone through a short-skirt phase during the War Years. The advent of synthetic fabrics and yarns revolutionized the clothing industry. Sweaters and sweater sets of Nylon, Orlon and Banlon in soft pastel colors were very popular and worn with skirts, and as pants became more and more acceptable for women's wear, with slacks and later pant suits, with matched pants and jackets.

There was a little joke back then between Connie and I that we still recall sometimes today and have a little laugh! It was while she was still attending Allindale and I was in training at Grey Nuns' with hardly a cent to my name. I had many grandiose plans what I might do with all the money I would be making when my training days were behind me and I would finally be earning a substantial wage as a nurse. I promised I would be able to buy her Banlon sweater "sets" (plural-no less) and other nice items of clothing we had always longed for as girls. Needless to say, after I graduated, several major purchases with monthly payments, like my shorty muskrat jacket and stainless steel cookware, put my generous plans for gift items to my sister in an "indefinite holding pattern", and I don't recall ever presenting Connie with those sweater sets as promised so long ago!

Bathing suits weren't much of a priority for us while we were growing up, having very little opportunity to get to a beach or pool, with the dug-out water being forbidden. Katepwa was our nearest lake and we would sometimes venture there for a Sunday afternoon some summers. As mentioned previously, there was always swimming lessons offered at the dam beach in Wolseley each summer holidays, and Mom even offered to drive us back and forth so we would learn to swim, however we were never brave enough to try it, for which I am sorry now. I don't even remember owning a bathing suit until I was at least 10 or 12 years old. It was a burgundy/grey on white cotton with an elasticized top and a little skirt, not form fitting. I also recall having a stretchy, form fitting one of turquoise with white trim that I wore to get a beautiful suntan lying on the lawn at the farm one summer. I recall receiving another beautiful gold, satiny bathing suit for a birthday gift one year from my aunts, and being forced to try it on by Aunt Alice and Audrey against my wishes, as I was painfully modest and shy, especially about having to model it for everyone present also! It seems to me it didn't fit very well and was taken back and exchanged for a more suitable and useful gift.

I remember a rather painful recollection I have about going on a holiday with Aunt Elsie to the Marlin cottage at the Lake (I think Katepwa) prior to beginning school, and having no bathing suit at all, except a pair of white cotton panties Mom had sent along for me to wear in case I went in the water, which I guess she thought was doubtful. Well, it turned out there was a family staying in the cottage next door that had a little girl almost my age, that befriended me wanting to play and go in the water. She seemed to be an only child and spoiled, having everything a child could want for toys, clothes etc. She couldn't believe she had met up with someone who didn't have a bathing suit, and I recall nearly dying of embarrassment having to finally don my "one-piece suit" if I wanted to have any fun playing in the water! I guess it didn't seem very important to grown ups to cover a little chest back then, but it would have meant all the world to me on that holiday to have had a proper bathing suit to wear—it still saddens me to think of it. Why didn't we think of a t-shirt covering I wonder now? Having learned from my painful experience it seems to me Connie had bathing suits at a much earlier age, and often wore them to play in, like a summer play suit. I recall a pale yellow one in jersey-like material and later a little floral skirted one with orange trim.

My account of bathing suits that may have been in style for ladies back then is rather limited, as to my knowledge Mom never owned one or at least one that fitted her as we were growing up. I recall seeing pictures of her in what appeared to be a knitted, black form fitting one as a young woman, and I seem to remember Aunt Elsie having a floral cotton one with a shaped bodice and a skirt. Of course with the advent of stretch fabrics, many more fashion options were available for the manufacture of more stylish and form-fitting bathing wear.

I recall my teachers at Allindale being among the ladies I admired the most while growing up, for their manner of dressing as well as for their independence at such a young age. I remember Miss Audrey Adams always wore bright dresses and skirts often with a navy blue blazer overtop. Miss Jeannine Railton wore stylish skirts and blouses a lot with lovely black wedged slip-on shoes and often a kind of zippered smock in a pretty pale coral color that looked so nice with her dark, long wavy hair. Having her as a teacher for two terms I suppose of all my teachers I admired her the most for her style, poise, manner and crafting abilities (taught me to crochet—Mom still has the blue colored doily). Miss Mary Thompson, later Mary Brown, who married local farmer Ivan, and remained in our district and in our lives to this day, was right up there with my favorites—I especially always liked her strap-over sandals—it seems to me she had a white and black pair. Miss Edna Nelson also remained at Allindale for two terms, always wearing the latest styles of the day we could emulate and admire. Although I didn't particularly like Miss Clark's teaching methods, I recall she had a lovely royal blue suit she often wore with a cerise colored blouse that I just loved, because of its color.

I have mentioned previously, the naughty childish delight I seemed to derive from scrunching up the skirts of my lovely silk dresses and biting a little hole in the lot. I seemed to have many of these dresses in pastel shades of pink, blue, white and pale yellow, with little white collars and cuffs, often smocked across the chest, with large tie belts at the back. I'm sure I had some cotton ones as well, that must have required a lot of upkeep and care on Mom's part, as well as fixing all those bite marks! (I think I even got spankings that didn't help)!

I recall many lovely outfits of clothes we had as girls that were gifts from a favorite uncle (Grandad Teasdale's brother), Wilfred Teasdale, or Unky as we fondly called him. With the help of Aunt Alice, they had wonderful shopping trips when he would come to visit each summer from Vancouver, B.C. where he lived. He would first stop in Regina, and take in the races at Exhibition time, and supply all the funding for these shopping expeditions. Then he would arrive in Wolseley, visiting Gran for a while and always spending a few days staying at our farm, bringing those wonderful clothes gifts along with him.

Some of the outfits I recall he brought me over the years—all of them favorites were: a lovely lawn cotton dress with very pale pastel horizontal stripes with a little white lace collar and front button closure, that I called my "rainbow" dress"; a hunter green corduroy jumper with gold buttons and a crossed-over front closure, that went with a pale yellow cotton striped blouse; another jumper in brown/orange plaid fabric, with a pleated, butterfly skirt; a striped white/pale burgundy dress with a pretty pique front; a dress in brown and red plaid and a rounded-yoke front of eyelet; another pleated skirt in plaids of yellow/blue/black/white and my very favorite reversible pla≈id pleated skirt in turquoise/pink and blue shades that I wore a great deal with all my sweaters and blouses as it went with everything. I recall a pink sundress with shoulder ties and pink pique fabric dresses Mom made us for a church picnic that unfortunately was rained out, and we never took off our coats!

An Allindale school friend and I ordered matching dresses from the catalogue one winter. I dearly recall they were comfy to wear being made of a soft-brushed cotton/rayon blend with plaid trim on collar, the tie at the neck and on the short sleeves. The skirt was "wagon-wheel", and fell in graceful ripples from the waist, having a border about 3 inches from the bottom of the same plaid trim. My friend's dress was red and mine was a medium blue, and we would often plan to wear them to school together so we could "twirl" the skirts at recess—being made like an 180 degree circle they would flare out even with our little waists, making us feel a little like ballerinas! (The nearest we two ever got to dancing like these wonderful ballet ladies we only saw in pictures or movies).

A little pink suit I wore when I was 5 or 6 years old was a very favorite outfit. It was made of a pale coral-pink wool blend with a multi-colored squares pattern. The skirt was pleated with shoulder straps from the waist, while the collared jacket was elasticized at the back with gold button trim. I had a white blouse with blue buttons and embroidery on the collar that Gran Sexsmith made for me that I always wore with it. A photographer's picture taken by the local photographer of Connie at about 6 months wearing a little white silk embroidered dress and myself at 6 years, in this same suit, captured how we girls looked then for posterity. It seems to me when I outgrew it, Connie then wore and liked this little pink suit as much as I did.

Piano recitals were always important occasions, held each spring while we took lessons, and always required a new dress. At our first recital, I remember Connie having a lovely pink nylon dress covered with little flocked dots, lacy front and tie at the back, when we played a duet together called Little Birdie. I had a princess-line dress in pale floral-flocked nylon with a zipper back and high neckline that I wore for the occasion. We felt like two little princesses getting up on the stage in the Wolseley United Church to perform, wearing our pretty new dresses and playing together. It is a fond memory for me to this day. Subsequent recitals in years following must have required more new dresses, but this one stands out most, because it was first and because of our duet.

It seems to me a fabric called taffeta, a rather silky, shimmery kind of material, with a ripple-weave, was popular as we grew up, and I think perhaps our mother or aunts had garments made of it, although I don't recall Connie or I wearing it. I recall cotton pique and plisse that looked like cracked ice.

I remember having accessories bought for us by Aunt Alice, who living in the city, was often more aware of stylish changes, from being able to shop in Regina stores, than we had any idea about, and we always appreciated her keeping us "up-to-date", so to speak. The sock pins mentioned previously were her idea, and also many colorful, pleated silky neck scarves school girls were wearing at the time. These pretty little scarves could be coordinated with any outfit, as they came in any number of colors, and I must have had twenty or so at the height of this fashion. They could be secured at the neck with a clasp or slide type of closure, and I recall I had a pearl ring one made in three tiny rows of faux pearls, and a gold looped one that I still have today, as well as all the little scarves. Laundering of course, ruined the delicate tiny pleats that made the scarves so attractive, but they could still be worn and useful afterwards. Another accessory that I recall Aunt brought us were pom-poms—also worn at the neck of a blouse or sweater at the time, by school girls. These were made of white rabbit fur sewn into a ball and attached to a colored, velvet cord, with another matching fur ball attached at the other end. She brought Connie and I each one of these pom-poms, one with a red velvet cord and one with yellow that we interchanged with each other, depending on what we were wearing that each color would coordinate with.

Belts were also a popular fashion item back in those years, because of longer styles of dresses and skirts that seemed to look best belted. Either self-belts or leather, suede or patent were common, as well as some made of a new material—plastic. Cinch belts, also popular at the time, were made of wide medium stretch elastic, in a variety of colors and always had an ornate gold, silver or beaded closure. I recall Mom always saying these cinch belts were like a god-send to me, helping me hold up my skirts and later my slacks, as I was built like a "bean-pole" (straight up and down) with not much of a waist or hip line! I remember having a navy one that was perhaps three inches wide, and a narrower one of red that was my favorite, that I wore with all my skirts.

Women always wore earrings for ornamentation, often with matching necklaces. A pearl necklace, one or several strands of good quality pearls often with matching earrings was all the jewelry some women owned, reserving wear only for good. It seems to me rhinestone jewelry became common about this time, and was often worn by brides as gifts from their grooms. Brooches and bracelets were also worn, much as today. Ear piercing had not yet made a common appearance, and most earrings were screw-backed and later clip-on. (I think some elderly ladies of European descent had pierced ears at the time, however, I have no knowledge of the procedure involved to procure the actual holes). It was common while in nurse's training to "operate" on each other with hypodermic needles from the hospital, to "pierce" ears, however, I was never brave enough at the time to allow my ears to be punctured, given all the grief these girls had during the healing process!

Mom had a passion for earrings and always wore them for dress-up. I recall her pearl ones from Dad were favorites, as well as a medium green circular pair with a swirl pattern. Silver and gold "dangle" earrings made quite a fashion statement at the time, and Mom had several pair of them, again gifts from Aunt Alice. I still remember helping her look for one at the Indian Head hospital site where there had been an explosion around that time, that we had visited out of curiosity, and she lost one of her dangle earrings. Unfortunately, we never did find it and she had to retire the other one out of necessity. Another pair of silver earrings with three little tear drop shapes, suspended from a central ornate bead worn on the lobe, were also favorites.

I can't remember my first earrings or even when I began wearing them, but much prefer pierced earrings with dainty designs that I wear today. Screw-backed ones were all right, but clip ones always gave me a headache! Heather was only nine when she persuaded me to get my ears pierced along with her at the mall! Now both daughters have had their ears pierced in several places, besides the lobes, and even Michael had his left ear lobe pierced and wore a single stud in it, as was popular for young men's ornamentation too. Originally, the particular ear pierced also denoted the young man's sexual orientation, with left being heterosexual and right being homosexual, but I am told this no longer seems to hold as much credence as it once did; Michael no longer wears the earring now.

The women known to me back then wore limited jewelry and adornments because of their simple farm life—style, involving lots of hard work. Most ladies had a diamond engagement/

wedding ring set denoting their marital status; the plain wedding band always being worn for everyday and the diamond one only accompanied it for special occasions when going out. I don't recall Mom ever wearing any other rings, however, both Grans, especially Gran Teasdale owned and wore several rings with stones, and a gold one made like a buckle, all inherited since by her daughters. She also owned a darling brooch given to her as a gift by Grandad Teasdale, I think when they were married, making it special to her and she wore it often. It was three fine horizontal strips of gold joined into a backing, topped with a flower, centered with a little pinky-mauve stone. I recall admiring it often, hoping someday she would bequeath it to me, her first grandchild, and I am almost sure she would have granted it, if I had asked her. She wanted me to have the 23rd Psalm embroidered picture that was dear to both of us from my Confirmation days. As it turned out, Gran passed away not naming this special brooch for anyone, and after a struggle of who should have it, Aunt Dorothy Teasdale ended up with it. That she seems to treasure it and wears it whenever they visit, helps a little.

With regard to rings, I recall receiving a black diamond from Gordon in our courting days that was a real treasure to me, as they were very popular at the time. The black diamond was always highly polished in an inch long elongated vertical shape surrounded by an ornamental gold mount. Signet rings were sometimes worn by men and ladies back then for better wear. Watches were also only for dress-up—I recall Gran Sexsmith always wore a wrist watch with an expansion bracelet (a new concept at the time), very dainty and delicate, and I was always enthralled with it, and the fact that the expansion could stretch and then retain its original shape again. I can't say as I remember Gran Teasdale ever wearing a wrist watch, but Mom had a fine gold one, a gift from Dad, she sometimes wore for good, when it was in working order, but it didn't have that expansion bracelet I was so taken with! I recall fondly my first wrist watch was a gift from Uncle Wilfred, and I felt very honored and grown-up whenever I wore it, that he would bestow such a fine gift on me. It was gold with a black squarish face; the bracelet was made in double strands of gold non-stretch metal, held under delicate prongs at each side, curving into a single loop that held the watch, joining again around the wrist into a hook and flip-over closure. I wore it all my late girlhood and teen years, until Gordon bought me another delicate oval shaped gold one when we were first married.

Watches, rings and bracelets were favorite toy items for little girls back then, and I can recall Connie and I owned our share. She especially loved to play "dress-up" as a little girl, and was always putting on lipstick—bright, red on those sweet little lips, and she could really put it on well. Sometimes I would join her in her imaginary little dress-up world, but our age difference always seemed to put a void between us then.

As mentioned in the hair care pages previously, barrettes and hair ribbons were often worn by girls in those days, to keep hair in place, whether worn long, in braids or short. Colored and ornamental combs were sometimes worn by ladies, for dress-up. Perfume was reserved only for going out, and then sparingly, a dab behind the ears, or on wrists. I recall Mom having a midnight blue bottle with silver decals and a little rubber stopper/dabber top called Evening In Paris. Gran Teasdale always loved Lavender fragrance and wore it sparingly. I also recall receiving perfume in a little crown-shaped bottle, with a fine lawn handkerchief, as mentioned previously, my first Christmas gift from a boy while attending Allindale. Another bottle of perfume received from Aunt Ruby as a gift to carry in my new leather purse was special too.

Handkerchiefs were in common use by all the female gender back then, as disposable tissues weren't common. Kleenex provided the first tissues, followed later by many other brands. Lace borders or embroidered ornate designs were often featured on hankies for good, while plainer ones served for everyday. I remember "health inspection" each morning at school involved showing clean, neatly cut fingernails on a clean, pressed handkerchief on desktop to the "monitor", of the week, (It didn't seem too hard a task for the girls in attendance, but for rugged farm boys a bit more of a challenge, and they often got a poor mark on their inspection!)

With regard to sleepwear for women and girls, I can recall preferring pajamas of flannelette for myself as a girl, as I always seemed to be cold back then, and Gran Sexsmith made many a pair for me over the years, as she did for Connie and Dad as well. Mom preferred to wear short nightgowns, of cotton or later on nylon that she ordered from the catalogue or bought in town. I remember "Baby Doll" pajamas became popular for girls as we grew up, and were still popular as girls' sleepwear when our own girls were growing up. These p.j.'s consisted of a short blouson top and roomy, romper type of short pants, coordinated in pastel colors in cotton or nylon with pretty trims, buttons, lace and usually short-sleeved—very comfortable for sleeping, I recall.

Housecoats were made of chenille or cotton in long or short styles, usually with a shawl collar. Satin housecoats with quilted collars and trim could be purchased in fancier styles for ladies, but none of the women I knew wore such luxurious lingerie—only in the movies. By the same token other silky and satiny sleep apparel wasn't very practical for farm life back then, and fabrics that were more serviceable and more easily cared for were the norm.

I remember a style of housecoat that seemed to become popular just as I went in nurse's training, the mu-mu, as I recall making myself one out of a pastel blue/mauve/white cotton fabric to wear, in addition to my pretty mauve, silky quilted housecoat I also got new for this phase of my life. A short-sleeved float-type of covering fell in full gathers from a yoke at the neck, into a knee-length housecoat. It slipped over the head, without any closure at all, and I remember wearing mine a lot while off duty, and about residence.

Slippers were usually made of leather with fur trim, much in the style moccasins are made today. I think knitted slippers were also worn some, and I seem to remember Gran knitting us pairs of those also, especially after nylon yarn became available, which of course rendered them easier to care for.

Babies wore cloth diapers, hand-sewn of flannelette and long nightgowns of this same fabric. Gran Teasdale would often feather-stitch dainty embroidery on the necklines or yokes, and cuffs, I remember from Connie's baby days. Knitted booties, sweaters and hats were popular for going out doors for warmth and of course lots of blankets, Esmond being a popular manufacturer I recall back then. Apparently this same Gran knitted me a beautiful white shawl at the time of my birth that was also used for Connie, and a little for our children. Because it was such an heirloom, and not easily laundered being made of wool, I felt very protective of it, and have it stored carefully even today. With the advent of stretchy terry cotton, domed sleepers were a definite boon to baby wear, leaving nightgowns far behind, although I still recall using some for Heather as a newborn. Bunting bags of fabrics available then were worn on babies for outdoors.

I don't seem to have made any mention of luggage or suitcases up until now, and since they seem to be kind of an accessory to clothing, will be mentioned briefly here. There was not the emphasis on "matched sets" that there is nowadays, with several pieces for various needs made of leather or other synthetics now available. Since farm people rarely stayed away from home for any length of time or even overnight, there wasn't much need for luggage. I recall Mom and Dad owning a black leather patterned case of medium size that had silver closures and divider compartments that clasped shut and inside pockets. I myself remember a little black case of simulated leather with blue patterned paper lining that I took my belongings in while visiting Aunts etc., augmenting this with the one our parents owned when Connie and I both went visiting. I recall Gran Sexsmith owning a pretty brown set as she traveled about visiting Uncle Lloyd's family in Ontario quite often, and Aunt Alice and Uncle Don owned matching luggage with grey domed covers, I suppose to protect the finish (probably leather). Both grandmothers seemed to make do for "over-nighting" with their faithful cloth shopping bags, mentioned previously.

A dearly prized possession, my new green colored box-type suitcase with kind of a silky red/green shot material inside, pockets and divider, bought for me when I began high school, seemed to me back then about the best thing a girl could own, to carry clothing and possessions back and forth from home to Gran Teasdale's where I lived during those years. (Gordon recalls this suitcase being "very heavy" most of the time, when he was lifting it about in our courting days, and claims even empty, it was unusually heavy!) I recall Mom owning a small black trunk for storage, with a lift—out compartment, and of course the two blue wooden trunks in the basement used also for storage. Her cedar chest with drawer was always a favorite item she owned, used for storing special clothing/linen items, permeating them with that heavenly cedar aroma. A little green suitcase with compartments and dividers bought for Mom as a gift in the mid—sixties, has been a faithful companion to her on her many visits to Regina over the years—it has always amazed me the number of items this case is capable of carrying, so neat and compact!

As always, styles and fashions came and went during our growing-up years, just as they always have. Because of our simple farm life and limited resources, the memories I have recorded of clothing and accessories people wore and commonly made use of back then may not necessarily be a complete representation of all the fashion-customs of those '40-'50-'60 years, but only those I was aware of at the time, or am able to recall now.

It would be easy to assume from the previous account with regard to procurement of the necessities of life and the farm "work-oriented" environment we grew up in, that there was little effort made to enjoy life and have a little fun now and then. This is not the case at all—there were certain, short breaks in the tedium of work days that we all looked forward to and enjoyed.

Special occasions were always celebrated with family, namely Christmas, New Years, Easter, Thanksgiving, etc., as well as Birthdays for family members, most often celebrated with cake and candles. Several summer events were almost always attended, namely the Sports Days in Wolseley and sometimes Sintaluta, Ellisboro Picnic on July 1, an occasional day at Katepwa Lake, or Indian Head Experimental/Forestry Farm, and the Regina Exhibition and Grandstand show. Sunday Church attendance at St. George's, Wolseley, either in the morning, or Mom's and my favorite evening Evensong Service, and short visits to Gran Teasdale's for lunch following morning church were a fairly regular outing, especially in summer.

Saturday night shopping was another summer "ritual", often followed by taking in a show, in the early years at the town hall, and later at the local drive-in. Community dances at the district schools or in Wolseley or Sintaluta Hall were especially popular, as our family all loved music and dancing. As previously discussed, get-togethers at family members homes, or with friends/neighbors, often ended with a sing-song, especially on the Sexsmith side. Other fun events were school Christmas concerts, Field Days, Music Recitals, Vacation Bible School, occasional weddings, holidays with Aunties, and for me the many crafts I enjoyed as a girl filled many happy hours, as they still do today.

Because we went to town almost every Saturday night in summer all the years we were growing up, I will discuss this popular outing first. Dad especially looked forward to this little "get-away" each week, stopping his work early that day, so we could do chores, get ready and leave for town shortly after supper. The idea was to take our produce of cream, eggs and butter, etc. to town for sale and pick up groceries for the week. Local merchants seemed to enjoy this opportunity for increased sales and a visit with local farmers as much as the farming community did, and from May to September, extended their schedules 3 extra hours each Saturday night to accommodate everyone. (6:00 p.m. to 9:00 p.m.).

Farm children used this opportunity to shop for a few treats with a bit of spending money (earned, saved or given by parents or grandparents) and to meet up with other farm/town children their own age, for a bit of socializing. Young girls (approx. 8-12 yrs.) especially loved to link-up, often five or six to a group, cruising the streets, chattering, chewing bubble gum, giggling and showing themselves off in their latest outfits, to anyone and everyone, especially any unsuspecting boy or boys from farms, town, or surrounding towns, that might be about!

Saturday afternoon, in preparation for this outing, Mom would draw Connie and I a warm weekly bath in the portable, galvanized steel tub previously mentioned. She would then take a turn, and one of us would wave Dad in from the land with a towel from the back porch, so he could bathe after chores. The original water was used for all of us with kettles of hot water added until everyone had finished. A simple supper, for quick clean-up was usually planned. Everyone got quite dressed up, loaded up the produce and headed off to town in the current family car.

We would take the mile-and-a-half/Main Road route, where the roads were all graveled, or else the road south past the school and travel about one/half way on the paved "black-top". Dad preferred this route, as there was less chance of dirtying up his nicely polished car. Occasionally we would take the "Church Road" to town, that was more or less a narrow, dirt country road past the former Alexander Church site, so we could see how everyone's crop along that route was growing, etc.

I can still recall these many drives to town quite well, the beautiful golden sun setting to the west, the pale, blue evening sky, crops on each side of the road in various stages of growth, depending on early or late season, and just the idea of going somewhere, and doing something different from the usual during the long summer school holiday. However, the "anticipation" of the up-coming evening often gave me a stomach ache in those early years—I think it had to do with bathing and going out in the cool night air also, as even today this combination of events will give me an upset stomach, especially if I am tense or nervous! ! Looking back, it seems I was the type of young girl that was afraid of my own shadow, especially in that 8-12 year age! (Over the years, I've become somewhat braver!)

Perhaps there would be letters from pen-pals or relatives, or parcels from catalogue orders, as we only got mail when we went to Wolseley Post Office for it, perhaps we would be able to persuade Mom to buy us that special clothing item we had been longing for. There would be an opportunity to buy our favorite comic books, treats, or later on movie star magazines, and also the opportunity for socializing with our peer group. Although looking back, I was quite shy, never wanting to venture too far from Mom's safety net while she shopped, especially in younger years, to join these "girl-forays", which tended to aggravate my stomach aches even more!

Later when Connie was older, we would strike out together on our own, on some shopping mission, or would sometimes meet up and walk with those giggly girls, namely Alice Baker, Aileen Rein, Donna Jackson, cousin Audrey, Dianne Pow, Linda Hextall, etc., and sometimes girls from town like Judy Lewthwaite, Lynn Tubman, etc., also known from church. As I grew older, I would love to visit the craft/sewing/knitting areas of local stores, forever feeding my crafting interests. But, best of all, perhaps we would be able to take in a treat at the Chinamans Restaurant, visit Gran or attend a show. One of these events usually pre-empted the other, but we did our share of all, as I recall.

Our visits into town on a Saturday night usually began with a stop at the train station platform to unload the cream can for shipping, and pick up the empty one, to the candling station to drop off crates of eggs and pick up the previous week's cheque, and empty crates, and then to the post office, to pick up mail, usually containing the previous week's cream cheque from Elkorn or Broadview. These two cheques added together, were Mom's grocery allotment for that week. What a time she would have deciding what she needed most, and there wasn't usually enough money to buy all she had on her list, and Dad just didn't seem to like to augment these cheques unless absolutely necessary. I guess it was their way of budgeting, buying necessities only, although she confided to me once that she wanted to buy a lovely ham displayed in the store so bad, the thought crossed her mind to steal it, although of course she never would have.

Because Mom loved peppermints, Louis or whatever clerk was in attendance, would always manage to drop a gratis bag into her box of groceries, along with her order. A big bag cost .25 cents back then I recall, but even that amount, was sometimes unmanageable, Her favorites were the ones with the solid cream centers, not sugary. I suspect a green package of Doublemint gum also found its way into the grocery box most weeks as I recall Dad always chewed a half stick of Doublemint gum, until in frustration, after getting his dentures, he quit, as it stuck to his false teeth! We kids didn't care for it as was no good for blowing bubbles, just like some other popular gums—Juicy Fruit, Dentyne and Chicklets. We preferred colored gum-ball machine gum with prizes or Double Bubble.

It seems to me the local town residents also enjoyed this weekly influx of farm families into town, as many of them came "downtown" for the evening, either to shop for a few things or else

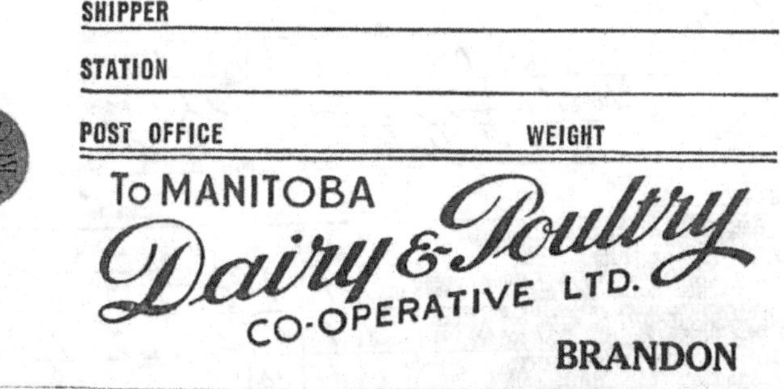

The thin wire that came with the cream can tags that I used for crafting whenever I could snaggle some!

There is a place where Sunday dinner is still considered family time.

Where people know all of their neighbours by name. And go to sleep at night with just the screen door closed.

There is a place where people have time for hobbies. A place where values refer to a way of life, not the cost of possessions.

It's the kind of place most of us think of whenever we take the time to actually stop and think. A place some say is hard to find. And maybe they're right.

A verse that reminds of the simpler, slower-paced days of our youth.

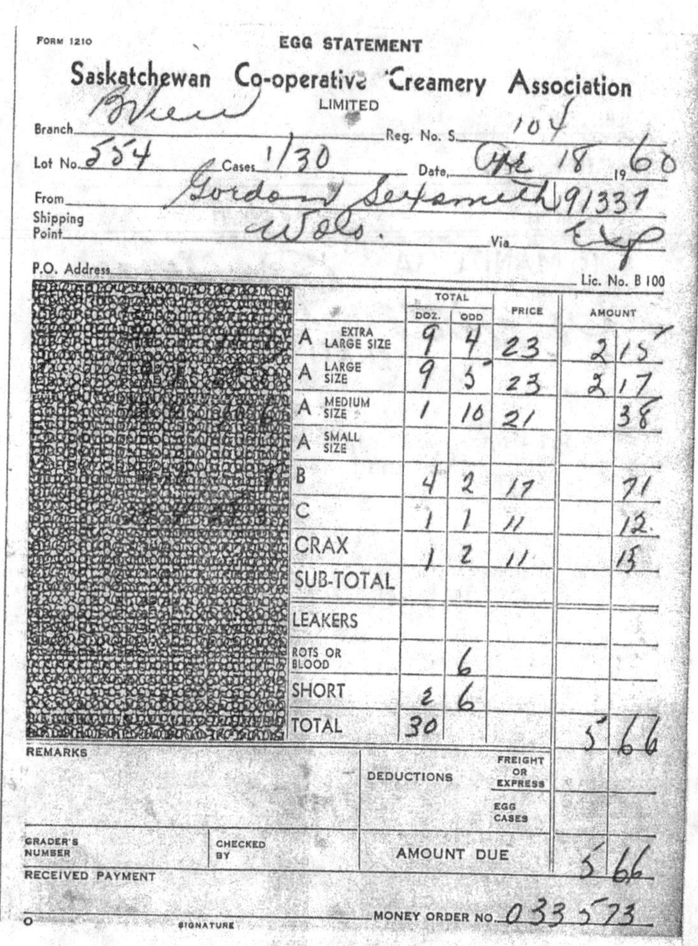

FORM 1210

EGG STATEMENT

Saskatchewan Co-operative Creamery Association LIMITED

Branch B'view Reg. No. S. 104

Lot No. 554 Cases 1/30 Date Apr 18 1960

From Gordon Sexsmith 91337

Shipping Point W'olo. Via Exp

P.O. Address Lic. No. B 100

	TOTAL DOZ.	TOTAL ODD	PRICE	AMOUNT
A EXTRA LARGE SIZE	9	4	23	2 15
A LARGE SIZE	9	5	23	2 17
A MEDIUM SIZE	1	10	21	38
A SMALL SIZE				
B	4	2	17	71
C	1	1	11	12
CRAX	1	2	11	13
SUB-TOTAL				
LEAKERS				
ROTS OR BLOOD		6		
SHORT	2	6		
TOTAL	30			5 66

REMARKS

DEDUCTIONS FREIGHT OR EXPRESS

EGG CASES

GRADER'S NUMBER CHECKED BY AMOUNT DUE 5 66

RECEIVED PAYMENT

SIGNATURE MONEY ORDER NO. 033573

CUSTOMER'S STATEMENT

Egg Cheque; Cream Cheque

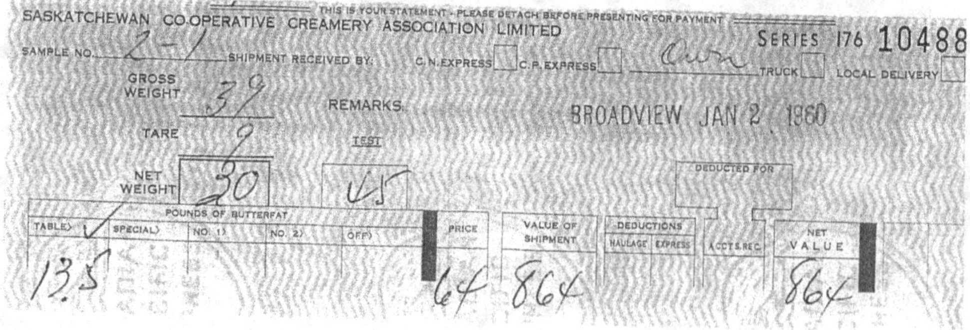

THIS IS YOUR STATEMENT – PLEASE DETACH BEFORE PRESENTING FOR PAYMENT

SASKATCHEWAN CO-OPERATIVE CREAMERY ASSOCIATION LIMITED SERIES 176 10488

SAMPLE NO. 2-1 SHIPMENT RECEIVED BY: C.N. EXPRESS C.P. EXPRESS Own TRUCK LOCAL DELIVERY

GROSS WEIGHT 39 REMARKS BROADVIEW JAN 2 1960

TARE 9 TEST

NET WEIGHT 30 45 DEDUCTED FOR

POUNDS OF BUTTERFAT TABLE)	SPECIAL)	NO. 1)	NO. 2)	OFF)	PRICE	VALUE OF SHIPMENT	DEDUCTIONS HAULAGE	EXPRESS	ACCTS.REC.	NET VALUE
13.5					64	864				864

just to visit. Dad especially liked this chance to chat, sometimes on the street corners on his errands to hardware, etc., or while Mom ordered her groceries, he would visit and share a joke or two with the clerks, namely George and Louis Dureault, Clarence Rein, Elsie Patzwald and even Chris Riehl over on yard goods side would get a kick out of his visit, shy as she was back then, with her cute little foreign accent. Stan Cole, owner/ operator of the store named after him (Coles), where we always did our shopping back then, was always in attendance helping the clerks in shoes and clothing department, always a gentleman, very pleasant to everyone, and later Jack Biram became manager, and was of a similar nature. Later on the store was known as Robinsons, as that chain had bought it.

Prior to the days of cash registers, Ralph Hodgkins, managed all money transactions in the old, original store, from his lofty little elevated office at the back, opposite the doors. A cash cable system of long, slender wires, led back and forth from the store departments to Ralph's office, with a little silver canister that conveyed the money and transaction bill. Change and a stamped "paid" bill were returned in a few minutes, in a similar or the same little canister, for the customer.

I can recall the ceiling in the old store had very ornate panels of patterned metal painted white, with suspended electric lights with shades, and I think the original floors were wooden, darkened with age, linseed and years of traffic, that were swept with dustbane as we did at Allindale.

Once in a while, if Mom was looking for a certain sized box, or we needed to use the telephone to call Gran Teasdale or something, we would venture into the "back" of the store and peek at all the high bunks of groceries stored there. It was a breath-taking sight to see that many food items at once—all the bulk fruit (especially bananas like they had hung on the tree) and vegetable produce, boxed and canned goods, as well as wooden barrels containing items now packaged in sealed plastic bags as individual units, like nuts, rice and other staples. Vinegar also came in a barrel with a tap, to fill customer's bottles.

Out front on the grocery side of the store, grocery orders were filled and boxed or bagged from stocked shelves behind the clerks, as the customer read the items off her list. A hand-written itemized bill was also prepared by the clerk, in a pad, with a carbon to make a copy. The original was later shipped with payment, up to Ralph as already explained, by cable wire. Mr. Cole was known for his benevolent attitude to those unable to pay, and it was said during the earlier years, he would often extend credit to customers, so they wouldn't go hungry. If they could, they paid later, and more often than not, the bills were just "forgiven". Thankfully, our family was always able to pay cash for things we bought. Dad was always very strict in this regard, with himself, and we knew it extended to us all. He always said if you couldn't pay for it, then you didn't need it! Wouldn't he be shocked at the amount of "plastic" transactions that go on nowadays!

With the grocery shopping completed, Mom would usually head across the street to Mr. Knight's Butcher shop to purchase her meat order, augmenting what we had frozen at the locker plant of our own farm grown meat (discussed previously). Wieners, sliced ham, bacon and the occasional roast were her usual purchases, and we kids always got a raw, peeled wiener to eat right there for a treat. I can still see Mr. Knight slicing the thin, pink slices of ham from a huge square or round original one, and how good it tasted for a treat at home. He knew how much we liked sweetbreads, and saved us some when he was butchering, which was often. It was always cool in the Butcher shop and smelled of sawdust, I recall.

Occasionally an item had to be picked up from Mr.Chesney's hardware just down the street, where Walter Chapman or Mr. Chesney would provide expert service, but Dad usually went there, unless it was an item he and Mom had to confer about. Next was a visit to the Oldfield's Drug Store back across the street. I recall it being my favorite stop, as they had no end of fascinating items for sale besides drug-related supplies. This shop always had a certain medicinal-perfumed type of smell, I recall, and for the longest time, had suspended lamps from the ceiling, surrounded by a spiraled cascade of silver stars, that always fascinated me then. School and craft supplies, film and developing, of course the pharmacy in the back of the store, all drug supplies, jewelry and gift-ware items, all manner of candy, gum and best of all comic books and movie magazines were all offered at this store. Counters and tops were made of glass, housing jewelry and other "untouchables".

I remember Mr. Oldfield would wait on customers, sometimes, if he wasn't busy in the pharmacy, or else a clerk by the name of Molly Biram was kind and helpful. Later Arnold McOuoid became assistant pharmacist, and eventually bought the business, calling it then by the McQuoid name, as it is still known today. We used to make our favorite purchases there; Double Bubble gum, wrapped in a waxed-type of paper, with a comic inside, just like it is packaged today, for a penny each. Neilson's mini-chocolate bars were 2 for a nickel and also a favorite. Bassett Lozenges, a flat, linseed tasting, powdered, brown colored-rectangular shaped cough candy, were a particular favorite of mine as well as Winter green Lifesavers. Penny vending machines offered enticing trinkets and round bubble gum.

With shopping completed the collective decision would be made to either go for a treat at Wing Yuen's Restaurant, or pick up Gran and head for the show, in earlier years at the theatre in the town hall, but mostly at the Drive-in in the years I remember best. The upcoming show would always be listed in the News (local paper) and if it was one starring our favorites Rock Hudson, Robert Wagner, Jane Wyman, Natalie Wood, or one of the Esther Williams movies always involving her swimming, there was no contest—the show would win! However, if we didn't care about the movie, the family treat at the Chinaman's would win out.

Looking back now, it was probably touch and go if we could afford a treat or show back then, however Dad seemed to think it was quite important—of course, as children, we were always in favor too! Because of huge fans, the restaurant was nearly always cooler on these warm, summer evenings than it was outside, and this was a definite plus, as no one had air conditioning back then. However, obtaining a booth was always a bit of a problem, at this popular place, and once in a while we had to sit on the round revolving stools at the counter, that Connie and I thought was great, (for twirling) but Mom and Dad didn't seem to like as much as a booth.

Floats were quite popular to order, ice cream cones and later on after freezers came along, Popsicles, Revels, Dixie cups or Fudgicles. Dad would sometimes order a denver sandwich with fries on the side; it couldn't have been a case of "real" hunger, as we had just eaten supper a few hours before—however it was his idea of a treat to himself, and of course we were getting the sweet treats we craved as well. Mom usually had ice cream as I recall.

Ice Cream was a real taste sensation, dipped from huge canisters kept in insulated bags. Sometimes, by the time we went, it was all sold out or had melted, in very hot weather. Occasionally we would take Gran some ice cream in a little white folding box or if we were going right home, would order some for ourselves. We always laughed when they asked if we wanted our purchase in a bag, as with their cute Oriental accent "You want it in a bag?" took on such cute expression, we would often mimic it at home! I suppose they were always trying to conserve their resources, and if no plain bag was required to carry the purchase, it was a cost saving to their establishment. Vanilla was the only flavor available in the earlier years however chocolate was followed by strawberry and then many of the flavors we now know today. The rich, creamy flavor and taste back then though doesn't begin to compare with what is available today, or as I remember it anyway!

There were a number of establishments in town that we did limited business with, but tended to stay with Coles/Robinsons store over the years, for groceries and many of our other needs, even though Del White ran an IGA on Front Street (formerly owned by the Gibsons that were so fond of me as a little girl) and Lorne Sexsmith sold groceries on one side of his Marshall Wells hardware for quite a few years too. A lady by the name of Mrs. Matusko ran a small grocery/confectionary store just north of Rene's Style Shop, across from the lumber yard, but I don't recall patronizing her much either, except for the odd treat now and then. It seemed there was an affinity with Stan Cole and Jack Biram through the church we all attended, St. George's, and we were always pleased with the service as well.

In the early years there was an old post office on the corner of Main and Front Street that

I recall was remodeled over the years several times before the present location at the end of Front street was finally chosen for a new building. I have previously mentioned getting my leg caught in the grating in front of the old post office one Saturday night, while parading around with some of the other girls, and being "rescued" without much harm by a kindly gentleman bystander. A gentleman by the name of Frank Vincent capably ran this old post office for a number of years, although I only remember him from pictures. A box system with dialed openings was in place for a few years, and then a key system replaced this. It was frustrating to get to town on a Saturday night, and have a "parcel" card in your box, but not be able to claim it because the wicket part of the post office didn't remain open, in the evenings—one of the only businesses not to do so. Wilf Robertson, Ed Kaduhr and senior Mr. Kaduhr are the postmasters I remember best, as I called at the post office nearly every day during high school, for Gran's mail or to mail her letters.

The train station attendants were Mr. Ed. Foyle in the early years, and later Bruce Marlin and then Johnny Marlin. Tom Allen ran the garage at the far south east corner of Front Street where Dad always had his cars serviced, while Schlamps ran another garage and car repair at the far west end of this street. Ted Lewthwaite ran the Massey dealership on Main Street for a number of years, while Bern Folbar ran the tractor dealership, first John Deere and later Case, where Dad always bought his tractors. For a few years, Stan Biram had a photographer's shop (took Aunt Elsie's wedding pictures, and Connie and I as girls), and Marg Simpson always ran her beauty shop (where Gran had her hair done on a regular basis) close to the Royal Bank building, the bank being managed by Jay Thomson during the time I remember. The Faye Family also opened a beauty shop during my high school years, and were very popular with the young crowd because they knew more modern styles, and had the cutest sons also attending high school!

Another restaurant Undeeda Lunch operated on Front Street beside the IGA for a number of years, under the management of my best friend Phyllis Boyes' parents, Elsie and Bill. I recall sometimes having a snack or treat there in the early years, as well as at the bus depot restaurant run for a few years by a Mrs. Dunford, located by the new post office location.

Mr. Knight's butcher shop already mentioned, was augmented by the locker plant shop, under the management of Tony Gruber. The milk plant and dairy was run by the Binst family (went to school with son Roger), and the candling station lady that I remember was a Trueman girl, although I know there were others too. The Beaver lumber yard (I always liked to come along when Dad bought lumber or supplies here during week day visits to town—it always smelled so fresh and clean with so much potential for all that cut lumber just waiting to be made into something!) was run by a fellow called Bob Lyttle, and just down from there the telephone office was located on the corner.

Drs. Isman, Bergal and Turnbull were doctors in attendance that I remember during this time, operating their office downtown on Main Street—the waiting room being long and narrow, painted grey, with ancient medical pictures on the walls, painted wicker furniture and smelled of antiseptic. The hospital across the dam, accessed by the swinging bridge, was run by matron Miss Hemming (G.A. Leader also) and later Lucy Souchotte, while Helen Gibney (Mom's faithful, kind neighbor) was matron of the Lakeside Home, then the old brick facility with four bed wards, and a scary porched part that faced the dam where old men sat in wheelchairs and grabbed your legs with their canes as you walked by!

The cemetery caretaker was a dear English chap by the name of Tom Poulson, who had the endearing expression about the "Rydio didn't say it was going to ryan" ("the radio didn't say it was going to rain") expression that we all loved to mimic when not around him. He maintained the cemetery with great care, with a push-type mower and hand tools, from his little white caretaker's building, the door having a cute little round window in it that always appealed to me as a girl whenever we visited the cemetery to take flowers to graves, which was often. We never realized until years later that Tom was formerly Mattie Poulson's husband that came to our church, presenting us with many vocal performances over the years. Walter Chapman from Chesney's store boarded with Mattie for years, coming to church with her, doing her yard work, etc. He seemed to inherit her home when she passed on, continuing to care for the house and grounds until he passed on; a new and different house is now located there.

A few other businesses I recall were Grant Garden's tax and legal office, on Main Street, capably run by Grant and his sister May, inherited from their father John R., where Dad had all his business looked after. For as long as I can remember Mr. George Cripps ran the town office across from the lumber yard. Several elevators were run by Mr. Linton, Bill Conn and Bill Patterson, although I'm sure there were others, while the pool hall and barber shop was run by Alex Patzwald, the barber, and Bus Conn was the local dentist. Another dear elderly gentleman ran a shoe repair and leather shop for a number of years, a Mr. Bill Hudson—he and his wife also attended St. George's, and were both very musical, as mentioned previously. Several craft shops opened up over the years, which I especially loved to haunt, but there just didn't seem to be enough clientele in Wolseley and area to keep such a venture viable for long.

A fellow by the name of Stan Zaba ran the local Twilite Drive-in, built probably in the mid to late 50's—a new concept in movie-going, along with drive-in restaurants with car-hops, that quite soon after this became very popular in cities and some towns, with A & W leading the way. (Gordon always felt we owned part interest in the first A & W in Regina located at Albert St and 2nd Avenue N., because we patronized it so much, especially in my nurse training days!)

With regard to drive-in theatres, a giant screen was set up in a fenced enclosure that could be seen for miles. Speakers with volume controls were set up on posts beside rows of ramps in a semi-circle, to elevate vehicles, making viewing easier, especially for back seat passengers. The visual part of the movie was projected onto the giant screen from a projection/concession booth, while the audio part came into each car via the speakers. It was a neat concept and we certainly attended our share of drive-in movies over the years, as mentioned previously, following Saturday night shopping, often enjoying the show over a treat from the concession booth. Young people especially enjoyed this entertainment concept, as they could load up their cars with friends and head off by themselves to the drive-in alone for a few hours of enjoyment, without supervision or interference, although drinking/rough-housing was not tolerated.

The local pool room and barber shop was the hangout for local boys both after school and on Saturday nights. Since Dad never spent any time there (Mom cut his hair, and he didn't play pool), and women and girls weren't allowed therein, I don't really know what all went on there besides pool and hair-cutting! Probably could get a drink, or if not the Leland Hotel lounge/ beer parlor was just next door. I think for school-aged boys the pool room was just a gathering place—somewhere to go "to be cool", without roaming the streets like we girls had to! Strangely enough, pool halls have again found favor, now open to both male and female clientele, used again as a meeting place, and of course to play pool as well, but now are classier.

The French/Catholic population that mostly farmed south of town was always well represented on Saturday nights back then in Wolseley. The Bonnevilles, Coueslans, Dureaults, and Beliveaus to name a few came out for shopping and visiting with the rest of us, always "dressed to the nines" as Mom used to say, meaning very dressed up! Always very vocal, laughing and talking loudly to each other in French or to us in English, whatever was needed! A lesson in Bilingualism, although we had never heard of that word at the time! There was no animosity between us and them, that I can remember, although Mom always hoped we would never marry a Catholic, when we grew up, because their church services were all in Latin, and some of their beliefs not quite like ours.

The German/Lutheran population, which tended to farm mostly north of town, across the valley, were also well represented, like the Reins, Bakers, Fehlers, Patzwalds, Magels, etc., on those Saturday nights in Wolseley. There was always lots to discuss among farmers from different areas, with regard to farming, how the crops were coming along, the pattern of summer storms/rain/hail etc., how the yield or pricing might be for grain, and more or less the current state of things for that particular season.

Although it was never discussed per se at home, I always got the feeling that to be of English/Scottish/Irish descent, as we were, was viewed to be somewhat more superior in every way to being descended from any of the other nationalities. The various countries represented in the Wolseley area, from all parts of the British Isles, Europe and even the Orient made it a kind of melting pot of United Nations, never more apparent than on those Saturday night ventures. I suspect with WWII just ended, there were rather strong feelings of animosity directed towards, German/Japanese people in general, but not to anyone we knew in particular, but perhaps accounting for some of this enmity.

The Jehovah Witnesses or some such group (we often referred to them as the "holy rollers") used to hold revival meetings on the street corners (soap-box style) under a street light, usually down by the locker plant, singing rousing evangelistic-type songs with some preaching. I recall a very attractive young woman with glowing auburn hair used to be part of this group as well. There was usually a few curiosity seekers about, but never knew how many, if any, actually became involved or made commitments. We were curious as well, but not enough to join in the singing—I don't recall if they gave out any tracts or literature, as they probably would today.

So ends my account of these very popular Saturday night outings our family enjoyed along with so many others in rural Saskatchewan at that time. Gordon tells me that his family never attended Saturday nights in Neudorf, preferring to day-time shop. On one or two occasions he went by himself walking and on his bike, so I tend to feel fortunate now that we enjoyed these outings as a family. His family, on the other hand, probably attended more Sunday morning church services during summer than we tended to, although, as mentioned previously, we often went to evening church, or Evensong at St. George's, picking Gran Teasdale up and taking her along also, if she hadn't gone in the morning.

The other summer event that we seldom missed attending as a family was the Regina Exhibition and Grandstand show. It was always held in late July/early August, and we would arrange with Aunt Alice to get us tickets for the evening Grandstand. Quite often Uncle Wilfred would be visiting from B.C., as he and Aunt loved to attend the horse races that always accompanied this event. Everyone got dressed up to attend in those days.

Since the Traveler's Day Parade was always held on Friday morning, we quite often planned to attend that day, leaving home very early, to be in Regina, parked, and have a good place to watch the parade. Dad never cared for driving in the city, but as long as we came in on Victoria Avenue and all helped him watch for Hamilton Street, where we had to turn left to get to the Morton's at Claire Apartments, he was usually all right. We would quite often walk from there to see the parade, and then after lunch would head out to the fair grounds. The route was pretty easy in those days, before the Lewvan was made—straight west on Victoria and turn right on Pasqua and into the parking.

As children Connie and I were never much for the scary rides, preferring the merry-go-round, pedal cars, and boat rides. Since our teachers at Allindale often entered our art work in the school exhibits, we always made sure to tour the exhibit buildings to see if we had won anything. Imagine our delight and surprise when my finger painting of a bridge over water won first prize one year, and that was the first we knew of it, when we saw the red prize displayed on it there in the exhibit building. I recall Aunt Ruby often entered her handicrafts as well, and often won prizes also. Mom always said she would like to enter her homemade bread or home preserves some year, but somehow never did.

Dad always bought Mom a little sachet of lavender, as she loved the smell of it, and usually some chocolate fudge as she liked it too. We usually managed to make purchases from vendors in the Midway—something different every year—kewpie dolls or little furry imitation monkeys attached to a curved bamboo cane with an elastic are some of the things I remember. Uncle Wilfred bought us heart-shaped expansion bracelets one year, and had our names engraved on them right there at the booth. I recall hats with furry plumes, pictures taken with our faces in comical stands, folding Oriental fans, parasols, and other such trinkets we treasured over the years.

Dad always seemed to have a voracious appetite while at the grounds, and we often stopped for treats, or hamburgers, fries, hot dogs, etc. Mom loved fiddle sticks, and always managed to have one or two during the course of the day. We usually walked around as a family, spending the day touring the midway, rides and buildings. A display of the latest farm machinery always intrigued Dad, and he liked to spend a fair bit of time browsing through all those new implements, being more and more amazed at the size displayed and the new innovations that kept coming out each year—something we girls weren't too interested in back then, but were willing to spend the time with him, as he devoted all the rest of the day to seeing what we wanted, bringing us there, etc.

Occasionally Dad would be intrigued by some midway side-show that we would sometimes accompany him to; I remember going to view a dare-devil motorcyclist driving his bike round and round a vertically built round wooden housing unit. The patrons stood on viewing platforms around the perimeter at the top. The rider began at ground level, and as he climbed higher and higher on his bike and went faster, centrifugal force kept him from falling—it was exciting to watch, very noisy, with a strong exhaust smell but also rather scary—I always worried about what would happen to the poor rider if he fell—caring little girl that I was! I think we ventured into the house of mirrors once or twice, viewed the fat lady and occasionally went on some rides. One year I remember Dad going on a ride called The Mouse that was new that year; it seems to me we were with Aunt Alice and a friend, that we had met up with by chance. The silly ride was suspended high above our heads on a kind of roller-coaster track, and Dad confided to us later at home he was scared skinny, but didn't want to let those gals know at the time, as they had coerced him into going and they made him sit in the front of the car! He talked about it for years afterward, and we sometimes teased him about it also, trying to get him to go other years!

Around supper time, we usually headed for one of several dining halls that used to be run by various church or charitable groups back then. These buildings were only used at Exhibition, so were out of necessity simply built out of rough wood, with a roof, whitewashed or painted, and have long since been torn down. They had long receiving hallways where people lined up to get their food, all prepared cold plates of sandwiches or cold cuts and salads that could just be picked up. Pie and ice cream was always offered for dessert, as well as beverages or pop in great tubs of ice. When everyone had their selections picked, and placed on trays, it had to be paid for. We then sat at long wooden tables and benches covered with oilcloth cloths where we would be able to eat. It seems to me these suppers were quite tasty, and preferred by our parents, as a good nutritious meal, seated, and out of the sun, however, we preferred the burgers and fries from the vendors always set up along the south side of the grandstand building.

With supper behind us, it was usually time to find our places on the grandstand for the evening's entertainment. This was always a very classy show, performed on an open air stage, with top singers and comedy groups, high-wire dare-devils, and Dad's favorite the Manhattan Rockets dance troupe. The show usually opened with these dancers dressed in colorful feathery dance attire, and of course showing lots of curvy bodies and beautiful legs. There were perhaps 25 of these lovely gals dancing a routine that always ended with them joining arms and kicking their legs high in the air in time to the classy music, supplied by the orchestra sitting in the pit immediately in front of the stage.

The show was always conducted by an affable, often comical emcee, dressed in a tux, very dapper and part of the production. The various acts were always entertaining, and usually the head-liner entertainer saved for the middle of the show. Some of the top names in attendance I recall were Bobby Vinton, Bobby Cartola, the Everly Brothers, etc. Often a heavy guy-wire was suspended over the roof of the grandstand for the final act, sometimes tight-rope acrobatics on bicycles with long balancing poles, or motor-bike riders in black leather! This was always the most exciting part of the evening.

The grand finale was always a thundering, dazzling fireworks display—quite a few in the sky in front of the grand stand and always stationary ones on the ground. If it was a special year, as in 1955, when the province was celebrating its 50th anniversary, this was recognized in the fireworks display. We always knew they were over when the one showed of the Queen—this would usually be about 10:30 or so, and everyone began leaving the stands. These shows were always well received and well attended, advance tickets being sold at Gilles Agencies on Hamilton Street back then. Occasionally "rush" seats could be obtained for the evening from a ticket office beneath the grand stand, but we never liked leaving this to chance, and as mentioned previously, had ours bought early by Aunt Alice for the best selection. Later on, when Gordon and I were both living in Regina, we would get ours and some for Mom and Dad on the same evening.

The close proximity of the then Grey Nuns' Hospital to the fairgrounds as seen especially well from our grandstand location back then, always sent little shivers down my spine. Those red brick stately buildings seemed to stand for healing and suffering, emergencies and sickness, none of which was too appealing to a small child. Little did I realize back then that very same hospital would one day become the place where I would learn my life's-work and meet my husband to be! I can still recall working nights on the D wings of the hospital, as a nurse-in—training and preparing the patients for the noisy boom-booms of the fireworks following the grand stand shows, especially if there was a south-east wind that carried the sound right towards the buildings! (What memories that would bring back of all those years when we would be in attendance at the fireworks and grand stand shows).

We usually headed home shortly after the grand stand show was over, sometimes stopping for a snack from one of the many vendors still hawking their food. One year we had car trouble, and had to stay overnight unexpectedly, while we waited for repairs. I recall the rest of the family stayed by kind invitation, at Bob & Phyllis Chisholms,(Mortons'friends), while I had to remain behind at the Morton's apartment, because I was used to staying there in summers, etc., and Connie was still little! As I recall we were able to get home next day without further incident, and the only time any unforeseen event marred our many visits to the Regina Exhibition. Looking back, I remember it being something we always looked forward to each year, especially Dad. I think it was because he was denied so much as a young lad, out of his parents being poor farmers at the time, or just not being inclined to want to attend. I remember him relating to us one time when he and Mom were old enough to be courting, and wanting to attend the Exhibition, so they must have had a means of travel. His Dad offered him a nickel (.05 cents) to take along to spend, that I suppose would have had a lot more value then than it does today! However, Dad said he might as well keep it, and as far as I know, he and Mom went anyway, without this "spending money"! What they used for money, I never remember hearing, unless he had some saved back they used, from his employment on the farm back then, helping his Dad.

I remember it being preferable to attend the Exhibition earlier in the week if possible, especially in the early days, and we would sometimes forfeit the Friday morning parade for this very reason. The grounds were all dirt or graveled back then, not paved, and covered with sawdust or wood shavings for the week to keep things cleaner. What a mess if it happened to rain, and as the week progressed, a lot of litter was generated by people in attendance. Garbage and refuse was not picked up on a regular basis as it is now, by service club volunteers, and it just tended to accumulate in garbage cans or right on the ground. The worst was old discarded corn cobs, gobs of fallen gum or candy floss, etc. that had to stepped over and around. If it was hot weather, of course, the aromas got rather high as the week progressed, making for rather unpleasant surroundings by the end of the week!

The grassy park area in the centre of the grounds, opposite the grand stand was always a welcome haven, especially on hot days, as so much of it was shaded by buildings and trees, even back then, and continues nowadays. It seems to me we just had to sit on the grass then, but now lots of benches and picnic-type tables have been added. I can't recall if the decorative fountain was always present in this park, but the sight and sound of the running water is pleasant and relaxing.

So, over the years, the Exhibition grounds have changed a great deal from those days when we attended as a family each summer all those years ago. New and impressive buildings have been added, different parking, paving of roadways used on the grounds, better facilities for vendors/public, and lots more horse racing, several times a year. Royal American Shows from the States always provided the Midway back then, while Conklin shows, also American, now has the contract. New and exciting rides and attractions have come and gone, with a whole separate section for small children's rides apart from the rest of the Midway being a welcome concept I'm sure, for everyone involved with these members of the fair-going crowd. We rarely miss going over to Exhibition Park, as it is now called, each year during Buffalo Days/Exhibition time, and enjoyed attending with our children when they were young, keeping this popular summer outing as an annual expedition we all still enjoy!

Perhaps the next event I will reminisce about will be Ellisboro picnics, always held each summer on July 1—Canada Day or Dominion Day, as it used to be called, and an event we usually always took time to attend. It was held on the fair grounds adjacent to the little town of Ellisboro in Qu'Appelle Valley north of Wolseley, and north-east of our Allindale farm.

For as long as I can remember, Robin McLean, local farmer and benefactor to this annual picnic, very ably conducted the events of this popular get-together, along with many willing volunteers from the town and surrounding farms. I think the valley locale definitely set this sports day apart from the ones held in the towns at their wind-swept, open sports grounds each summer. The one at Ellisboro always seemed like a "picnic", because the grounds were always freshly mowed prairie grass, complete with the odd gopher hole! The whole area (perhaps two city blocks) had around the circular perimeter especially to the north west, many natural bloughs of trees, providing shelter and shade, while a short distance away on all sides, the green/ grey valley hills rose gently in the summer sun, providing all in attendance with a lovely view. A beautiful relaxing day, filled with socializing and goodwill, in scenic surroundings. It was always well attended over the years, first by local residents and farm folk from the surrounding area, and in later years by many folks from town, and even Regina, as it was such a good chance to see everyone, at least once a year.

There was something for everyone to enjoy at Ellisboro! Several local mainline ball teams were always in attendance, competing for a winning place and trophy or money, on one of the three diamonds located in the north and east areas of the grounds. One always had to be aware of fly balls from these games, perhaps accidentally hitting a person or car parked around the eastern perimeter of the grounds!

A cocoanut shy was always located to the mid-western side of the grounds, with a few fence posts pounded into the ground to demark the area, with loose ropes suspended from these posts. Tarps strung along the back in the trees, stopped the thrown balls from becoming lost, while three similar fence posts with nails driven in the top provided make-shift stands for the cocoanuts! Dad always loved to try his hand at knocking off a cocoanut for us, and quite often succeeded—three balls for a quarter, or something like that. We would sometimes have him break it there, so we could savor some of the milky fresh cocoanut right at the time. Usually the "milk" inside had mostly run away from the nail hole poked in the end to secure the cocoanut to the post, but sometimes a bit remained, that was an extra bonus to drink right then and there! Otherwise we would stash our "treasure" in the car trunk to enjoy on future days at home, when we would have a better chance to get at the cocoanut's snowy white interior with spoon or fork.

Even sweeter than this memory is one of attending this picnic with our children, towards the final ones being held in the late 70's, and having Michelle and Michael each try their hand at throwing a winning ball in the cocoanut shy! They would have made their Grandpa so proud—could he have been in attendance that day—they each knocked off their own cocoanut and proudly carried away their prize to open and enjoy, just as we had done back in the old days! Needless to say it was a very proud moment for me, and brought back a flood of bitter/sweet memories. (Because of their small size, I know the attendant let them stand up closer, but they still had to be accurate, with enough thrust and focus—I don't ever remember us being able to try this popular stand as children, but maybe we were just too shy). A fellow named Barry Garden usually ran this stand, I recall.

Races for all ages were another popular event that took place in the early evening, during an interlude in the ball games. A good runner could earn their summer's spending money there! A first prize win usually earned a dollar, second .75 cents and third .50 cents. As the ages went up, so did the competition—and sometimes the prizes. Prize money was collected (in Mr. McLean's straw hat) throughout the day from those in attendance, and always all given away to the runners. Three-legged races, sack, potato and wheel-barrow races were some of the novelty events offered to take part in. Mom related how she always ran in these races as a young girl, earning her share of prize money over the years, and I followed in her foot-steps! I loved to run as a girl, and was as speedy as a young deer, preferring to begin at the end of the line up of participants, rather than in the middle somewhere, to be slowed-down by the girls around me. I could motor best in sock feet, on the grassy field, but those poor socks proved to be a laundering challenge next wash day!

Most people in attendance came to watch the races, and cheer on their children and relatives. An area right in the middle of the grounds, (free of gopher holes) was usually chosen, and then roped off for start and finish line—the finish line being moved farther and farther to the south as the ages went up. Races began for little ones, right on up to adults, separate for male and female. It was allowed for a person to run in age groups older than current age, and I always did so, usually winning. Novelty races followed, Joyce Malo and I teaming up a few years, for three-legged, wheelbarrow, etc., as we were of similar age and both in attendance, although we were never really friends, otherwise.

Horse shoes were often played by the men in attendance, the pits usually dug for this event at the treed north end of the grounds. This popular game went on throughout the day, and the clank of the metal horse shoes being tossed against metal rods was a familiar audio sound to all in attendance. Dad often played, seeming to enjoy this bit of entertainment, and was quite good I seem to remember.

A wooden concession stand located on the little knoll to the west of the grounds close to the cocoanut shy stand, did a roaring business throughout the day. It was again manned by local volunteers, wearing money aprons, making change as necessary from there. All manner of treats were available, as well as soft, drinks kept in huge tubs of ice that soon turned to water in the heat. Ice cream was usually available in the early part of the day, before it too, melted. Slices of watermelon lasted most of the day, and were a popular crowd pleaser! Drips of pink juice around little mouths was a common sight as I remember.

It seems there was no need for security or policing of the crowd at the Ellisboro picnic grounds back then. Children ran about everywhere, in twos and threes or groups, without parents' constant supervision. The crowd was mostly known to each other then, and everyone looked out for everyone else, including children—it was very friendly and congenial. There were no cars allowed in the grassy central area, except an occasional one to drop off supplies or an elderly person, in which case they got permission from Mr. McLean or his crew of volunteers, and could only drive 5 m.p.h. or less! As mentioned previously, parking for vehicles was along the open, eastern perimeter of the grounds, and in later years, when attendance increased, the west perimeter by the trees was also used, all this conducted by more volunteers, again under Robin McLean's capable direction.

The only other permanent building on the grounds besides the concession booth, and ladies and gents wooden outhouses, was the kitchen/supper booth, located just south of the concession one, with the open, sloped area and some trees, off to the west in between. The cold plate evening meals served from this booth were well known, with all the food except perhaps the sliced ham and cold cuts being supplied and plated by the local Ellisboro ladies. Every kind of homemade pie imaginable was available to buy for dessert, as well as hot or cold beverages. I'm not sure how they managed this, especially in the early days, before electricity. I suspect a lot of the food was prepared immediately before-hand in surrounding homes, and just brought over at supper, and probably gas stoves heated water for hot drinks, etc. The area all along the north side of this booth, but still under the roof, was open for serving, and patrons lined up for their food along this counter, being assisted by the friendly, helpful local ladies and a few gents. A very nominal fee was paid at the east end of this building, again collected by several local ladies/gentlemen with cash boxes, seated in the shade at tables.

There was some seating in this building with long tables and benches, but most families preferred to sit on blankets they had brought from home, spread on the grass by their cars, or else more wooden benches and tables were placed in the grassy sloped area adjacent, to the food/concession booths, for this purpose. This meal was the highlight of the day for many in attendance, and indeed, some came to the picnic just for this delicious meal, and a little visit with friends and neighbors, in the cooler, late afternoon and evening of the day.

In the later years, it seems to me a small entertainment section was added for young children, located off to the west part of the grounds, around the cocoanut shy area. There was a merry-go-round and a small ferris wheel, as I recall, but even though I'm sure the young patrons appreciated this addition, it just didn't seem in keeping with the simpler, less commercialized days of the original venue of Ellisboro picnic.

After the races were completed, and twilight was approaching, another one or two ball games and more visiting and reminiscing usually ended the day for most participants. However a dance always concluded the picnic, held in the hall east of the grounds, with music supplied by local musicians or a local band. I remember Mom and Dad relating to us how they always attended this dance, and always had a good time, even though it was usually hot in the hall, and everyone there had spent the day at the picnic, so wasn't usually a dress-up affair. However, I don't recall us ever staying for it as a family when we were young. I do remember attending one picnic and dance during high school with a current heart-throb, who was also playing on one of the ball teams taking part in the tournaments at that picnic, and having fun there.

Finally, as with all old-time, favorite things, the era of Ellisboro picnics came to an end in the late 1970's or so. Since it was entirely run by volunteers living in the area, over the years, perhaps interest waned in keeping it viable, and of course Mr. McLean couldn't go on running it forever, as he became older. To me, he was a very big part of Ellisboro picnic, always welcoming people as they drove in at the entryway, from all regions of the valley and beyond. Then later he gathered the money for the races, etc., visiting with everyone, young and old, and always keeping things running smoothly. Each year when July 1st comes around, all of us who had the privilege of attending those picnics over the years, remember back with fondness tinged with sadness, to a time when the simple pleasures of getting together for a day of visiting and fellowship in this idyllic valley setting, on Canada's Birthday was enough to give us enjoyment, and the desire to return year after year.

Summer visits to the Indian Head Experimental/Forestry Farm weren't as high a priority as the two previous events listed, but were family-type gatherings that we all enjoyed. The "Teasdale" side of the family was mostly involved, over our growing up years, this event taking the form of a family picnic. Since all the ladies of the family loved flowers and growing them at home, the numerous, gloriously colorful flowered beds, were of particular interest to them, and the men and children simply enjoyed the day visiting with family members, and touring the grounds, barns of purebred livestock, and trial plots of different grains, and new varieties of vegetables. There seemed to be endless manicured lawns, between the neatly spaded flower beds and gently curving graveled paths, on which to play and frolic, especially at the Experimental Farm. The Forestry farm seemed to be more involved with what else—trees! This operation raised and made available wind-break hedges and trees to farmers for nominal amounts, to avoid soil erosion, etc. and still does to this day, as far as is known.

Gran Teasdale, our family, the Mortons and sometimes the Wilson clan would join us for these outings, each mother bringing a variety of cold meats, potato salad, buns, other salads, desserts, fruits and beverages along from home, as there were no food outlets on the grounds. It seems to me there was a kitchen available, especially in later years, where people could heat water for hot beverages, and picnic-type tables to sit at. However, mostly we just picked a shady spot and laid out several blankets brought from home, then spent the later afternoon sitting on them, eating and visiting. Many families from the towns and surrounding areas would gather for picnics at these two "Farms", especially on Sunday afternoons, to enjoy each other's company in pretty surroundings, making their visits there as entertaining as possible, sharing each other's company and food, away from the cares of everyday life even if just for a few hours. Our family picnics now sometimes held in Wascana Park remind me so much of these outings.

I do recall going for one last visit to Indian Head Experimental Farm with Mom and the Robins when our children were very small, having supper in what seemed like someone's private yard on the grounds, but no one seemed to mind we were there, and we did enjoy their picnic table! Also, another time when Gordon and I were going together, the family met for a picnic at Indian Head; we were invited, but unable to attend due to our work schedules. Apparently, it was one of the more eventful, funny picnics, we were told later, because half way through their supper it began to rain but everyone elected to stay out in it and continue eating. Dad put newspaper over him to keep the rain off his summer straw hat, and some funny incident involving a cake or pie seems to come to mind, but not being present, I have forgotten how it all went—sorry now we missed it!

Usually, over the course of the summer holidays, both Wolseley and Sintaluta held Sport's Days. These events were sponsored by local Chambers of Commerce and/or service clubs for the entertainment and enjoyment of local town and farm people. July seemed to be a favorite month for these Sport's Days, and tended to be held on or near the same date each year, so as not to interfere with the ones being held in surrounding towns, as often people would attend in their home town as well as in neighboring towns, although I don't recall we did, usually only going to the Wolseley one.

They often began with a parade in the morning, on the downtown streets, but the main activities took place at the fair grounds, usually a large, open, grassy area at the edge of town, complete with an oval racetrack, high racetrack watch tower, grandstand, concession stand, ball diamonds and bleachers, kept and maintained solely for such events. Often a little midway would be hired to provide entertainment for the younger crowd, while harness races and ball games were always popular with the adults in attendance. Again a lot of visiting was part of the agenda, as most folks in attendance were known to each other, or at least acquainted. Of course, a hot sunny day was always most conducive to a good attendance, and for the most part the weather tended to be fair and especially hot. If it was windy, a lot of dust blew around the grounds from the dirt race track. I expect harness races were always a big part of the Wolseley Sport's Day because several influential horse enthusiasts like Dr. Isman and Joe Sanderson lived in Wolseley.

The location of the racetrack, dissecting the fair grounds between grassy area and grandstand created kind of a dangerous situation for pedestrians during each horse race, and extra care and attention had to be paid to keep the track free if there was a race in progress. I recall one year an incident occurring where a fellow unknown to us was injured in this manner, crossing the track at the time of a race, and coming in contact with a cart, horse and driver. We were always even more careful after this, and it seems to me each side of the track was more carefully policed and no pedestrians were allowed to cross during a race after this incident.

Apart from these few remembrances, I am not able to recall any outstanding memories with regard to Wolseley Sport's Days, or any in other surrounding towns either for that matter, because we rarely attended them, and only the Wolseley ones occasionally. I think children's races were sometimes held, but not with the same prize money available at Ellisboro. Mom and Dad not being at all interested in the horse races and only Dad in the ball games, our family seemed more inclined to making Ellisboro their one summer outing most years, as the gate and other prices continued to escalate, and we always seemed to have a better time there, probably because we knew more of the people attending, etc.

Very occasionally, "a trip to the Lake" (Katepwa) was planned for a Sunday. We would go even though neither Connie nor I swam (not because we hadn't the opportunity to learn, as mentioned previously), and of course Mom and Dad never ventured in the water, and didn't even own bathing suits that we ever saw them in anyway. However, we liked to tan and puddle around in the water, and usually had fun for the day, wishing we could return oftener. Sometimes we met other family members there for a picnic, along the same idea as the Indian Head picnics, or sometimes we just got hamburgers, hot dogs or fish and chips from the local order counter. No close relatives had a cottage there then, except the Bowers (Aunt Gladys's family)—we were invited but never seemed to go.

(In memory, I recall a one day visit to Katepwa when Heather was perhaps two years old. We thought it would be a nice outing for Mom, recently widowed, and took her along for a visit and picnic supper. I'll never forget Mom brought along the fixings for a full-scale dinner, complete with fresh garden peas she cooked up beside the car on her little gas stove—home away from home! We sure thought it was cute, but it made her happy, and spending the day with her precious first grand-daughter gave her much pleasure also.)

Connie and I would "sun-bathe" at home on the lawn in summer, laying down a blanket and playing a game of naming cloud shapes. I recall loving the deep blue prairie sky even back then, staring up into it and the clouds, imagining far away places like Egypt, with camels and pyramids, and remotely dreaming of going there someday. Little did I realize then that some 30 years later, in 1984 at age 41, that "pipe dream" as Gran Teasdale used to call day dreams, would become a reality, when Gordon''s company incentive trip would be to Egypt with a Nile Cruise and visit to Cairo, where we did indeed see many pyramids and even rode on camels! Who says dreams don't come true?

One particular summer when I was about 11 or 12, I owned a rather stylish turquoise colored, form-fitting bathing suit with white trim and piping. I determined I would suntan every sunny day to obtain an all over tan befitting my new suit and budding feminine figure! The effort required sweating buckets I recall without the benefit of a cool shower following, but I persevered, and by the end of summer I had a real nice tan that I recall my favorite uncle Clippie admiring—this made me really happy, even though the rest of the family thought it was a waste of time, he had noticed, and it mattered to me then.

Both Aunt Elsie and Aunt Alice did their best over the years to see that Connie and I had a "little holiday" with one or both of their families over the summer, and looking back it must have seemed to them we led a rather boring life, with nothing but endless sameness to fill our annual holiday from school. However, I don't remember feeling bored or deprived in any way. Connie and I had each other to play with, or we would get together with cousins to play. We did help out some with the garden and produce and in later years and the lawns, etc. Also we always had Saturday nights, Drive-Ins, Ellisboro and Indian Head visits to look forward to, as well as Exhibition. I always had my many crafts to keep my mind and fingers occupied also, and dearly loved spending time creatively, a pleasure I still enjoy to this day, whenever time and circumstance permit.

Visits to the Wilson farms, wherever they were living, at Sunny Hill or their farm in the trees, (somewhere south of town) were always a pleasant change, as for the longest time they had no children, and spoiled us on our visits rather indulgently. In the early years, when Connie was too young to stay away from home, I visited them alone. I recall on one of those early visits, there was some kind of picnic/outing at the local school where Aunty taught and we attended it. Clippie's niece, Betty Ann Hinton was also in attendance and we chummed around together that day, sharing her wintergreen lifesavers one by one until they were gone. Another time, a severe thunderstorm came up, during the day, while Clippie was away from home. I had never known an adult that was so petrified of thunder and lightening as Aunt was, hiding her head under the cushions on the couch until it passed, while I bravely stood guard; no one at our house was afraid of storms—Mom and Dad used to watch them from our many windows, predicting their course, etc.

Aunt Elsie had many girlhood treasures that she let us admire and play with, taught us new songs, with actions, and to play cat's cradle with string. It seems to me Borden's had just brought out Elsie the Cow as an advertising gimmick with their new sweetened condensed milk product, on one of my early visits, and I remember coloring books and recipes Aunt made from that milk tasted extra special! I have already mentioned the visit to Lake Katepwa Aunt Elsie took me on, as a young girl, to the Marlin cottage, and not having a proper bathing suit to wear. The fact that she wanted to take me with her on that holiday, was what counted most though.

In addition to these visits to the Wilson's, summer visits to Aunt Alice's apartment home in Regina became regular occurrences, when we were a little older, and could stay further away from home without tears and wanting to go home. The first time, Connie and I went for two whole weeks, getting a little taste of city life! I remember the constant hum of the traffic on busy Hamilton Street, even during the night, was different and hard to get used to at first. Shopping was fun, and visits to the Museum and other points of interest, as well as visits to the park across the street and to the corner store with cousin Bob.

Several years the Morton family rented a cottage at Regina Beach, Daweville by name from a lady Uncle Don knew, and we were invited to stay there with them. I recall we had to drive down a steep, curved, inclined road to access the cottage, and all along the graded sides of the road, bank swallows lived with nests in holes they had made. What a neat place to have a house—much different than the barn swallows we knew from the farm, with their mud houses built in the rafters of the hen house. Aunt Alice made delicious stews in her new pressure cooker and we picked wild strawberries, flowers and little cactus while they golfed, a favorite pass-time for them.

Looking back now, having had our own family, I can appreciate more the extra effort it must have taken for these two dear aunts to share their summers with their two little nieces, but they did it willingly and happily, and we appreciated it a lot. By the same token, both these families, especially the Mortons along with Gran Teasdale, were frequent Sunday visitors to our farm home, over the years, always remaining for supper. We always loved to see them, and everyone had a nice visit, as well as allowing the Morton's son Bob some "open space" as he was growing up in an apartment in the city, before they owned their own Regina home.

Birthdays were always cause for celebration, with cake and candles, cards and presents, even for adults. I hardly recall a childhood birthday that wasn't celebrated with relatives present, a favorite birthday supper and much jubilation. I will never forget my 10th birthday party celebrated with family as well as a party just for school friends and cousins. Even boys were invited and we had a wonderful play time, including a barn dance up in our barn loft, singing and clapping the songs we had learned at school as well as the dances. It was at this party many lovely gifts were received, including the box of plaster-of-paris white wear molds ready to paint Isobel had made for cousin Wayne to give me, as mentioned previously.

Over the years, the Birthdays of Gran Teasdale, Aunt Alice and then Connie, all born in December on the 4th, 20th and 5th respectively, were celebrated in early December with a family get-together, usually at our home. Madeira cake, trimmed with toasted almonds, was Gran's favorite, so was usually the cake of choice, with white, chocolate or marble being added over the years, for other family members not as keen on the Madeira one! Gran's 7Oth Birthday party in 1959, held in the form of a come-and-go tea at her home in Wolseley, while I was in high school, and her 80th celebration at St. George's parish hall, in 1969, when I was expecting Heather, are special remembrances.

It never occurred to me back then, that all families weren't in the habit of celebrating the birthdays of their family members, like ours did, with cards, presents, parties, guests, cake and candles, especially for the children anyway. Gordon relates to me his family never made much to—do of individual's birthdays, for which I feel sad and sorry, especially when he and Helmuth were youngsters anyway. Surely one day of the year could be set aside as a fun day one could rely on for his or her birthday—we have always made sure of this for our own children, and have had many happy celebrations in many varied locations, (Great Skate roller rink, Centre of Arts, Wascana, McDonalds, etc.), over the years, and many specially decorated cakes, with many little guests from neighborhood and school, as well as family members.

Many other occasions were cause for family get-togethers, back then, especially Christmas and New Years. Most years Christmas was spent with Mom's family, because Gran Teasdale wanted us all to be together—being together was paramount. We were often invited to spend it also with Dad's side of the family alternating either at Raymonds or Uncle Herb's homes as they had the largest houses for such a large family affair. I recall we would often go for New Year's celebrations rather than Christmas. After a massive turkey dinner with all the trims, much visiting would take place, as well as games of cards and finally a good old sing—song around the piano. It was a good chance to visit and play with cousins, some of whom lived farther away, like Sintaluta and even Regina.

Christmas Eve was usually spent with final preparations for Christmas Day, final shaking of presents, and a late night trip to Wolseley for midnight Communion at St. George's Church, with a visit at Gran's house beforehand. Looking back, those cold, snowy, star-lit Christmas Eve's spent with family at Church are a favorite childhood memory for me, the nativity scene, carols and Bible revelation of the true meaning of Christmas filling all our hearts with peace and joy. The anticipation of the events about to happen the very next day, presents, special foods and family gathering together adding to the pleasure we all felt.

We always had a live Christmas tree, purchased in town, set up in a huge, heavy triangular shaped steel base Dad had made and trimmed with bright glass baubles Mom had got in Fort William, as well as those made at school each year etc. The parcels from England were always eagerly awaited, always arriving in plenty of time to savor the contents that had to be listed on the front for postal purposes. My very favorite Rupert Books were always sent from Aunt Elsie and Uncle Norman Fisher, while Aunt Mary often sent scarves, handkerchiefs, brooches, diaries, purses, mint cakes and pink sugared mice, with string tails. Everything from England had a special smell, kind of musty and old but because the gifts had come from so far, they were special in their own rite.

Christmas traditions like stuffed turkey, Trifle, Gran's plum pudding, mince meat and Christmas cakes she made each year from her very own English recipes, all ingredients carefully measured by weight on her special scales, served with brown and white sauce (later hard sauce from the Hodgson's recipe), holly on top sent from Uncle Wilfred in B.C., brandy poured over it, burning with a blue flame, and Christmas crackers to pull, at each place setting, are all favorite memories we still try to incorporate to this day in our annual celebrations.

As mentioned previously, all Christmases during our childhood were preceded by our favorite Allindale School Christmas concerts that hold special memories for all who attended and took part in them over the years. The Christmas I received my new doll carriage, maroon with white trim and a fold down top, remains a vivid memory, along with many others. Being "home" for Christmas was of the greatest importance, and all family members strived towards being present, in the early years to Gran Teasdale's home in Wolseley, and later to our farm home. I recall riding in the sleigh box pulled by horses one year to attend, and when Connie was a new baby, taking our old blue Chevy to town with her all bundled up in the wicker wash basket (car seats weren't invented as yet). Mom and I had gone on ahead into Gran's house, and all relatives present, were so glad to see us, jubilant we were all safely together, we temporarily forgot about Dad carrying in the precious baby bundle in basket, and he had to knock to get in! Spending Christmas apart from family during nurse training years was perhaps one of the hardest adjustments required in the whole regimen, and one I resented greatly, even though realizing someone had to keep the hospital operating for the patients, also away from home and ill besides.

Another Christmas Eve, when I was in high school, and sang in the United Church Cantata Choir, arrangements were made for our group to sing several Carol selections live on CK television. What a special event, happening on a special night—it seems to me several of us girls got car rides there and back with other adult members, and I seem to recall our group went with Lorne Sexsmith, and it being a lovely, clear, moonlight night, as we returned.

I have memories of singing at the Carol Festival in Regina with the RGNH Glee Club, during my first year of nurse's training. Mom and Connie came up on the bus to be present for it. Later back at residence, where a special city bus had brought us singers after the performance, I was desperate for a visit with them and had to get over to Mortons, where they were staying for the night. I hailed a ride with a class-mate's boyfriend, and had time for a short visit prior to residence curfew, brought back there by Uncle Don Morton. These are some of the special remembrances of Cristmases past. Another favorite memory is of making a roast duckling dinner for Gordon and I on my little hot plate stove and oven at Andris home before we were married, and having to work evenings that day, so I rested while he did all the dishes! Of all the occasions of the year, Christmas definitely had to the one all of our family held most dear over the years.

Spring and Easter always seem synonymous because they fall so close together. Although Easter never seemed to have quite the same traditional celebrations as Christmas, attending Church and being together afterwards for visiting, Easter egg coloring and then exchanges, egg-pacing matches (rolling colored, hard-boiled eggs along the floor, from opposite sides of the room, trying to crack opponent's eggs without cracking your own—a game from Mom's childhood), hidden Easter chocolate treats at Grandma's house, and sometimes a new Easter outfit or hat are some of the things I remember about Easter in those early years. Searching for crocuses on the hills or railroad prairie banks, seeing the first crow, meadow lark or robin were also some family-oriented things we did together.

Thanksgiving at the end of the harvest season, was often celebrated first at church, with St. George's being beautifully decorated with the bounty and produce of the summer and fall. Often a turkey, pumpkin pies and mounds of rich, whipped farm cream graced our table as family once again got together for visiting and to give thanks. Of particular interest of course, to farmers, was having the fields of grain safely harvested and in the bins, stooks made into stacks or stored in barn lofts. It didn't always happen that "all was safely gathered in" as the hymn says, just because thanksgiving fell around the second weekend in October, as so many variables, mostly the weather, being such an important factor, just as it is to this day!

Radio played a big part in the day to day lives of farm families back then, as an information and entertainment commodity. Almost every household had at least one or two radios—a smaller one on a shelf in the kitchen for the homemaker to listen to as she went about her chores and housekeeping, or for family entertainment during mealtimes, etc., much as some families have a small kitchen T.V. today. A larger radio was usually found in the living room or parlor, as an item of furniture, often a console, floor model of fine wood, and even sometimes in combination with a record player. An aerial on the roof of the house and attached to the radio via small wires, (at our house threaded through the east front room window), resulted in much improved reception.

I recall our family owning two radios as we grew up, located in the front room, sufficing to be heard all over the house, as it was small, so we didn't need a kitchen one. The first radio I remember was a console model, standing on the floor, made of highly polished wood with speakers in front. When this radio wore out and could no longer be repaired we bought a wooden table model, that Mom kept on a nice wooden table—shelf with drawer and end racks, bought especially for this purpose. It seems to me both radios were of quite high quality, and were played extensively each day, as Mom loved music playing in the house during the day, and for the news, etc., and during the evening we enjoyed certain shows. It was our family's one main link with the outside world, in the absence of a telephone, and we were able to keep up with the weather, as well as local and world-wide happenings, just as we do today, with T.V. giving us pictures to go along with the events!

The radio stations I recall that were available at the time were Regina stations, CKCK at 6:20 on the radio dial, with one of the early announcers being Jim McLeod, (who later went on to be a T.V. broadcaster for many years), and CKRM dialed at 9:80. CJGX Yorkton, Mom's favorite, always played Country Music and was also the home station of announcer Joe Hatcook from my Amateur Hour days, located on the radio somewhere between CKRM and CHAB Moose Jaw, located at 8:20 on the dial. We used to listen to an afternoon show from this station hosted by a comical fellow Cy Knight, called The Mail Bag. People could write in Greetings and Song Requests that he would read over the air, commenting here and there—it was very entertaining, and had an old-fashioned sounding accordion music theme I recall. BBS Watrous tuned in at the extreme left side of the radio dial at 5 something played mostly classical music and had interesting artsy-type guest interviews, readings, etc., that we rarely listened to.

Mom preferred the stations that played the Hit Parade songs, popular at the time, like Eddy Arnold's Red Roses For a Blue Lady, etc. I can still recall Gran Teasdale having trouble understanding this song title, not figuring the "blue" to mean sad, but the actual color! We sure laughed as we explained it to her! I assume the hit parade songs that changed each week were governed by record sales and popularity of requests to be played, etc.

Day-time soap operas were broadcast right after lunch every week-day, sponsored by Procter and Gamble products. It seems to me there were four stories running, in 15 minute segments each day, with the entire broadcast lasting an hour, allowing time for airing commercials, just as our T.V. soaps of today, (only there was no remote to mute them on command if desired)! Ma Perkins was one and Pepper Young's Family another, I recall, with the last story involving a women Carolyn, a father Miles and a young son Skip, although I don't remember the name of this one. The first story it seems to me changed often and I have no recollection of it or its name, however the last three were long-running and had quite a following. From all accounts, these shows were done in the broadcasting studios quite often live, and heard as they were being performed, as opposed to taping and recording nowadays. Voices had to be projected with additional clarity and depth, in conjunction with an active and well articulated sound department, as the audio part was all listeners were getting over the air waves, with the video part being imagined from what was being heard. It must have been quite an art form back then.

Another afternoon show I came to like a lot as a young girl was especially designed for young listeners called Cuckoo Clock House, a half-hour show being aired at 3:00 p.m. every Sunday afternoon. I can still hear the little theme song in my mind and recall there was a kindly male narrator with a voice sounding something like Mr. Dress-Up's our children were so fond of on T.V. There was a story section, where he would read part of a new children's book to us listeners, encouraging us to watch for the Title by such and such an author, next time we visited our local library. Of course, the nearest and only library we ever visited was the one available at school, although in Wolseley there was a well-organized library located in the town hall, looked after by local folks, where we could have borrowed. Also on this show were recipes young people could try, experiments with simple household items and sometimes crafts, usually explained by a guest crafter. There was opportunity to write to the station with comments about the show, and it seems to me I did write once in a while. I was sorry when it went off the air sometime during my girlhood years.

Another favorite week-day show was the Happy Gang with congenial host Bert Pearl—a long-running broadcast from Toronto, featuring Blaine Mathey, Kay on keyboards and Bobby Gimby, who later went on to Broadway fame with his Seventy-Six Trombones, etc., and as an entertainer in his own right. Many other musicians shared the spotlight for the hour of music and friendly, wholesome banter. Mom and Gran Teasdale especially loved this show, and wouldn't miss it if possible. It aired locally close to noon, and was always on while we had our lunch, if we happened to be home on a week day from school. It seems to me Gran had an 8 x 10 glossy picture of the whole group comprising the Happy Gang she had sent for and she proudly displayed it and kept it to look at over the years, her favorite being Bert Pearl. Their "Keep Happy With the Happy Gang" theme song is still familiar in my mind also.

In the evenings, Lux radio theatre provided hour long drama presentations once a week, sponsored by who else—the Lux hand soap makers, the one we always used at home. As I recall, these shows were especially well done and received and this show enjoyed many long years of popularity as we grew up.

Boston Blackey, a detective-type show ran for a number of years, as well as the Edgar Bergen-Charlie McCarthy Show. It was of special interest, to me after receiving my Charlie replica from Albert Murrell, Mom and Gran's neighbor and friend when Mom and I lived at Gran's house during the war years. Amos 'n Andy, Fibber McGee and Molly, the Lone Ranger with Tonto, and Who Am I? with Monty Hall, were programs I recall we liked to listen to. Often the boxing matches were broadcast, and as a girl I took an interest in one particular boxer named Rocky Marciano, and especially liked to listen when he was one of the contenders—he was nice looking (there were sometimes pictures of him in newspapers and magazines) and he seemed to win a lot. I think my interest in boxing stemmed from relating to the boxers being punched in the nose a lot and having consequent nose bleeds. As I have mentioned previously, as a girl I was subject to this affliction of epistaxis, often on a daily basis in summer, and I felt a certain affinity with the contenders because of this—weird eh? At any rate—when the boxing matches were on I listened attentively! Of course Dad liked hockey, sometimes the baseball matches and was always interested in the news, weather and daily grain prices.

Gordon reminds me to mention that in the early days prior to electricity, radios were battery operated, and couldn't be operated for long periods at a time without running the battery down. Larger console models housed a large car-type battery, so were able to be run longer than smaller radios that used flashlight batteries. So if a special program was airing, battery provision had to be ensured beforehand.

We didn't get a television at home until way after everyone else, probably because of funding, however lots of people in the district and in town had sets. It became popular to be invited over to watch certain shows that quickly grew to be favorites like Ed Sullivan's variety show, Country Hoedown, etc. In high school I recall Gran and I being invited over to Relfs (neighbors across the street) to watch Rifleman with Chuck Conners as we both liked it a lot and Perry Como's show, as Gran liked him so much. During World Series in fall, Lykes (Gran's neighbors to the south, up the hill) invited us there to watch over the noon hours as that is when those broadcasts aired. Then Gran invested in a T.V., so we could watch whatever we wanted when homework was done. She was always very kind and wouldn't allow herself any viewing time either, until we could both watch (after homework).

At weekends when I was home during high school and we finally got a T.V. at home, we always watched Zorro while having supper on Saturday nights, and later of course Dad watched hockey, really enjoying this weekly broadcast. Once when I was half-heartedly watching with him, I mistook the "Replay" sign they showed for a player's name—we sure laughed and Gordon still teases me about it to this day! Dad also loved to watch the songstress Juliette's show that aired live, immediately following the hockey games. Occasionally, if the hockey ran late or into overtime, her show was cut back—then Dad would really be disappointed. Bonanza, Perry Mason and CannonBall were popular.

I also remember a funny incident involving Mom and the early days of T.V. in our area. It was decided by CK-TV to visit the towns around Saskatchewan and feature them on a weekly show. Video was collected by film crews and interviews with local businesses and residents. An interviewer Hugh Delaney, that always gave the local weather forecast with the local news from Regina happened to be coming out of the Robinson store just as Mom was going in for groceries one day, during the time Wolseley filming was being done. This broadcaster was very funny, always calling himself Hudel Aney, like his name sounded when said quickly. On meeting up with him at Robinsons Mom exclaimed "Well there's Hudel"—just like she knew him! I guess he burst out laughing and shook her hand, glad to meet one of his viewers that obviously liked him and felt she knew him by his nick-name! These shows were very well received and most interesting, as we learned so much about the many towns we had only heard of before.

Some evenings after homework was done or on Sunday afternoons, we would have a sing-song with guitar, and later on the piano, with just our family. As mentioned previously, Mom and Dad both liked to sing, and Dad especially knew the words, both verse and chorus to a myriad of songs he was only too glad to teach us. It was during these times, from listening to Dad sing harmony that I realized I had this singing gift also, and finally he said I became better and truer at it than he, so whenever we sang in public in later years, I would sing the harmony and he the melody. He would sometimes get his mouth organ out of its box in the top drawer of the dresser, and give us a little tune on it. He dreamed of someday owning and playing a more expensive harmonica; unfortunately, in this life anyway, was never able to realize his dream.

Dad taught me how to cord and play the fine Hawaiian guitar he had saved for and bought, as a young man, and I was eager to learn this skill. We spent many happy hours singing to its accompaniment in the earlier days when he played it, and later on after I learned to play. Cousin Dwight and his Dad Harold used to like to sing with us on their visits for haircuts, etc., and Dwight and I sang the song "Sometime" in harmony accompanied by teacher Audrey Adams at the town hall once for some benefit, when we were both in public school.

The piano also provided me with endless hours of enjoyment for lessons and recreation. I recall in addition to all the music we acquired with the piano, we also had quite a nice collection of our own books and a lot of sheet music Aunt Alice would buy for us at Hatton's Music store in Regina. Songs from current movies and popular hit parade tunes like Ivy Rose, Seventy Six Trombones, Paper Roses, Old Cape Cod and He'll Have To Go were some favorites I recall.

I also played the piano a lot by ear—I always knew if I had a chance, I would be able to play by ear, from being able to pick out and play little melodies on Gran Teasdale's piano, when we visited her. Kitty, My Pretty White Kitty, is the one I recall plunking out first—little did I know then we would someday own two beautiful white cats, when our stray Kitty chose us as her new family!

We also learned to dance at home with Dad, twirling around to peppy tunes on the radio. He loved to dance, and seemed to delight in teaching us the Fox Trot, Two Step, Old-time Waltz and Polka while we were young, and of course we wanted to learn! Then when we went to dances as we were older, first at school and then at the halls in Sintaluta and Wolseley, we knew how to dance and loved every minute of it! It still saddens me that Gordon's family denied themselves this pleasurable pass-time, because of its association with drinking and carousing—consequently to this day he derives little pleasure from dancing, much to my dismay, even though he has tried for my sake. Dad had a dream of someday dancing in a lavish ballroom to a fine orchestra, especially Guy Lombardo & The Royal Canadians or Lawrence Welk, with him dressed in a tuxedo with tails and Mom in a long gown. Perhaps when he and Mom are together in heaven, they will be able to realize this dream someday, if we dance there—who knows—sure hope so!

On long winter evenings while we were growing up, we would often play games like Checkers or Chinese Checkers, and simple card games like Old Maid, Rummy and Snap, with regular decks of cards. There weren't the specialty card games now available—I recall adults playing a new card game Canasta, and whenever we went visiting for an evening it was "The Game of Choice" to play. People also played Bridge and Whist as well as Crokinole and Darts or Ring Toss—we had a board in later years that we all enjoyed playing with each other and visiting cousins. In some homes card games were forbidden on Sundays but not ours.

Dad was very keen to help us with our homework, and me especially with my writing skills. It is because of his persistence and guidance, I think, that I possess the fine hand-writing I do today. We had a scribbler with an old-fashioned scene on the front, of a lady in front of a thatched house that I still have tucked away in my favorite keep-sakes to this day. In it we practiced my writing, making tails on the endings of letters, getting the slant just so, using the written alphabet letters printed on the sides of our free-standing toy blackboard, as a guide. For a man, Dad had quite good hand-writing, and he was determined I would also. We also did drawings—tracing our hands, opening the thumb and little finger just enough to look like a dog's head, side-face. Mom even took time once to make a drawing in this book, of a little baby girl in blankets, that I colored. Mom's abilities at drawing/water color painting were special.

Writing to several pen pals during my girlhood years gave me much pleasure and took up some of my spare time. They were mostly from the eastern provinces,, Terry Lorenzetti from Rawdon, Quebec and Joyce Veary from Lac Megantic, Quebec and a Wendy Kemp from Australia, are the ones I remember best and wrote to the longest. I submitted my name, hobbies and request for pen pals to The Family Herald newspaper we subscribed to at the time. Because I had mentioned I collected stamps (but only on a very small scale and local level) I got lots of letters from other collectors wanting to trade, much to my surprise. Another sent me little ornamental broach and earring sets made of a kind of brightly colored heavy foil-like material in the form of tropical birds with springy tails, in silver, cerise and pale mint green. The idea was to sell these sets for this person, keeping a small commission for myself. It seems to me I did sell some of them, but with my limited customer base, had to return the rest, realizing very little profit for my efforts! (The letter from the Yates in the Maritimes [mentioned previously while discussing hired hands] also arrived at this time).

In addition to Family Herald our family also subscribed to the Western Producer, Reader's Digest and the Wolseley News. Any other publications that we wanted to read had to be bought off the magazine racks in the drug store. I always longed for ladies magazines but Mom never seemed to want to subscribe to any—either cost or lack of time to read them or from lack of interest, I was never sure. I also longed for an up to date set of encyclopedia for use at home, and later on when Connie needed them, our parents did buy a set of Britannica ones in a case, but when I lived at home, we only had Gran Teasdale's set she had bought many years before, on time, from a traveling salesman, so the information was very out-dated, but still better than nothing. I guess this is why owning a good set was such a priority while our own children were growing up (and they and their school friends made very good use of them too).

I had a passion for Movie Stars during my formative years, fueled by all the drive-in movies we went to see during that time. I had stacks of movie magazines, bought with money squirreled away as allowance—they became more popular for me to buy than any sweet candy treat or gum, as I grew older. I made scrap books of my favorites, and spent hours pouring over their romantic, high-profile life styles, dreaming of what it would be like to actually meet one of them, especially Robert Wagner. He was my absolute favorite movie star idol. When he married another favorite actress Natalie Wood I recall thinking it was great. Then her mysterious death on that boat they owned and him taking up with Stephanie Powers really disturbed me and my opinion of him was shattered. Other favorites were Tony Curtis, Janet Leigh, Rock Hudson, Jane Wyman, James Dean and for singers Pat Boone, Tab Hunter, Roy Orbison and Elvis a little, although not to the extent that Connie and her generation idolized him. Although Mom kept a lot of childhood treasures for Connie and I in her little house, I'm not sure about my movie star collection, as I haven't seen my scrapbooks since high school years—perhaps downstairs stored in the blue trunk—someday when we go through all those things we'll know I guess.

Although pets didn't play an important role in our childhoods, we always had a dog and lots of cats. The dog I remember best, that seemed to endure through all my time at home was a male, brown and white mongrel dog simply named Boy or Buoy. His home under the step, winter and summer was his territory and it was here he stored his accumulated treasures (see previous pages). Buoy would growl and bare his teeth if this make-shift home was infringed upon—otherwise he was a well-behaved and good dog, loyal especially to Dad. He followed Dad wherever he was working, with his tractor, fencing, taking the stone boat with Babe, etc. As a pet, we never really played with him much, except when he was a puppy and cute. The cats were preferable to us, especially Connie and she spent many happy hours in their company in the barn.

Zeke was our first cat, a birthday gift from Audrey to me soon after we moved to our farm. This poor cat met with a kind of sad demise. He had a habit of sleeping in the hay beside the cows for warmth we assumed. Alas, one night he was smothered when the cow accidentally laid on him. We then acquired a mother cat with Tabby stripes, we simply called Mamma. Dad loved this cat as she was an excellent mouser and kept the loft and barn free of mice, teaching her subsequent litters of kittens her skills to do the same. This cat seemed to be the mother of all the kittens ever born on our farm, including my favorite male named Poody, white with grey tabby markings. Farm animals were never altered back then.

Gran Sexsmith had a dear old pet tabby cat called Tigger that seemed to be ancient to Audrey and I as we were girls playing together. He sat on the kitchen window sill that faced south most of the time, sleeping and dozing the days away, not wanting to be bothered with anything or anyone, except Gran. Even with his huge, adult male cat size, he would still like to sit on her knee and be petted—he would even purr a bit for her! In later years, he got really crotchety, finally dying of natural causes when he was past 25 years old, or more, which saddened Gran a great deal in her old age. She was very frail by then, failing in physical and mental health, making her home with Herb and Ruby on the home place, as Grandad had stipulated in his will.

An orphaned jack rabbit Dad brought home from the field lived with us one summer. We were immediately attracted to this soft ball of fluff, wanting to be friends, but as he grew up Mom was the only one he would allow to care for him, and we finally let him go in the neighboring pasture in fall.

Gordon relates how he and Helmuth had a little wild orphaned deer they called Billy for a pet one summer when he was a lad. He used to pasture with the cattle as he grew older, so they tied a little bell around his neck so they could hear his whereabouts, and he would come when they called to him. Imagine their dismay when they found Billy's bell and rope—all that was left of their little pet, after hunters accidentally shot him in fall. Gordon and Helmuth raised lambs when they were boys, selling their wool at shearing time, and later on the grown sheep for profit. They also hunted gopher tails and crow legs when the government made funds available in an attempt to limit their numbers. Gordon relates he and his brother also trapped muskrats for their pelts to sell for profit, using a series of trap lines for this.

As related previously, Connie and I had our share of dolls over the years, and I enjoyed making clothes for them as I became older and my sewing and knitting skills improved. I recall each receiving large black and white panda bears as gifts from Uncle Wilfred one Christmas that we proudly displayed on our beds, all the years we were growing up. Because I was older when I received mine, I rarely played with mine, so he stayed very clean and nice, sporting a green satin ribbon at his neck. However, Connie's saw a lot more active play and became soiled, especially the white parts! It seems to me hers had a yellow bow at the neck that also became bedraggled over the years.

However, another beautiful gift of an ornate, old-fashioned bed doll, from Uncle Wilfred to Connie, was preserved in its box until she was older, and I believe is still beautiful to this day. A Hiawatha Indian doll and my little blue teddy bear received from Dad when he was overseas when I was about 2 years old were some other favorite toys I remember. A red table and chair set, wooden doll high chair, toy stove and cupboards made of metal, as well as a little canister set of white with red lids and decals have endured through the years and now live at our house, where they were enjoyed by our children, to be passed on to theirs someday. (Thank goodness for the attic over the garage)!

At about the age of 8 or 9, I "discovered" the mounds of yellowish-tan earth or clay at each end of our recently excavated dug-out in the pasture. (see earlier pages for dug-out description). I think I was attracted to it, because of its different color and texture, compared to the usual dark, crumbly soil found elsewhere on our farm. At school, we often studied about far—away peoples living in different lands and climates who used this miraculous clay material to make artifacts still studied and admired in our time. Here, on our own land was clay "in the rough" for the taking!

It seems to me the school library had books on pottery and using clay to make things, and so armed with this knowledge I knew to gather this damp clay, haul it home, mix it smooth with a bit of water and proceed with all imaginable creations. I know that when I handled it, the consistency and tenacity of it was very fascinating. I hauled it back to the house yard (never working in the house as it was too "dirty" Mom claimed), fashioning it into pots, bowls and vases for our play house and circular beads and squares with holes, later threaded for jewelry. After slowly drying in the sun on planks, any cracks were patched with a thin water/clay mix. After this had dried, each item was painted with water colors and later a coat of shellac gave a glazed, shiny look.

I had no way of knowing then that firing clay at high temperatures after painting it with a glaze would give it a non-porous durable quality suitable for everyday use. Mostly, the items were used for pretend food anyway to grace our table in the play house and be stored on our wooden shelves there. I once shared one of my clay bracelets with a friend visiting from B.C. She seemed to like it—purple and white square beads, I had joined with my faithful cream tag fine wire, I was always squirreling away from Mom, and she sometimes had to use string or binder twine to tag her cream cans for shipping!

I always had the feeling I could have had quite a flair for being a potter and longed for a wheel someday and "proper" clay to work with. Nowadays, a child showing promise in this direction would quickly be enrolled in classes at the community level or in specialized classes, to nurture this talent, if indeed one existed. However, back then on the farm there was neither the opportunity nor the inclination on the part of parents to do such things.

Years later, after Heather was born, I did enroll in a community beginners pottery class, being held west of us in the old treatment plant basement. I had limited success at throwing a few pieces and "hand-building" a plaque and tiny triangular candle holder. Glazing was an area we only had one class in and our teacher did all the firing—so much for my pottery experience then. Gordon has an old fly wheel he always intended to make into a simple potter's wheel for me, that would have been foot powered. However, now with new electric ones, this would be preferable. The fall of 1995, Warren's mother, Shirley and I attended another beginner pottery class at Pasqua Rec. Centre that I thoroughly enjoyed, remembering some of my previous skills at the wheel and also doing a lot of hand building. Perhaps we will take another class soon at the intermediate level. Having a room or spot, set aside with a wheel and even a kiln would be the ideal way to pursue this talent, and perhaps I will again someday.

As a girl, I had a lasting and abiding fascination in shells and anything to do with the sea and oceans. Probably because we grew up on the land-locked prairies, the thought of vast bodies of water filled with creatures of the deep, and especially the pretty shells some of them produced, was a total amazement to me. Mom had a beautiful conch shell painted with a harbor scene on its outer edge, that Dad had sent her from his wartime travels in Europe. Its inner swirls were the most delicate pink, as far inside as could be seen, and if held up to the ear, definite ocean-like echo sounds could be heard—(or did we just imagine them?)! I also received a smaller orange and rusty shaded shell of a little different shape from my Daddy during those war years that I fancied I could also hear the ocean sounds from. I treasure it still today, as well as a little wooden jewelry box, topped with a decorative shell design on its hinged lid, he also sent me. Norma Luther, friend from Allindale had a similar, but larger jewelry box, with shells on the lid, I always recall admiring when I visited her in her tiny room at the top of the stairs of their farm home.

The only shells I was able to find naturally on the prairies, were washed up at the edge of ponds and sloughs from snails. They were a bland grey or brown shade, but perfectly and exquisitely shaped similar to Mom's large conch shell from the actual ocean. I would bring them home by the score; wash out the mucky contents, always hoping the snail that had used it for its home was long-gone! I would dry them and paint them with left-over paint-by-number paints I had saved, fashioning them into decorative tops for jewelry boxes or fastening screw-type earring backs on them, bought at the local craft stores, for earrings. They were terribly fragile, and shattered easily, but that was never a deterrent to my fascination with them.

I have just mentioned paint-by-number paints—these were a very popular craft for me in my girlhood days, and I painted several sets—all gifts from family and friends. I recall a pair of roses in vases, spaniel dogs, and a pair of harbor scenes. The color of paint supplied in little plastic lidded pots, in the kit, matched the numbers on a printed cardboard faced with a heavy canvas-like material. A colored replica of what the finished pictures should look like, one or two fine brushes and a little bottle of turpentine for cleaning were all supplied. It seemed to be a new concept at the time I was a girl, and I loved painting these paint-by-number pictures, and all the uses I found for the left-over paints afterwards! I recall always loving to look into Audrey's kaleidoscope, with its myriad of colored shapes, while visiting her, and also playing pick-up sticks at her house.

Creating artificial flowers at first from crepe paper and later from little squares of a new product on the market and in the craft, stores at the time, wood fiber, were also a special pass-time and craft for me back then. How-to books were available, for the self-taught, and I recall making several little pink roses, wrapping the stems with stretch adhesive, incorporating leaves, etc., I later fastened a brooch closure to and wore on blouses and dresses for trim that seemed to look quite nice and realistic. Wood fiber was quite easy to work with having the feel and pliability of real flower petals.

Knitting, crochet, embroidery and sewing were crafts I picked up along the way from Gran Sexsmith, Gran Teasdale and teachers, that I seemed to have a natural bent for and really enjoyed doing. Craft kits with shells and another with a little loom and rounds of stretchy cotton fabric in different colors, along with a little metal hook, allowing me to weave place-mats of different designs, were other projects I enjoyed as a girl. I recall sending for many stamped doilies and runners in sets, for embroidering from the Family Herald magazine. They came with the floss to work them, as well as directions and needles. Mom still uses some of these in her home today.

Kits of ink and rubber stamp designs as well as a set of stencils allowed Connie and I a wide range of possibilities in art-work we could make. I was fascinated by the glorious cerise-colored water that resulted when Mom boiled fresh garden beets in Fall and try as I might to write with some of it, the glorious color always turned a dull-brown shade when it dried on the paper—thus my ongoing joy at the myriad of colored pens available today! Jet black India ink was used for highlighting and outlining. Colored pencils in boxes had made their appearance, and were put to good use at school and for play at home. Crayons seemed to be available in more and more colors, offering a rainbow of pastels to make coloring even more pleasurable, as opposed to the basic colors available earlier. I always loved coloring, outlining with the sharp point first, and then filling in with soft, lighter textured shades. Even when our children were young, I still enjoyed coloring with them. Perhaps someday soon, there will be grandchildren that would like

Grandma to color with them! I recall faithfully keeping a diary all my girlhood years.

I enjoyed a bit of carpentering as a girl, going to Dad's garage, using the vice for holding projects, etc. I liked fret-sawing, having been introduced to it at school. I recall using Dad's fret-saw to make a little frame out of quarter round for my copper tole picture for G.A. (too bad Ivan hadn't come along sooner with his mitre-box!) I also recall making a small knick-knack for the play house, patterned after some Dad had made for Mom, cutting, sanding and varnishing it myself.

Connie and I enjoyed skating in winter as girls. Dad would kindly clear us ice space in the large slough adjacent to the barn in early winter, and kept it cleared for us all winter long. Of course the water froze right to the bottom in this shallow pond, and the resultant cracks in the surface were our biggest bug-a-boo for falling! Occasionally, on Saturday afternoons in winter, if our family was going to town for groceries, we would take our skates along and skate during the free-skate time at the Wolseley rink. There was even music to skate to and no cracks to make us fall! We also enjoyed sleigh riding down the many slopes in yard and bloughs, or being pulled behind the stone boat when Dad and Babe made trips to the dug-out, etc. In spring, we used to like to make little boats out of half a walnut shell, complete with paper mast stuck on a toothpick, secured in the bottom with wax or plastersene. It was great fun to race them along the many little rivulets of water that formed beside the lane—I still think of it every spring, when the water starts to run. (Some memories bear repeating).

From the previous account, it is easy to determine our girlhood days were filled with many, varied endeavors, with our parents, with each other as sisters, and independently. For me then as now, there never seemed to be enough time to fit in all the possible crafts and interesting things there were to do each day. School, work and the business of living always seem to get in the way!

Several treasured items that have been handed down over the years, come to mind and should be recorded. I have previously mentioned having Aunt Martha's miniature sad iron, complete with detachable handle. A small wooden three drawer chest she also owned, I have painted white and now use to store my sewing notions, as it easily sits on my machine cabinet arm. A small jack knife with bright, multi-colored handle was given to me by Aunt Elsie, as well as a tiny cuticle tool with a green colored bone-like handle. The little jack knife was never found, after I threw it out of the barn's half door one dark, rainy night (just to see if we could find it the next morning—what a fool thing to do Dad said, as one of the cattle could have injured their foot on it, since I couldn't remember if the blade was open or not when I threw it!) A silver tea service from England, complete with tea-pot, creamer and sugar bowl has been handed down from Mom to myself, and I expect in time, there will be more items like this to treasure, inherited from her.

A Belleek cup and saucer, given to Gran Teasdale's safe-keeping by Mrs. Horde, prominent Wolseley lady, for me as a little girl, is now safely stored here as well as several Nippon china pieces bequeathed to me from Gran Sexsmith. A tiny pair of manicure scissors given to me as a girl by Gran, following one of her many trips to Fort William to visit Uncle Lloyd's family, are also treasured—I wonder if Audrey still has her identical pair Gran brought her at that time as well? I have previously mentioned my Charlie McCarthy replica, a childhood gift from Albert Murrell, former Wolseley neighbor and valet to Mr. Sargeant that Mom has housed for me all these years.

From Gordon's family, Michael, being the only grandson, inherited a little steam engine that burns real fuel, makes steam and whistles, that had belonged to Helmuth and Gordon as boys on the farm. A mechano set with many pieces, has found a home here as well. Our daughters and I inherited many household items and keepsakes from both Grandma Issel and Mom Schroeder.

As we come to possess these cherished mementos of the past, they serve as timeless reminders of where we have come from, and someday, many will be passed on by us, to our children and future generations, hopefully, to be treasured by them as well.

Along with all the activities related to enjoyment and entertainment just discussed, we also enjoyed attending church and related activities, evenings of supper, cards and visiting at neighbor's farm homes, especially in winter, and attending functions at the school and in the towns like dances, plays and concerts, etc.

One winter, when I was still in public school at Allindale, and perhaps about eight or nine years of age, Dad was invited to take part in a Minstrel Show being put together in Sintaluta by local talented people. There must have been a driving force or cause, perhaps a fund-raising, Farmer's Union, or perhaps just for the fun and pleasure both player-participants and audiences gleaned from such a venture.

At any rate, this show stands out in my mind as a shining highlight at the end of another dreary winter. I recall the production was staged in Spring, as our lane and the grid roads were muddy. We had to leave our car at the lane's end and walk to and from the buildings to attend, or perhaps Dad did that and Mom and us girls walked out and caught a ride with some neighbors that were going. Dad was never much for attending anything in the towns when the roads were muddy, mostly because of his precious vehicles, and not wanting to dirty them! I recall Mom and us girls attending a piano recital one spring, because Audrey was playing in it. Uncle Herb was willing to drive us and them, but had left the emergency brake on (while we stopped on Gran's hill sloped property in town), and then we slid in the ditch on the way home, because the brake was accidentally left on, causing his green Ford car to skid! Dave Livingstone rescued us with his tractor, I recall, as we were on the school road in the ravine east of their place when we hit the ditch—it seems to me there was water in the ditch as well!

Anyway, this particular spring, Dad had no choice but to travel back and forth on these muddy roads to practices, etc., as this minstrel show was a big production for a small town! Preparation of songs and skits, costumes and music went on a goodly part of the late winter. Dad and Ed Thompson were asked to do a little two-man play, and I can still recall helping Dad learn his lines for it, from a script book. It was staged on a darkened street, on a corner by a lamp post, and seemed to centre around a case of mistaken identity, as I recall.

Of course, all participants in the show had to be portrayed as Negro, so make-up and/or black masks played a big part. Straw hats, bow ties, bright shirts, white gloves, dark pants and suspenders made up the men's costumes, while long, dazzling calico skirts, bright flowing blouses and turbaned heads with bangles at neck and on wrists, completed the ladies costumes.

The show was made up of a great deal of singing, as well as the little plays and skits. A mixed chorus of perhaps 20 to 25 people sang many Negro Spiritual-type songs and provided the beautiful background humming and accompaniment for individual singers, while accomplished pianist Vic Sexsmith provided the main instrumental background. One particular number, Sleep Kentucky Babe, sung by Vic's wife, gifted songstress Marion, remains in my mind as my favorite number in the whole show. She held a blanketed baby doll in her arms, as in her beautiful voice she sang it this lullaby, with the chorus singing and humming softly behind her, while swaying in time to the music. I recall being very proud to be related to such a fine lady, with such wonderful talent and ability. Hearing her sing this same song, later at one of our many Sexsmith sing-a-longs at Raymond and Isobel's home, etched this beautiful memory in my mind still further.

This minstrel show production was so well received in Sintaluta, it seems to me it was presented there on another occasion, as well as taken to several surrounding towns like Wolseley and Edgeley (another small town) over the next few weeks. It probably helped to raise a lot of funding, as well as being a special time for all those who took part. Dad loved the singing, one of his favorite pass-times, and all the comradery. He never liked his play too much, as didn't think it was very funny or good, but he and Ed gave it their best shot anyway. Mom always seemed to be a bit envious of Dad's participation and all the evenings involved in practice, etc., but seemed to enjoy the production in the end. I know I sure did and the fond memory of this Minstrel Show remains dear—a real credit to the many talented persons involved from Sintaluta and surrounding communities, so many years ago.

Family vacations weren't as common then as they have become today; apart from the "day" trips just previously recorded, with one unscheduled overnight stay in Regina that time our car broke down at Exhibition, we never spent time away from the farm as a family. There were always cows to milk and be fed as well as chickens, pigs, cats and the dog. Occasionally Uncle Herb would be called upon to do the milking if we were inadvertently delayed in homecoming; however the rest of the chores just had to wait. The only people we knew who went on holidays were either retired or well-off. Both Grans visited family and friends across Canada from time to time, Gran Teasdale visiting Mrs. Stutters and Unky in B.C. and Gran Sexsmith going to Fort William to visit Uncle Lloyd's family. Both traveled by train, the most reliable over-land means of travel in those days. Gordon reports his family took an automobile trip to Cascade, Iowa to visit family friends, the Hackeys when he was about ten years of age—quite an unusually long car trip for a farm family at the time.

So concludes this section on how our farm family and others like us, managed to enjoy a few simple pleasures and activities that helped maintain a bit of balance between the farm-oriented work ethic and the enjoyment of life.

I have purposely chosen to discuss modes of communication last because it is the medium through which all information is shared. Without being able to communicate our thoughts, memories, feelings and what we know and experience, it is lost. As explained when I began these jottings, it is through these remembrances being written down that I hope to share the era of our childhoods that has now passed into history, with future generations and whoever else might be interested.

At first family histories were recorded by word of mouth, or the spoken word—telling others our history and how things used to be as in folk tales, folk lore, (ie. The movie "Roots") what their heritage had been. However, often in this method of recording, some parts were forgotten and details changed over the years.

With the evolving of alphabets from signs and symbols, the written word became a more efficient means of communication and the recording of history. In days gone by, runners and carrier pigeons were dispatched to communicate important messages over long distances. Smoke signals aided first family ancestors of this nation to communicate messages over long distances. Long hand writing using quill pens and ink later gave way to lead pencils and fountain pens and still later ball point pens, and ever-sharp pencils, in common use today. The telephone, typewriters, computers, word processors, voice mail, fax, Internet and e-mail are some of the modern and convenient ways we now use to share information around the globe in seconds.

Tracing family trees has become a popular means of tracking family histories and several cousins including Audrey and Elaine have done commendable jobs researching and recording the Sexsmith family tree presented at well-attended family reunions in the 198O's. Family

Bibles were commonly used in early years to record births, marriages and deaths, and are still a useful source of information in tracing family histories. Public archives, church records, libraries, Genealogy societies, and museums all have their place in recording family histories. However, long lists of who is related to who aren't very meaningful without background data on what these people felt and experienced, as well as some of their joys and sorrows.

It saddens me to think that the opportunity existed to find out more about our family history from both Grans Sexsmith and Teasdale while they lived, and about their early years. No one back then felt their memories of those years gone by, hardships experienced etc., were of very much importance and just as well forgotten. Apparently, Grandad Teasdale is our only ancestor who made an attempt to record some of his thoughts, feelings and the way he perceived things on his arrival in Canada from England. A notebook exists wherein he recorded some of his early experiences for Gran, his future bride still back in Kirkby Lonsdale, so she would have some idea what life would be like when she joined him on the Prairies in 1914 in Winnipeg and they were wed. They farmed on several rented homesteads north of Wolseley and ended up on the Chew farm in the Allindale/Mount Crescent area where their eldest daughter Margaret, our mother, was courted and later married by the neighbor lad living "across the dam" Gordon Sexsmith, our father.

Sending letters via the mail system was probably the most common means of communication in the early years and while we were growing up, for sharing of personal information as well as running the business of the country. Telegraph was a quicker mode of sending information by Morse code, being received in the form of a telegram, usually at the local train station in small towns like Wolseley. During the war years, it was often the only means loved ones had of knowing the whereabouts or status of those off at war, as letters were often delayed or even confiscated and never received. Air mail letters, written on blue, tissue-thin paper were less expensive to send by air and also quicker than regular mail and always used for overseas postage. Letters received from England even today are still almost always written on this type of airmail paper.

The telephone, so much a part of our daily lives and taken for granted today, only existed for our family down at Uncle Herb's house, where we had to go to use it, or in turn when any messages were received for us on their telephone, they had to come to deliver them. Even in my teen years, while I lived with Gran Teasdale during high school in Wolseley, I was still petrified of this modern contraption if it rang, and if I had to answer it if Gran was busy at the moment, or it happened to be for me. Heaven forbid, if I had to make a call on it! Gran was very patient with me, teaching me how to proceed and finally I did master use of the thing to some extent. (How could I possibly have known then my work each day would revolve so completely around using the telephone in my nursing work at busy physician's offices, and skilful use of it would become almost second nature to me!).

The telephone of my childhood looked much different to the sleek, touch-tone, color co-ordinated models capable of so many options like call-forward, call-waiting, voice mail, hold, remote units, record-keeping of past callers, as well as visual display we are all familiar with today. (Who could have predicted the present popularity of portable cell phones?) A rectangular wooden box suspended on the wall in a hallway or other strategic place in the home, housed the silver two-bell-system on top for ringing, and the black, extended mouth-piece for talking into. An entirely separate ear piece in a 6-inch long horn shape, attached to the telephone box by a covered half-inch round cable, and when not in use hung suspended from the left side of the telephone box by a silver, receiver clasp attachment. A little crank on the right side of the box called "central" at the telephone office in town to place a call, or the desired number of rings to call a neighbor. (No wonder I was afraid of it!)

Of course, these telephones were always mounted on the wall convenient to an adult male's height and too high for kids or even the lady of the house to reach! A stool of suitable height for sitting down while talking into the receiver offered the caller the best comfort. Party lines were "the norm" of the rural system; each home had a separate ring, but by quietly lifting the receiver, eaves-dropping was easily and entirely possible and indeed often done, as all subscribers were hooked up to the same line from the individual towns. (Only recently (1988) in some rural Regina areas has this obsolete system now been eliminated). A long ring going on for 15 seconds was a "neighborhood alert" call and everyone picked up their receiver for the message, ie. fire, community announcements, etc. The rectangular box housed telephone cable and lines as well as a battery needed to make the bells ring when an incoming call was being received. Gordon tells me his family and the Maurers, nearest neighbors on the corner, were instrumental in establishing the rural telephone lines to Neudorf, their nearest town.

Not owning a telephone was always a bone of contention in our household, and even more so for the neighbors, never being able to figure out why we didn't make the effort to get "hooked up" once our farm home was completed. We were closer to the Sintaluta line and it would have been less expensive to be hooked up to it, however, since we conducted most of our business in Wolseley, we would always have been calling long distance there, when placing most calls. The extra expense of hooking up to the Wolseley line always seemed the biggest deterrent, cost-wise, and Dad just didn't feel it was something we really needed. The few times we needed the telephone he felt, didn't warrant the cost.

During high school, I tended to disagree with him entirely, as when I came home from Grans for weekends, the time when dates were arranged and all activities were taking place, I was unfortunately incommunicado! Also when Dad passed away suddenly in 1968 and we girls were both away from home, it would have been so comforting for Mom to have the telephone for communication. Thank goodness, when she moved her house to town the following summer, a telephone was installed—a first for our 1ittle home!

Next in line to the box-type wall model telephone of my girlhood, came the type that sat on the desk or wall with a cradle for the receiver all on one unit. There was a rotary dial system on the front, with round slotted holes with the numbers from 0 to 9 printed beneath, for the caller to dial their number. The higher the digits in the number, the longer it took to dial, as the rotating part had to return to its original position before the next digit could be dialed—it was tedious. (The touch-tone telephones of today are much more agreeable and time-saving to operate). All telephones were black back then, as opposed to the pastel shades to match all decors of today.

A CB radio system installed sometime while I was in high school, to communicate between district farmers was of some help and less expensive to set up than the telephone. Mom and Dad seemed to get quite a bit of use out of it, especially talking back and forth to the Browns, etc. when they were more involved in our farming operation. In fact, Mom still has hers in her home in Wolseley, and occasionally uses it still to call out to the Allindale district, just to keep tabs on how things are going, especially since telephoning the Browns involves a long-distance call to the Sintaluta line—the greatest deterrent, to having a phone in our home all those years ago!

Even though several more pages of personal memories will follow, this page ends the formal record I have chosen to keep for posterity. I dedicate it to all the predecessors of our families, who have gone on before us, but I especially wish to remember both dear maternal and paternal Grandmothers, Gran Sexsmith, Agnes Mary (Donald) Sexsmith, and Gran Teasdale, Ann (Taylforth) Teasdale. Their constant, abiding love and devotion to me as a child and into young adulthood helped shape and mold me into the person I am today. Their gentle discipline, kindness and Christian virtues are forever locked in my heart—I am indebted to them for their positive influence over my life—God rest their souls until we meet again someday in Eternity.

May 4, 1996.

Memories of Gran Teasdale

Of my two grandmothers, I seem to have more of a wealth of memories of this maternal Gran, probably because I came to know her best when I was at more of an age to recall her many attributes, while I lived with her during my High School years from approximately the Fall of 1957 to the Summer of 1961. Although we also lived together with Mom, during my very early childhood, while Dad was overseas, I have only vague and fleeting memories of this time. I seem to recall her being rather stern and "too proper" back then, not seeming to know how to become emotionally bonded to a small child—not like the loving bond I felt for Gran Sexsmith from the earliest days.

However, during those high school years, we developed a very special, loving relationship with each other, based on kindness, mutual caring and respect. I shall never forget those days spent living in her cozy cottage home with her—she providing a home and gentle guidance for me, and I in turn companionship for her, a respite from many, long years of widowhood, and a "reason to be" so to speak. I didn't realize it at the time, but during those formative, impressionable years, this little lady, Gran Teasdale, had a very positive and influential effect on me personally and spiritually and I will be forever grateful for the opportunity I had of knowing her so well at that time, and the benefits this association afforded me.

It was during this time, I learned of her early life back in England and of her coming to Canada to begin her life here. As mentioned in my notes regarding Gran Sexsmith, if only we had talked of how she felt at those different life stages, and recorded it then, while they lived, how much easier it would have been to put things down now. However, I shall document what I know and remember of this dear Gran also.

Gran was born Ann Taylforth at Kirkby Lonsdale, Westmorland in England's beautiful northern Lake District on December 4, 1889. Her father was Head Master of the local National Grammar School (Church of England), while her mother died in childbirth while little Ann was very young, and she was raised by her sisters, Mary and Alice. She seemed to lead a rather sheltered life, attending school, meeting John Lister Teasdale, also of Kirkby Lonsdale, whose father was head coachman of the Royal Hotel Stables. The two young people became engaged to marry, and since it was always Grandad's dream to come to Canada to farm, it was decided he would precede Gran here to become established. Two sibling brothers also came to Canada around that time, Harry (Richard Henry) to Preeceville, where he was killed by a run-away team of horses, and Wilfred, who farmed with Grandad in the Wolseley area, until Grandad's passing.

Grandad first procured work on the Bell Farm at Indian Head, and then in the Wolseley area for Mr. Perley, land owner, eventually working a rented farm a short distance northwest of Wolseley (later Henry Moss's farm), and later worked the Chew farm in A1lindale district.

In 1914, Gran traveled to Canada, by arduous boat and train rides to Winnipeg, Manitoba, to meet Grandad, where they were married on August 4 of that year. They journeyed by train to Wolseley and went to live in a new house at the Moss farmstead. Gran became a "farm-wife", a rather radical adaptation for her, having grown up in a little English town under rather pampered circumstances, but her strong English constitution prevailed and in spite of heart-wrenching bouts of home-sickness for her beloved family and England, she managed to raise her four children, three daughters and a son, Margaret, Alice, Elsie and Harry.

Gran loved the farm way of life, probably remembering the many stone-fenced farmsteads of England, providing a loving, stable home-life for Grandad, managing to provide a meager living for their growing family, as they moved to the Chew farm. There was always a longing to return to England for a visit, to their beloved English roots, but they were never able to save enough funding for the return fare.

Poor health forced Gran to become bed-ridden a great deal of the time, while Aunt Elsie, their youngest child was small, and our mother, Margaret, being the eldest daughter, and a very capable homemaker, even at an early age, kept the busy household running. Gran eventually had to have major surgery in Regina, during the "dirty thirties" when farming was in a disastrous slump. Eventually, she recovered, and they came home, hoping to pick up their lives again and proceed.

However, Grandad, overcome by the stresses and strains of mounting medical bills and no farm income, died suddenly in July of 1939 of a heart attack. Their dream of owning their own farm someday was shattered, and out of necessity abandoned. Gran moved to the home she would occupy for many years in Wolseley, while son Harry and Wilfred joined the Air Force in support of the war effort. Alice went to Business College and work in Regina, Elsie lived with Gran for high school and later went to Moose Jaw to Normal School to become a teacher, while our mother Margaret, engaged by then to our future father David Gordon Sexsmith, went by train to Fort William to marry him, where he worked in Canada Car, before going overseas.

Gran's love of good food well-prepared, led her to hone her culinary skills to a fine art, setting certain family traditions with regard to food that we still adhere to today, especially at the Christmas season. Plum pudding, Mince meat tarts, Christmas cakes topped with thick almond paste and snow-white hard icing are examples, as well as layered Christmas trifle. Christmas crackers complete with hats, prize and fortune are still "a must" at each place setting for Christmas dinner, as they were on Gran's table for all the Christmas dinners she hosted over the years. It was while living with her, that I developed a better appetite than I had ever enjoyed as a young girl, and came to appreciate eating as a pleasure all its own, even though the "art of cooking" would elude me for sometime yet!

Embroidery was her needlework preference, delicate feather-stitching her particular forte. She spent countless hours working at her embroidery, especially pairs of pillow cases. Looking back, her eyesight must have been excellent, even in her later years as she often worked on her needlework in the evenings, with only an overhead light in both kitchen and front room for illumination; she wore wire-rimmed glasses all the time I knew her, similar to Gran Sexsmith's, the style of the day.

Although I can't recall her knitting much when I knew her, Gran must have enjoyed this craft as well, as I have proof—a beautiful white knitted shawl she apparently knitted for me as a baby—first grandchild and all! As we were growing up, Angora wool became popular for home-knitted articles of clothing, and I recall Connie and I both having grey knitted angora bonnets with pink trim, that tied under the chin, that Gran had knitted for us, with matching mitts, to keep us warm in winter. It seems to me she also knitted men's socks, for her family with cable and diamond designs, (Clippie insisting his be yellow), and I recall her knitting me a royal blue cardigan sweater with grey trim, on which she ended up lining the sleeves with white, silky fabric, because I found the wool too itchy!

Gran loved her garden, birds and nature in general, and spent a great deal of time out in her yard each summer, enjoying her passion for growing things. Gladiolas, and Sweet Peas were her particular favorites that seemed to respond to her loving touch; she loved to plant new bulbs each spring, with ruffles and different colors preferred. Mounds of white baby's breath, an expanse of glorious, orangey California poppies at the eastern end of her garden, trumpet-throated Nicotine (the Hummingbirds loved), and Mignonette were also some of the flowers she always seemed to grow, as well as some vegetables.

Probably her beautiful, peaceful yard had a lot to do with the many birds that visited in summer. I have mentioned elsewhere about the Robin that nested on top of her milk box right by the back door shed, not being the least bit frightened! Jenny Wrens often nested under the eaves at the front of the house, their darling singing bringing much joy, while Hummingbirds often visited, especially in early morning. Morning Doves often came to the rink area and meadow beyond, their plaintive call always causing Gran to comment "Hark at the Doves", probably reminding her especially of England.

In winter, sparrows and chickadees came to the back door, for her faithful hand-outs of crumbs, and her little Ede-Adee" phrase she talked to them with. She never failed to shake the tablecloth outside, following a meal, "for the birds" she would say, to share the crumbs! Magpies were the only bird she seemed to dislike, claiming they were cheeky and brought bad luck—she never liked to see one, and crows fell into a close second, as they "were robbers" of the song-bird's nests, and should confine themselves to the country, which they mostly did back then.

Gran was always "an English lady" and being "proper" in manner and dress was very important to her. She insisted on nice, clean house dresses to do her morning work, with an apron tied at the waist (always tried to hide her apron for pictures), which she often made herself. After her afternoon nap, which she took daily while I knew her, she would tidy herself up in another clean afternoon dress and have her tea, and usually a sweet, a cookie or muffin, etc. Gran always wore shiny, laced-up oxford shoes, the style of that day, for ladies like her and Gran Sexsnith and wore gloves for gardening and chores in the yard. She had her hair done at Marg Simpson's Beauty Salon weekly, with a perm and blue augment to her white, straight hair, that she kept quite short and neat. She wore signature brightly colored mesh hairnets for head covering for housework and chores, with pretty feathered hats for church and a "babooshka" for yard chores in winter. The one "luxury" item of her wardrobe, mentioned previously, the black Hudson Seal coat Gran wore in winter was a gift from Aunt Alice, I believe.

Even to her closest friends, Gran was known as Mrs. Teasdale, and they by Mrs. and their sir name to her, but never by first name—only Gwen Lowe, her good neighbor to the south, up the hill, probably because Gwen insisted on it! Perhaps this is why at her funeral, we were all so shocked to hear the well-meaning minister, Rev. Pat Tomalin, address Gran by her Christian name of Ann, as we had never before heard her referred to as such. We half expected to see Gran lift up the lid of her coffin, and scold him right then and there! Going to church each Sunday was a top priority all her life, and from her bounteous, garden flowers, she was often happy to provide St. George's altar with floral adornment over the many years that she was a member. She reverently helped care for the altar and brass polishing and in earlier years she was active in the Afternoon Branch of the Women's Auxiliary. Although Gran didn't profess to be a singer, she often hummed little tunes and snatches of hymns to herself while doing her housework or out in her yard.

Out of necessity, Gran was always frugal, as she claimed "she never had nothing", as a long-time widow living on a meager pension, but to all who knew her, she was wealthy in the things that really counted—putting God first in her life, she was spiritual and devout without being pompous, kind, considerate and caring with many friends at church, and in the neighborhood and community. It bothered her so in later years, when many friends and acquaintances passed on, and she remained. She would often ask "Why is He leaving me?" and then would content herself that the Lord had something left here on earth for her to do yet. Given the poor state of her health in earlier years, I suppose it surprised her to have lived so long following this. While I knew her she always suffered from hypertension, the occasional bout of depression and epistaxis and varicosities in her legs, for which she always wore support hose, but otherwise remained in relative good health.

I especially recall her penchant for saving string, probably because back then, it could be put to so many uses before the days of tape, glue, staples and stickers. No piece, however short, was ever wasted or thrown away, but was wound onto her ever-present "string-ball" that lived in the first kitchen cupboard drawer, behind the kitchen door.

Cleanliness was next to Godliness in Gran's books—she especially liked clean, shiny shoes, and claimed you could tell a lot about a person by their shoes! Gran liked things neat, and orderly, like any proud English lady, however, by her own admission, her dining room table often acted as a "catch-all" for saved items, and every once in while a major clean-up had to be done. Otherwise, she kept her home tidy and well cared for, with the help of her children—most often our parents, when it came to maintenance, like wall papering, painting, cleaning stovepipes, etc. She always joked that since her bed and bedroom was located right directly above her huge soft water cistern in the basement, and the floors being so old and creaky, she may end up in a "watery grave" someday, which thankfully never happened!

Only in the later years, did Gran finally agree to have sewer services put into her home (in the spare bedroom), managing for years, as we did on the farm, with her outdoor outhouse in summer and canister-type in basement for winter, cistern and pump for soft water, and pails of water from the common well beside the rink for drinking water. By the time I lived with her, she had put in cold running water for drinking, at the kitchen sink.

Gran liked her fire-wood stacked neatly against the lattice fence, (often buying it from reserve Indians that called by in Fall), that divided her yard from the next property to the south. We recall fondly Gran's reference to her "ginnel"—the walkway beside her house made by this lattice fence. (I was thrilled when Gordon made our patio fence of lattice, just like in Gran's yard). She always liked to rake her garden refuse and leaves in fall, calling them "rubbage", instead of garbage or rubbish, and burn it in the trusty steel barrel, she maintained at the east gate of her yard just for this purpose, before the days when fire laws now prohibit such burnings. (I can still recall this burning smell every fall in a nostalgic, sort of way and I miss it). Gran kept a green painted wooden rocking chair just outside the back door to sit on during hot summer days, on the carpet of Creeping Charlie that always blanketed that area of her yard. To this day, anyone who transplanted plants from her yard, from our family, all have this baneful ground cover in our yards now too, although, because it reminds me of Gran, I hope never to be totally "rid" of it! My California poppies. Sweet Peas, Glads and Nicotine are equally dear to me for this same reason.

However, most of the legacy left to us by our dear Gran Teasdale was far more meaningful and precious. She was revered by her four children and their families, all their days and indeed by all who knew her. In 1960, she made one last trip back to her beloved birthplace in England, accompanied by her brother-in-law Wilfred and thankfully, was able to visit with her sister Mary, other family, and some of the haunts of her younger days. However, she was glad to return to Canada, realizing it was now her home more than England—if only she and Grandad could have returned together for a visit, so many years earlier—this was always her life-long wish, and always made her sad to speak of it. (Gordon and I were thrilled to meet cousin Mary and tour Kirkby with her and brother Bill Fishwick in 1984, when we visited England—I felt as if I'd visited with Gran being with Mary—life and buildings appeared much the same as always).

Gran maintained her own home with dignity and steadfastness until unable to do so, at which time she spent her final days in the care of our mother Margaret, first in Mom's home, and then in the Lakeside Home at Wolseley. She would not have wanted to linger as she did in the bed-ridden state of her last several years, not being aware of her life or surroundings, but finally her tasks were completed, and the Lord called her home. Another chapter had ended in the book of this life, but we were all blessed and privileged to have known this fine lady, our Gran Teasdale.

FOUR GENERATION PICTURE

Taken at Mom's Summer 1970. Nana (Ann) Teasdale, Grandma (Margaret) Sexsmith, Mother, (Carol) Schroeder, and Daughter, (Heather) Schroeder. (All are first-borns except Nana, who was the youngest in the Taylforth family.

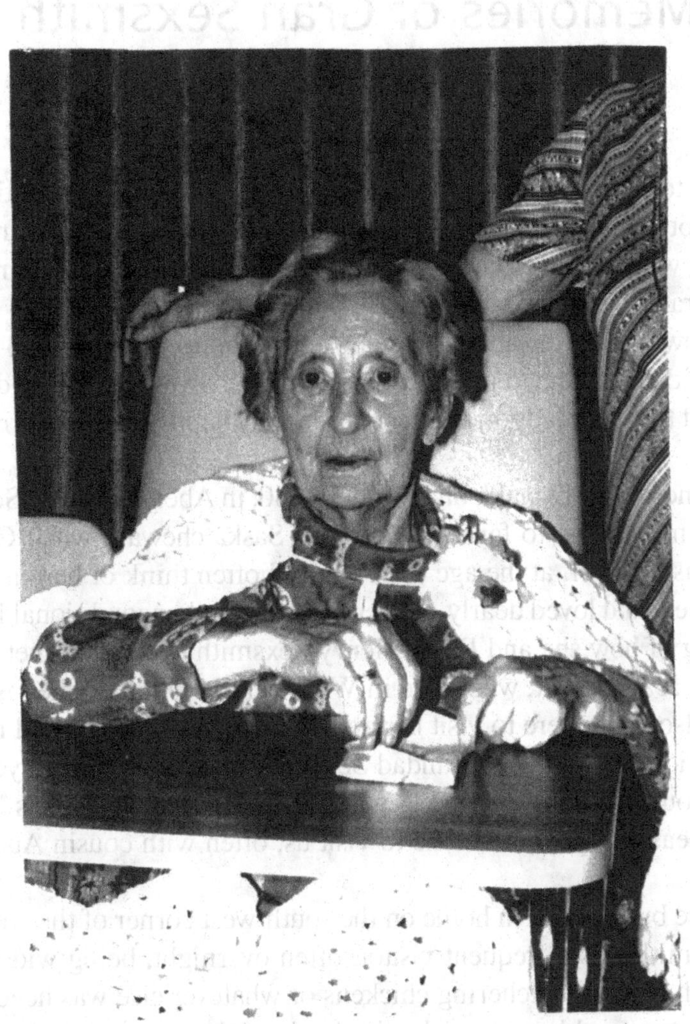

Gran Teasdale on her 90th Birthday celebrated at Lakeside Home with all her children and grandchildren present. December 4, 1979.

Memories of Gran Sexsmith

Very little is known to me about this grandmother's early life, and as mentioned before, I am eternally sorry for not asking or taking note of this while she lived, so that now it could be recorded. On checking with cousin Audrey, who has our family tree recorded in detail, she knows almost nothing of Gran's early life either.

Only having known Gran for about 17 years from approximately 1944 until her death in 1961, was not a great deal of time to get to know a person, however, I will endeavor to put down what I do know about this dear lady, of whom I have many happy memories from my childhood, and younger life.

She was born Agnes Mary Donald, on March 5, 1880, in Aberdeenshire, Scotland to Scotish-Irish parents. The family came to farm in Northern Saskatchewan, when Gran was five. She passed away in August of 1961, at the age of 81 years. I often think of her on March 5, and still miss this Gran we knew and loved dearly, for her kindness and unconditional love shown toward us. We know nothing of how she and David Henry Sexsmith (Grandad) met. I know she had a sister, our great Aunt Jean Gouett, who lived in Waubashene, Ontario; she visited Gran here on occasion and Gran also went there to visit her and husband Al, who worked in mining.

My first recollection of Gran and Grandad Sexsmith is during the War years when I would have been three or four years of age, living with Mom at Gran Teasdale's home in Wolseley while Dad was overseas. They would come to visit us, often with cousin Audrey in tow, so we could play together.

Later on, when we built our farm home on the south-west corner of the south half of section 17's land, Gran Sexsmith was a frequent visitor, often overnight, being widowed in 1948. She would help Mom with sewing, butchering chickens or whatever else was needed. She seemed a multi-talented lady, very capable and quick with loads of energy, even in her advancing years. She never seemed too busy for her grandchildren, and would always include us in whatever she was doing, as opposed to Mom, who always seemed too busy to allow time for us to learn and help her in her tasks.

It was during this time I recall Gran fitting me for my pink flocked, long nylon dress and matching long silky slip I was to wear as flower girl at Aunt Elsie and Uncle Clifford Wilson's wedding in October 1948, when I would have been five. I remember I loved the way the fabric smelled, so new and crisp and felt a bit itchy. However, when the silky slip was worn underneath, only the sleeves itched me a bit.

The other preparation for being flower girl for this wedding Gran also had the skill with which to assist Mom. In order to curl my straight, medium length, fine blond hair into the ringlets, deemed appropriate for the occasion, Mom and Gran had to wrap my hair, while wet, around long strips of flannel cotton. As related previously, this tried and true method resulted in lovely-shaped ringlets, however the worst part was having to leave these multiple wrapped "curlers" in my hair overnight to achieve the desired results. I recall having a terrible time getting to lie down on them and crying to have them taken out. Thank goodness we have pictures recording the end result! (In spite of the struggle, I'm glad to have had such an honored part in that wedding.)

Gran loved her garden, always growing lots of pretty flowers she often shared with Mom, (before Mom grew her own) as well as a vegetable garden. Two areas west of the house were allotted for garden space—a large strip running north and south, bordered by huge cottonwood trees on the west, and a second long strip on the west side of the trees. A huge front yard with lawn, was bordered on the east by mauve Lilac bushes and north and west by Caragana bushes. Flower beds by the house contained lots of Sweet William, Iris, and purple Sky Rocket. Red and pink Geraniums always filled her windows. The distinct smell of geranium leaves on gardener fingers still reminds me of Gran Sexsmith to this day!

Many of my memories of Gran seem centered at the sturdy brick farm home that she and Grandad built, and Aunt Ruby and Uncle Herb had upstairs rooms in the northwest bedroom and southwest room that served as a living/kitchen area. Later on, although Gran always maintained her large bedroom downstairs, off the back entrance stairway, her living quarters moved to the upstairs southwest room where Herb and Ruby started off, and they inherited the remainder of the house. It is in this room that I remember Gran treated Audrey and I to heaping bowls of oatmeal porridge for breakfast, on mornings after I had stayed over night, to visit with Gran and play with Audrey. Gran would allow us to pour loads of rich farm cream over the porridge and then as much wonderful brown sugar as we wanted, (and much more than our mothers would have allowed, we knew!) Then she would exclaim "Now pitch in tucker and get your feet wet!" meaning pick up spoons and get eating, before it got cold.

Gran had many life-time treasures, pictures, and china stored in this living area, and often marked these items on the back with a name written on adhesive tape, so it would be given to that person "when she passed on", as she used to say. She seemed to change the recipients' names from time to time, but it was through this arrangement that we all came to inherit the things that were dear to her in this life. I recall two pieces of Nippon china in perfect condition and several pictures I came to inherit in this manner.

Then of course there were all the articles of clothing she made for each of us on her trusty Singer treadle sewing machine, without benefit of a pattern or guide. She could look at a picture and make up the garment with her own pattern cut out of brown paper. I have mentioned some of this clothing elsewhere in these jottings, as well as my lambs wool quilt, still in use to this day, with several different coverings since Gran first covered it with the sailor-patterned material sent in error by the mail order catalogue. Doll clothes were just as important to her, and she made Audrey, Connie and I our share. Knitting was one of her favorite crafts, and she always seemed to have a pair or mitts or socks "on the go".

Gran often "set" clucking hens in little A-frame coops on eggs and Audrey and I would "assist" her in feeding the little chicks that eventually hatched, with oatmeal and mashed potato. The little chicks were so cute and fluffy and we adored them, and helping to care for them. I recall Gran taking us down into the ice-house located just west of the barn/henhouse door, to retrieve cold-storage items. It was always amazing to me that even in summer, it was cool and of course dark and damp down there, and blocks of ice remained frozen under the straw coverings. Cream, eggs and possibly meats and other perishables could be kept down there before the days of refrigeration. There was a small wooden enclosure on top with a door for access and steps built down to the base from the doorway. Gathering eggs from the hen house nests into a large wicker basket also seemed to be on our list of morning farmyard rounds. Audrey and I always felt pretty important that Gran would take us on all her farmyard duties and let us help her.

Gran always seemed to be in happy frame of mind and sang and kind of whistled hymns like "Down At The Cross Where Jesus Died" and "Precious Jewels" as she went about her work. Her relationship with her Lord seemed very important to her, as well as going to Church. Being founding members of Alexander United Church several miles up the "Church Road" south west from the farm, it was this church she and Grandad attended most of their adult life until it closed, and attendance was transferred to Wolseley, St. James. Membership cards in the Baby Band and Mission Band from the time I was born attest to the importance this loving grandmother placed on bringing her grandchildren to Christianity through Sunday School, and attendance at services when possible, even though we ultimately went to St. George's Anglican Church in Wolseley.

I especially loved it when Gran would come to stay at our house overnight and also if I went to stay with her overnight as we always got to sleep together. We would say our prayers together and then she would tell a bed time story or else we would write and draw on each other's backs, trying to guess what was being written, a game our own children dearly loved to play as well, as they were growing up. Gran taught us to play Cat's Cradle and would read to us by the hour from our story books. She taught me to knit, (a doll scarf in red, green and yellow, being my first project), and also the basics of crochet.

Another fond recollection I have of Gran was when she came to stay with Dad and I while Mom was in hospital delivering Connie. It was of course December, and she somehow got the furnace just roaring hot one day, trying to keep us warm. Dad always felt if he hadn't gotten home when he did, our little house may have gone up in flames—I can't recall, but given the year of 1949, it must have been the coal furnace. However, she did take good care of us and no harm came to us after all. Audrey used to drop in to visit on our way home from school, and Gran liked to give us a treat. She was reaching for something baked from the shelf above the basement stairs when she slipped and fell downstairs, with several thumps and a stifled scream. Audrey and I were really frightened and afraid to look, until Gran called out for our help, and then we realized she wasn't dead or hurt too badly. As it turned out, the gold wire-rimmed glasses she always wore had flown off during her landing, and she needed help to find them! Amazingly she was unhurt physically, thank goodness, as Dad was away in town visiting Mom and Connie at the hospital, and we had no phone.

Gran's generous nature was always apparent, especially where her grandchildren were concerned. She always had treats for us in her pockets, and often gave us quarters or fifty-cent pieces to buy our own treats. She always brought us gifts from her frequent trips to Fort William to visit Uncle Lloyd's family or to Regina to visit Aunt Gladys's family, etc.

Although we did not know her then, Gran's early life had much sadness and was filled with hard work, as was the lot of all pioneer ladies of that era. Three of her children Alex, Ida and Rachel died in infancy and a fourth child Martha, died in childbirth as an adult. She is known to have said of her young life she always had "a baby in her arms, one on her skirts (a toddler) and one in her stomach" (expecting). Fortunately, Grandad had the means to provide her with hired help in the house a good part of the time, which probably helped her keep her sanity and dignity for the most part. Her living children, Herb, Gladys, our Dad Gordon and Lloyd and their families brought Gran much joy. In later years, it was amazing how much Aunt Gladys and Gran were alike, especially with respect to their fine-lined facial skin, mannerisms and agility.

Tigger, Gran's pet cat was a source of great pleasure to her as they grew old together. He was a monstrous Tabby cat that loved to be doted over by his mistress. Nothing was ever too good for Tigger, and he lived to a ripe old age, sleeping under the footed cook stove or on the south window sill in the kitchen for hours on end—I think she had had him as a pet for many years before we knew her.

Gran aged very gracefully—she never seemed old to me, but was always full of life and enthusiasm, agile and slim all her life. Her hair maintained a good hint of medium brown mixed with grey, even to old age, and although her face was very wrinkled, her youthful and spry movements always seemed to keep her young. She sewed a lot of her own clothing, including the "pinafore" aprons she always wore over her everyday dresses for housework, and had the means to buy nice suits, hats, jewelry, shoes, purses and of course her lovely long muskrat coat and hat I still recall for its luxurious feeling.

Gran was affectionately known to all others as "Aunt Aggie", just as Mrs. John Sexsmith, her sister-in-law was known to us as "Aunt Katie", who was also a dear and kind elder to us all. Gran was very fond of our Dad, and he of her, always addressing her as Mother, and she affectionately referring to him as her Gordie—after all he was "her baby" for ten years, from 1910 to 1920, until his family position was pre-empted by the birth of Lloyd (nicknamed Bunty by his siblings). Only once can I recall Dad ever relating to us that he questioned her judgment on an issue that seemed to bother him even as an adult, was when as an older lad, no longer playing with his toys, she saw fit to pass them along to some minister's kids that were particularly naughty, and he knew wouldn't appreciate them or take care of them. I always felt kind of sad about this, for Dad's sake, I mean.

As a teenager, out of necessity to attend High School in Wolseley, I spent almost all of my time living with my other grandmother, Gran Teasdale, in Wolseley, only being home at the farm on weekends and during summer holidays. It was during this time I am sorry to say now, I kind of lost touch with Gran Sexsmith, who towards the last several years of her life, developed a bit of quiet senility, and seemed to live in her own little world. She was never hospitalized for it, and lived out her life, as she wished, at the home she and Grandad built as pioneers, as he had arranged for her in his will.

I recall with much sadness, even today, how I learned of Gran's passing, and the profound effect it had on me—my first real encounter with the death of someone who had meant the world to me. I was staying up in Regina with my high school friend Phyllis Boyes, who was working at Sask. Tel and living in a rooming house close to the downtown area. The idea was for me to find employment, following high school graduation, by dropping off resumes and arranging interviews. Phyllis, Diane McCall (also from home) and some of the gals they worked with had arranged to meet me on their lunch hour, on my second day in Regina.

Unbeknown to us, Gran had passed away that morning. My parents, wanting to get word to me as soon as possible, called Sask. Tel, giving the sad news to Phyllis to relay to me. Through no fault of her own Phyllis had to give me the this news immediately upon our meeting, on the street outside the chosen restaurant, somewhere on 12th Avenue, as it was across from Victoria Park I remember. Having to stifle my grief, so as not to upset the other girls' lunch was one of the hardest things I have ever had to do, having this huge lump of sadness in my throat, and being on the verge of tears. Nowadays, we would have brought it out in the open, for all of them to lend me their support, at such a sad time, however, back then death was hushed up and not discussed openly like it is today, unfortunately.

An era had ended, a chapter in the book of life closed, but the many memories of Gran live on in our hearts and minds, and also many of her traits and abilities live on in me, I am told, from time to time. I must admit, I feel glad and proud of this, for to be anything like this fine lady would indeed be an honor; I feel privileged to have known her and had her as my Gran.

So happy to have this photo of my Gran Sexsmith, as this is how I remember this dear lady looked when I knew her in my childhood.